God, Faith, and Reality

Sam Akowe

ISBN: 1522818308
ISBN 13: 9781522818304
Library of Congress Control Number: 2016901963
LCCN Imprint Name: North Charleston, South Carolina,
USA

Dedication

This book is dedicated to my late mother, Nene Ahewe Akowe and late brother, Mr Saturday Akowe for raising me after the death of my father in 1963 when I was barely 7 years old.

Contents

Dedication... 3

Acknowledgments... 6

Preface.. 7

Chapter 1   God and Science 10

Chapter 2   Wealth and Religion 22

Chapter 3   Individual Attitude 32

Chapter 4   Illiteracy, Poverty, and Bad
             Governance 42

Chapter 5   You Are the Architect of
             Your Fate 49

Chapter 6   Confront Your Fears.................... 55

Chapter 7   Creating and Identifying
             Opportunity............................. 63

Chapter 8   Success and Risk Taking 71

Chapter 9   Building on a Wrong
             Foundation.............................. 75

Chapter 10   Everyone Is a Gambler................ 79

Chapter 11   Pursuit of Greener Pastures......... 85

Chapter 12   **Do Not Believe in Miracles**............. 94

Chapter 13   **Tradition, Culture, and Development** 103

Chapter 14   **Time Forgives No One**.................... 113

Chapter 15   **Superstition and Blame Culture**....... 119

Chapter 16   **Success: Reality against Fiction**...... 127

Chapter 17   **Realistic Thinking for Positive Change** 135

Acknowledgments

First and foremost, I want to thank my family, particularly my children, for supporting me throughout the process of writing this book.

I would like to extend my sincere gratitude to Eze Chimalio, a colleague, artist/musician, writer, and friend, for his invaluable ideas, editing, and general support of me in completing this book.

My gratitude goes to a very special friend, Sunny Agwaze, for his belief in me and for generally supporting this project. Your invaluable advice and encouragement went a long way in helping me complete this book.

Thank you to my friends and acquaintances, who contributed by way of criticism or approval of the ideas contained in this book. Without your help, this book would not have been written.

~ *Sam Akowe*

Preface

The secret of success lies within every individual. However, only few realize this and explore all the possibilities available to them. While others lament the lack of help and support to excel, they fail to understand that they, too, possess the powers to succeed. It is just that their negative thought or action works against them in succeeding.

The majority of motivational books are written in an American or European setting and are designed for American or European readership. As a result, many of the illustrative stories used can lose some of their impact on Africans or other readers due to cultural/traditional belief and lifestyle differences.

In setting out to write *God, Faith, and Reality*, the author wishes to acknowledge a great debt to many of those American and European authors whose inspirational works have helped him in the preparation of his own book.

Sam Akowe's book highlights the various factors that contribute to individual success or lack thereof. He tells us that many individuals who are successful know exactly what they want out of life. According to Akowe, they plan and execute and are focused, whereas those whom success eludes appear not to know exactly what they want out of life. They are poor planners and lack focus. Furthermore, Akowe reveals that because many are in the wrong career, they are unable to excel even though, in their opinion, they work as hard as those who are successful.

Akowe insists that none of these erroneous beliefs are true. He opines that in life, wherever any individual finds himself or herself is a result of what they did or did not do. Therefore, everyone has the ability to change his or her misfortune to fortune if only he or she can focus on what he or she wants and works conscientiously to achieve that.

Every life-enhancing thing we see and enjoy—for example, air plane, car, television, telephone, item of clothing, and so on—all began with a simple positive thought. That being so, it is clear, that the secret of success is through our thought and actions.

Therefore, Akowe concluded that, it is incumbent upon every individual to think and act positively for realistic change to manifest in his or her life.

Eze Chimalio

Chapter 1

God and Science

Before now, I often wondered what to believe—
God or science. I grew up with the teaching,
understanding, and belief that God created
heaven and earth with everything in it. As an
African child with Christian faith upbringing, I
had no reason—or should I say, I was not
allowed—to think or challenge the assertion
about this and many other things I was taught. I
often hear statements like "God said this is so
and that is so," "According to God's
commandment, we shall not do so, say so, or
think so," and so forth. In other words, you just
do as God says according to the Bible, or as is
often the case, as the pastor, bishop, or any
church or other religious leaders command you
to do. I am sure many generations before me
within the Christian faith or other religious

teachings have grown up just like I did, believing these things to be direct command and unquestionable ways of God and therefore cannot and must not be challenged.

However, as I grew older, I began to look at things differently. I started to question statements and ideas that I previously accepted unquestionably as the truth and direct commandments from Almighty God. As I accessed formal education, knowledge began to flow through me. The process of acquiring knowledge—gaining more understanding about life and how things really work—encouraged me to raise questions about many things that I previously accepted as truth. My inquisitive mind began to explore many angles of life and seek answers to many questions I have about life itself. My quest to know why things are the way they are and why there is so much injustice in the world began to evolve. With what is happening around us today, I am pretty sure I am not alone in this thought that there is more to it than meets the eye. Much is going on that the Holy Bible cannot explain to the understanding of many, including myself.

My inquisitive mind began to search for the truth. I wanted to know why certain things are the way they are and why certain occurrences take place. Why do bad things happen to good people, and why do bad people continue to enjoy the rewards of their evil deeds while God just stands by and watches. I wanted to know why good people suffer so much, why they are so void of happiness, and why they suffer want most of their lives. I wanted to know why there are wars all around us, and why earthquakes, fires, floods, and other calamities take place all over the world as God just looks on. I wanted to know why certain people are so comfortable in life while others suffer. I wanted to know why many are born with perfect body and mind whereas others are born with grave deformity. I wanted to know why many people or countries are so different. I wanted to know why there are so many differences in places, people, and feelings that are experienced by many around the world. I wanted to know why this is so when according to the scriptures, we were all created equal. So far, I have been void of any answers to the numerous questions raised. The only plausible answer I can honestly conjure is that none of these statements is tenable. Please do not condemn me. Just hear me out.

I honestly believe to the extent that there is somebody or something greater than humankind. Yes, I do sincerely believe that. It is safe to say that God or something greater than humankind has created this world and everything therein, and God has bestowed upon us human beings the abilities to dominate all other things. Consequently, as human beings, we are able to create things and improve extant things, the environment, and the atmosphere to suit our needs. In this contest, human beings are able to construct buildings, create furniture, alter environmental features, and influence or alter atmospheric composition. Human beings are able to generally improve their own security by fortifying their surroundings to ward off any danger perceived either from environmental tendencies or outright threats or acts of aggression from other human beings or wild animals. Therefore, I believe that as human beings, we are responsible for the type of life we live, including how comfortable, uncomfortable, rich, poor, happy, or unhappy we are.

In sharp contrast, I believe that science has created a great deal of improvements to the world in which we live. Science has created and continued to improve on designs of facilities that add more quality to our daily lives. Furthermore, science is responsible for many things that have helped to sustain our existence and well-being. There are uncountable ways science improves the way we live our lives. To begin, without science, human mobility will be very limited. Without science, we would not be able to travel from one place to another. Without automobiles, the evolution of human transcontinental mobility could not have taken place. The advent of land, sea, and air transportation makes it possible for people from one part of the world to travel to another and also move goods in like manner.

Science has improved and continued to improve our quality of life. For example, science makes blood transfusion possible for those who have lost a huge amount of blood as a result of a serious accident. It is also possible for patients with bad or nonfunctioning heart, kidneys, or livers to have them replaced. Legs and arms can be amputated and replaced with artificial (sometimes functional) versions. Patients suffering from internal ailments or serious and life-threatening injuries are treated through open or key-hole surgery to repair damage or correct faults in the body. Difficult deliveries of babies are also eased through caesarean operations.

My thought is against the backdrop of beliefs contained in the Holy Bible, to the effect that only God can do all things. Consequently, people of the Christian faith rely on God's guidance in everything they undertake in life. I marvel at this approach to life by many people I know, especially the hard-core generation of Christians who believe in the ultimate power of God in all ramifications of their lives. These people are of the mind-set that success and change can be brought about only by God. Therefore, the normal routine in their lifestyle is to worship through singing of praises, prayers, and fasting. Where there is confusion of any sort in whatever they are doing—be it problem at work, feeling ill, embarking on a journey, deciding on type of job or career to pursue, both for themselves and their household, issues with family and extended family particularly among Africans and other developing countries—they turn to Almighty God with such forceful requests, believing that God will sort out the problems or issues in a miraculous way. I must say here that this is to a great extent pertinent to new-generation churches (mainly Pentecostal). The same cannot be said of most orthodox churches such as the Anglican, Catholic, and Baptist, to mention a few. Even though orthodox churches believe in the intervention of God in all that they do, they do so with caution and within reason.

Contrary to the attitudes of believers of the new-generation churches toward those of orthodox churches faith, God is central to their lives and everything they do. Therefore, their belief in God and His influence in their lives is never in doubt. However, their approach and application of Christian principles are very different to those of new-generation churches. For instance, orthodox faith still allows for people to seek medical help when they become ill. Members of orthodox churches access all medical help available in dealing with their ailments. They do not object to any form of treatment or diagnostic methods that medical experts may prescribe. They undergo surgery when recommended. They also accept blood transfusion, organ transplant, and indeed any form of treatment that will make them well again. While allowing medical experts to deal with their ailments, they still turn to God in prayers to augment the work of doctors. They ask God to bless doctors, nurses, or anyone else responsible for providing them with treatment. They ask God to guide them and provide them with knowledge, wisdom, and understanding to be able to care for them so that they can become whole again.

This is contrary to the attitudes of believers of new-generation churches who often reject treatment from medical experts, believing that only the healing hands of Jesus Christ would prevail on their situation. These people reject any suggestions to undergo medical treatment for their ailments. They do not accept any ideas of medical examination by doctors or other medical experts by way of X-rays, blood test, or any tests for that matter. They are encouraged, often blindly, by pastors who claim to have the powers bestowed upon them by God to heal the sick and raise the dead. I have personally witnessed this in the church I attended when I did not know better—situations when sick worshippers or visitors are called to the altar by the officiating pastor for healing exercises. Other pastors and highly acclaimed prayer warriors in the church are summoned by the resident pastor to jointly invoke the Holy Spirit upon the sick person(s) and pray very violently, rebuking the devil and banishing the spirit of sickness, death, and misfortune from the sick person(s). This is carried out in full view and appreciation of the congregation who are literally cajoled into an army of spiritual combatants simultaneously ͏sing loud "Amen" and "Blood of Jesus."

The belief in miracles is not limited to healing of the sick alone. It generally extends to virtually every aspect of life of the believer. Be it in the areas of jobs, poverty, riches and wealth, favors, challenging situations, and of course liberating faithful believers from the shackles of their enemies, God will deliver them through the Holy Spirit. Unfortunately, many die while still believing they have been healed and that feeling unwell is a state of mind. As recent as 2012, a story emerged in London claiming that a number of people of African descent died of AIDS. According to the story, these HIV-positive patients stopped taking their medication because a certain pastor told them not to do so, because God had cured them of the virus. These people stopped taking their antiretroviral medication because they believed they had received healing from God. They all died of course. They died of ignorance, not of the disease!

This pattern of behavior and blind faith is commonplace within the new-generation churches. Their belief that God will change all bad situations in their lives is unquestionable. If you are witnessing bad times at work, pray about it and God will resolve it for you. If you are not getting the job you deserve, pray and fast and God will deliver your ideal job to you. If you are experiencing financial difficulty and you wish the situation to change, just pray and fast and it will be done. The laughable part of it all is that when you fail to witness any change in whatever bad or unpleasant situation you may be in, the pastor often concludes by saying you have not prayed hard enough and that you need to intensify your prayers and increase the number of days, weeks, or even months that you need to fast. This is total nonsense! Rather than looking at their circumstances realistically and seeking ways of improving their lives, they hinge their fate on God who is the author of all good things in life to take care of their lots.

You should not be devoid of common sense. You have been robbed of your ability to think rationally and left with a false belief that with God all things are possible. I am not against God, and I am not anti-Christ. All I am saying is that we all acknowledge the existence of God and

His being our creator. However, you must not forget that you are created with abilities to achieve whatever you set out to achieve. As a creation of God, you are endowed with the ability to manage, improve, and choose your levels in life. You have the ability to make the choices about what you want out of life. Your good education and training will certainly enhance your marketability in the field of employment or creating your own wealth. However, the fact remains that you need to do well in whatever you choose to do. Maintaining good life habits and managing your resources well will put you in good financial position, good health, and good social standing.

As human beings, we are all endowed with the abilities to manage, improve, and choose our levels in life. It therefore suffices to say that you are the architect of whatever shape your life takes. Apart from the effects of diseases, illnesses, accidents, and other natural causes of which you have no control, you are responsible for your own actions—therefore, your life.

Chapter 2

Wealth and Religion

Wealth is not a derivative of any particular religion or faith; neither is poverty a product of ungodliness. Poverty is a product of poor education, poor economic awareness and climate, lack of opportunity, inadequate government policy to aid citizens, and individuals' inability to identify and pursue activities that would otherwise guarantee success. As a direct consequence of one or a combination of any of the factors mentioned above, many of us wallow in abject poverty and go through life barely surviving. Generations of those affected by this trend tend to continue the unbroken lineage of poverty-stricken families. On the other hand, affluent families and their descendants with guaranteed good education, commercial heritage, inherited privileges, good economic and political standing in society tend to continue to grow and multiply in their wealth. They should not be begrudged but appreciated for their generation's foresight.

As individuals, we are architects of our own destiny and what we become. That may sound like a shallow, harsh, and indeed unreasonable thing to say. However, the truth is that everything in life has a price. People spend years in educational institutions studying for academic qualifications or learning a trade that they intend to use in pursuit of their careers. Some end up working for organizations as employees, whereas others use their skills to create wealth for themselves by establishing their own companies or enterprises. In all, our level of success or lack thereof will certainly depend on our contribution: that is, how hard we work, the industry in which we work, or what we have to do and how prudent we are with our resources and accrued income. Therefore, the onus is on us to acquire the discipline, skills, education, and training that will put us in good stead to do that which will ensure success in what we do and influence upon the position we occupy economically.

So, it is right to say that you are the architect of your own fortune or misfortune. You are solely responsible for whom you become and the position you occupy in life. It is no illusion or surprise that those who waste their precious time, particularly when they are young and should be in a learning institution, or not focus on what they need to do to enable them to achieve success end up as failures in life. On the other hand, those who toil hard enough and meticulously plan their lives achieve set goals, elevate themselves, and occupy positions of respect and affluence in society. It is thus very important that you cultivate and nurture a life strategy that will secure your future. This you do through parental guidance, education and training, and generally being consciousness of those things that will assure you good character and success in life. The opposite of this is when you choose to be disobedient as a child, lazy, void of idea of what you want, nonresponsive to stimulus gestures or directives, rebellious, refusing to heed constructive criticism, and being antiauthority and antisocial.

When you fail to achieve your goals, your life is riddled with all sorts of problems ranging from poor finance to failed marriages or relationships, to unruly children, to poor health; indeed, every disappointment in your life, you develop the "give up" and "blame culture" syndrome. You resort to blaming everyone and everything around you, except yourself, as factors responsible for what you have become. You surrender all efforts to try harder, concluding that you are not good enough. You lie and wait for some kind of miracle to take place. This is the point where most religious people resort to God for salvation. At this point, nothing else matters except their faith in God and His promise of miracles, signs, and wonders. They have accepted that there is absolutely nothing they can do to influence any change in their lives. They have given up totally on everything and anything else, apart from God, to help them.

Many blame and condemn themselves saying that they are being punished by God because of their sins against Him. They believe that poverty, death, disease, sickness, and indeed every sad situation in their lives are caused by their sins. None of these is true!

Poverty, underdevelopment, and underachievement are evident throughout the whole world. There are poor and starving people in a number of developed countries in Europe and America. However, it is more pronounced in Africa. Also, there are poor and starving people in some second-world continents such as Asia. In some of these countries, there is high population, illiteracy, and poor economic and political dispensation. People are affected by lack of government policies to emancipate themselves from poverty, economic inadequacy, and political inadequacy that are tantamount to their overall state of want, underdevelopment, and underachievement. The lack of opportunity, individual development, and focus on what is required to succeed in life, have condemned most people to penury and failures in life.

As a failing individual, you now see God as the only way for change in your life. Consequently, you dig deeper into knowing God and doing His will. You do this with utmost surrender. You have stopped being yourself, subjecting all that you do to the dictates of your faith. You have now drifted totally into the "doing God's will syndrome." You have indoctrinated yourself into all sorts of disciplines within the teachings of your chosen religion and faith. This syndrome is synonymous with the Christian faith. Some followers surrender themselves to the point where they become zombies.

Having confined themselves to this frame of mind, many, particularly of Christian faith, become subjects of control of the Holy Spirit and spiritual leaders within the churches. They are fed with ideas and teachings that to be happy, successful, and rich, and to enjoy good health and financial independence, all depend on their level of faith and righteousness. This is arrant nonsense! People have been brainwashed and fed with negative thoughts about their positions in life. In fact, there are those who are made to believe that the reason why they have not been successful or continue to wallow in abject poverty is a result of what some pastors described as "generational curse." The generational curse, according to them, is also responsible for some of the ailments that some people suffer. Generational curse, they claim, is a direct consequence of some kind of sin committed by individual parents or further generations. Also, they claim that generational curse could be geographical. That means that your success or lack thereof depends on where you were born, how you were born, and whether people from where you were born had been cursed for some unexplainable reason. Consequently, the only cure for the so-called generational curse is "deliverance" by some powerful pastor or other gifted man of God.

The generational curse is broken down into many types and forms. There is barrenness, poverty, premature death, epilepsy, bad luck, and so forth. In short, anything and everything bad in your life is a direct consequence of generational curse. You are, therefore, told that the only cure is God's intervention through spiritual deliverance by a man of God—the almighty pastor. The process entails a catalog of endless fasting, various forms of self-denial, and prolonged day and night prayer orchestrated by self-acclaimed prayer warriors within the church and finished off by the resident pastor or spiritual leader of the church. Believers strongly believe this mumbo jumbo. They religiously follow given instructions so blindly and unquestioningly.

If you are one of these believers, it is no wonder that your life has not changed or improved in any form. You remain in your sorry state, continually increasing your level of fasting, prayer, and self-denial, still hoping that God will turn things around for you in His own time. You need to realistically assess your situation and employ positive action to change things. Do not remain sheepishly obedient to the teachings of the church, believing that with increased faith, prayer, and more discipline in line with the teachings of the Holy Bible, God will eventually turn things around for you.

It is disheartening to see people, even now, still believing in the unproven miracles of God and the biblical "manna from heaven." It never happened. Even if it did happen then, it is foolhardy to believe that it is still happening today. It is make-believe, an illusion.

It is no wonder that with the increased global economic depression and the resulting hardships that mushroom churches are springing up everywhere. This is more prevalent within African countries and communities all over the world. Instead of engaging in activities that will ensure political and economic liberation, they continue to pursue shadows, spending their valuable time in church and hoping that God will take all their problems away.

You need to wake up from your slumber and do the right thing for yourself. God is not coming to change anything about you—He has finished designing and creating you. The power to change things for the better was given to you when He created you in the first place. So, look inward and exercise the power you already possess.

All you need to do is change the way you think, and believe more in yourself.

Chapter 3

Individual Attitude

In life, individual attitude plays a significant role in the shape our lives take. There are positive and negative attitudes and much depends on how individuals see themselves. Therefore, it suffices to say that if you have negative attitude toward yourself, you will fail. This is so as you tend not to try hard enough in whatever you do, believing, you are not good enough. On the other hand, if you have positive attitude toward yourself, you seldom fail. It is therefore safe to say that you are what you think of yourself. If you believe you can succeed, you apply yourself and work very hard to achieve your goals. However, if you discount yourself as never good enough, you have already failed even before you started on anything you try to achieve.

Those who have a positive attitude toward themselves possess the can-do attitude. They never give up at the first huddle. They believe in their ability to do well and thus soldier on until they achieve their desired goal. Whereas those who have negative attitude toward themselves develop a can't-do attitude. They see every challenge as impossible. They do not believe they are good enough to achieve and thus give up at the first obstacle that confronts them.

People who are unsure of themselves find it extremely difficult to start anything. They procrastinate, defer, and discount ideas that are otherwise brilliant and success guaranteed. They have no drive, no inspiration, and no desire to achieve anything as they have no belief that they are capable, and therefore they feel no need to even try. They drift from plan to plan and from project to project without starting up any. When they do manage to begin something, they never persist to complete what they started. Among this group of people, you will find those with very bright ideas and creativity but who never start anything. They are full of excuses and would create reasons why it is not possible to achieve rather than find drive and desire to be successful.

The world we live in is not a perfect one. There are many obstacles and situations that will make it difficult for us to do things that we desire to do. Circumstances will prevail upon us to deprive us of doing the things we set out to do at a given time. Situations will arise making it impossible to achieve set goals at the time we set to achieve them. If you have a positive attitude, you will push ahead and find ways of overcoming any hardship, disappointment, or circumstances that may seem beyond your control. Because you have positive attitude and belief to succeed, you will break through and achieve set goals. Whereas those with negative attitude stop thinking or acting the moment obstacles surface. They give up and accept defeat. The can't-do attitude takes over, and they surrender to pressure at the slightest presence of challenge or misfortune.

There are circumstances that are very grave. Also, there are situations that may be caused by ill health, accident, and other misfortunes. Positive-attitude people will work around such situations. They will redesign their plans, choose alternative routes or courses to accommodate their deficiencies, and go ahead to achieve their goals. On the other hand, people with negative attitude surrender to the situation or circumstance. They cannot think of any other way. Their can't-do attitude takes over their thought, and they never seek alternatives to their original plan or method to achieve them. They blame ill health, accident, misfortune, or other natural causes for their failure.

This is the point where those with can't-do attitude resign to their fate and turn to a cheaper option—God. They give in to the pressure and seek the intervention of the omnipotent power of Almighty God to come to their rescue. Nothing else will work as far as they are concerned. Rather than focus on replanning and reappraising issues in their lives, they expend their valuable time in the church and other religious activities. They surrender their will power to a pastor or other spiritual head who takes over the rein and control of their lives. The pastor or spiritual leader now prescribes doses of powerful prayer sessions, endless fasting, or extensive rituals and sacrifices that will enable the Holy Spirit to take control and change their life situations. If you are one of these unfortunate people, you have lost the plot and you need to rediscover yourself. You need to regain control of your life.

Apart from prayers and fasting, you are also subjected to parting with the little money you have which could be used in executing project or business to the church in the name of "sowing seed." Sowing a seed in Christian faith is when money or valuables of varied nature is given or pledged to the church as a means of challenging God to turn your misfortunes into fortunes. In my opinion, this is nothing short of gambling, which God prohibits His children from doing.

As in the past, many come to realize much later to their own detriment that their situations remain almost the same (if not worse) as they faithfully commit their future to Christ God. Sadly enough, many remain in this inactive state for a very long time, depending on the individual's level of faith, without realizing that the only thing that can cause change in their situation is *to change the way they think*. You need to change your perspective on things; you need to start feeling positive about yourself. Above all, you need to identify what you are good at, plan well, seek information to enhance whatever you are doing, and working hard toward achieving your goals. Please do not get me wrong: I am not in the least suggesting that God does not exist—far from it. I do agree that God created "heaven and earth and all that therein," but that is as far as it goes for me. God created us all with the ability to add value to our being—in other words, create and improve factors in our lives to make life better for ourselves. Therefore, it is foolhardy for anyone to still think or continue to believe in the biblical notion that God will send manna from heaven above or miraculously change their lives just because they believe in the Lord Jesus Christ as their Lord and Savior. You need to wake up from your slumber and face the realities of life.

This belief has given rise to the epidemic of blind faith experienced by many today. People no longer think logically about solving problems in their lives themselves based on their individual abilities. Instead, they surrender all to Lord Jesus to sort things out for them. This is not relative to uneducated people alone. It cuts across class and status in our society. The question here, though, is: have we all gone mad to think God will come down from the heavens (wherever that is) and take over our troubles? Of course not! Yes, I know, the Bible says so. However, I have news for you. Your destiny is in your own hands. As the famous saying goes, "Life is like a bank account—what you put in is what you take out." It's that simple. If you spend your entire life (or a better part of it) pursuing negativity, you will end up with nothing (i.e., a broken and unhappy human being).

On the other hand, there are some smart people around to take advantage of the fools. They are called pastors, bishops, and so on. As the epidemic of blind faith takes supreme hold of our society, new churches are springing up everywhere. Many professionals, accountants, lawyers, engineers, pilots, scientists, and more who have failed in their individual careers have now found a new way to succeed in life. Suddenly, everyone is being called by God to serve Him, and as a result, people are starting their own churches. As the world's economies continue to suffer even deeper recession, church is now the fastest growing industry. You do not require a lot of capital to start one. All you need is a room in your existing home, a chair and table at one end of the room for the pastor, and a few chairs for five to seven members. The man is the head of the church while his wife is his deputy.

These churches usually start with members of the same family and a few friends desiring to invest in the "church business." Walking down the streets in your locality today, you will find different churches with increasingly unbelievable names, each coined from words from the Bible: New Wine Church of Christ, Breakthrough Pentecostal Church, Christian Church of God, and so on. These days, new churches are growing like weeds. With the current global economic crisis and breakdown of social order, the world suddenly needs a savior. Many are out of a job; many are divorced; many wish to get married (particularly women); many are dying from various diseases and sicknesses; many are homeless; many are fighting the demonic recreational drugs abuse; and many living in foreign countries seek integration. All these circumstances constitute a minefield for fake pastors. They target the above-mentioned circumstances, or those experiencing these circumstances for deliverance, miracles, and abundant God blessings. These deprived and vulnerable people troop to these churches in their millions worldwide—all seeking the face of God instead of working hard on their projects, businesses, and careers. Stop being a fool. The only person benefiting from this is the smart pastor, bishop, or those by other names.

The person who can change your unhappy situation is you. You have the power to do so. All that is required is for you to change the way you think. Start feeling positive about yourself, believe more in yourself, work harder, and remain focused on your objectives. You will experience great change in your life. Believe me when I say I was a doubting Thomas myself until I confronted the demon head-on. Altering my thoughts and feeling positive about myself changed everything for me. I read successful people's autobiographies, and I found that they did not achieve all that they did by a stroke of luck or through the miracle of God. They built their reputation and wealth through methodical planning, judicious execution, unwavering belief in themselves, and great focus. You are designed by God with all the attributes to succeed and be great. It is all in you. You only have to invoke it to work for you.

Think positive for realistic change.

Chapter 4

Illiteracy, Poverty, and Bad Governance

There is a high level of illiteracy and attendant poverty in most third world countries, particularly those in Africa. As a result, the population suffers untold hardships providing for themselves and their families. Furthermore, due to ill-governance, access to social infrastructures such as industrialization, potable drinking water, electricity, good roads, and environment and medical facilities are almost nonexistent in many places.

Third world countries, particularly in Africa, are still struggling to guarantee a minimum level of education for their population. Without basic education, development is remote. As of today, many countries charge educational levies for primary and secondary education. This prevents poor families from sending their children and wards to school. This is one of many reasons why in some countries today, girls as young as ten or twelve years of age are given out for marriage. Apart from obvious health implications, these children are condemned to a life of poverty from a very tender age; they are thus denied the opportunity to create a better life for themselves. Education is not the only reason why young girls are married to older husbands. There are also other causes based on cultural and religious practices. Even though it is not a universal fact, it is common knowledge that within the Muslim community, it is acceptable for brides as young as ten or twelve to be given away in marriage by their parents.

Poor education is mainly responsible for the lack of individual development in most third world countries. Consequently, there is a high level of dependency on the government, the rich and influential individuals in our society. What this means is that people depend on the government to provide them with everything from economic to social infrastructures. When this fails to materialize, they resort to the second option—God. This is the one reason why in many third world countries today, churches and other religious groups are springing up and taking over the lives of many downtrodden and vulnerable people desperate to succeed. Education provides unquantifiable benefits to individuals and nations. With education, people are able to source information that will enhance their personal development. Therefore, they will rely less on government and others to provide for them. For example, if the government of a country is forthcoming with sound educational system, citizens will avail themselves with the opportunity to engage in various activities that will enhance their well-being. They will avail themselves good education and training, seek and obtain employment, and also be able to create wealth for themselves by engaging in entrepreneurship. These are a few benefits that education can provide people.

Developing countries, particularly in Africa, are known to have large families. Apart from the average couple having as many as five to seven children, there is also the lingering extended family syndrome whereby a fairly wealthy member of the family is made to cater for the children of his brothers, sisters, uncles, and aunts (dead or alive). Consequently, this affects the supposed rich member of the family's ability to educate his own children to the level he would like, had it not been that he had to take on the responsibilities of other failing adult members of his family. As the trend continues, generational development and improvement of individuals' lives continue to elude most families.

To further compound the problems of underdevelopment, most developing countries, particularly in Africa, have bad governments. They are grossly responsible for non-development of both economic and political life in the region. From time to time, countries in the continent are at war with themselves. There are frequent coups and countercoups. As a result, economic activities are stifled. Due to grave political unrest in Africa, there is a high level of refugees in the region. This situation does not require scientific knowledge to understand that development in this environment will be retarded, if not completely stalled. This is not peculiar to Africa, though. The cancerous situation is also affecting some newly independent countries in Europe and Asia previously thought to be immune from political and economic instability, resulting in underdevelopment.

In all these, what is most lamentable is the belief among people in these countries that the multifaceted problems are caused by sins against God. Consequently, rather than face realities—that is, address issues affecting government nonperformance—African religious followers spend hours, days, weeks, and years praying for their countries. They solicit God to intercede for the country. They pray to God to annul the country's sins. What rubbish! You do not need God for solutions to your economic and social deficiencies. All you need to do is look inward to find solutions. God created you with abundant and inexhaustible abilities to succeed. Just tap into it. You can do this by first believing in yourself. When you believe more in yourself, you will depend less on others—government or some rich and influential individual—to succeed. You do not need God's miracles to turn things around for you either. Just open your eyes and believe in yourself more; you will be surprised to see that solutions to all your problems are right there at your fingertips.

Many African countries are rich in mineral resources such as oil, diamond, gold, iron, zinc, and many more. It is sad to know that many of these countries do not get the revenue accruable to them from the sales of their individual resources. For example, Nigeria in West Africa is the world's tenth largest oil producer. Therefore, Nigeria ought be the richest country in Africa and also rank as one of the financially stable countries in the world. Instead, corrupt politicians, government contractors, and crooked businessmen and women are richer than the country. Oil revenue goes into individuals' pockets instead of the national coffer. In the light of all these atrocities, what do Africans do? They turn to God for solutions. Africans should be bold enough to confront bad government for wrongdoings. I understand the brutality some African governments employ in ruling their countries. Still, unless we learn to stand up for ourselves, this trend will never be broken. It is time for you to leave God out of the equation and deal with realities yourself. You are only able to do so if you change the way you think.

Start to think positively and you will begin to achieve greater progress.

Chapter 5

You Are the Architect of Your Fate

Whatever shape your life takes, you are solely responsible for it. You blame your lack of opportunity and success on other people and circumstances. You wish for yourself a slice of good fortune. You look at people around you who are successful with a sense of jealousy and envy. You curse your ill-luck. Well, let me tell you something that you do not want to hear: *you are the architect of your own fate.* You need to take responsibility and control of your life. Opportunities abound around you; all you need to do is take them. When you realize how many opportunities you have missed and how much you could have achieved, you will be angry with yourself. Still, it is never too late to start something new, especially if it means a whole lot of change to your life.

Before you can change your misfortune to good fortune, first you have to discover who you are and what you are. You have to identify your personal qualities—your abilities and capabilities. Also, you have to acknowledge your limitations. This process will definitely help you focus on what you want to do or what you should be doing. At the age of twenty or twenty-five, many do not know what they want to do in life. Even at forty, many still have no clear idea what they want to do in life. It is surprising to find that when many are asked what type of employment or career path they want to pursue, they simply answer, "Any job will do." You should know what you want and desire and that will fuel your drive to achieve great things. If you have no preference as to what you want in life, it is no wonder your life is void of purpose and direction. You should be able to say to yourself, "I want a job as an accountant, legal adviser, political adviser, pilot, architect, and so on" (in line with individual educational or professional training).

The same goes for those aspiring to go into business ventures. As a potential entrepreneur, you should be able to say to yourself, "I want to invest in 'Jack' or 'Harry.'" It is not good enough to float from one line of business to another without focus or conviction and expect to make success of your endeavor.

Successful people know exactly what they want. When they plan, they are precise and direct. When they set goals, they make sure they are achievable within set time frame(s). They focus on their target with every fiber in their body because they believe in what they are doing. The end result is success—nothing short of it. Therefore, if you want to be successful in securing gainful employment or business venture, you must have a clear idea of what you want. It is no use wishing for a better life. Plan for it, and work hard to achieve it. Nothing will be given to you by nature, government, or people associated with you, safe for a few who may inherit wealth from family or other sources.

Understanding your profession, business, and indeed the environment in which you operate is vital for you to succeed. One thing is to attain qualification in your chosen field of endeavor; the other is to know how to apply yourself in order to maximize your potential. Also, it is well and good to be able to provide essential capital for your business; however, if you do not understand what you are doing, you will definitely fail. It is irrelevant how much hard work you put in or how much capital you invest. You need to have adequate information about how your business works, who your potential customers arc, and above everything else, the environment in which you operate. These are essential ingredients for a successful career or business to grow.

It is commonplace to find many seeking employment not to make good inquiries or research into the field of work they intend to go into. Equally so, someone venturing into any kind of business must first research into the business so that he or she is able to provide what is required for the business to not only succeed but to also be profitable. You need to know that it is not a sign of weakness or failure to seek information and guidance. In fact, it is a good sign that you are prepared to learn and intend to be great in whatever you chose to do. Also, it is all right to make mistakes. When you do, be humble about it. Seek support and advice so that such mistakes do not repeat themselves. We are in the jet age of electronic data revolution, and any information we require on virtually everything is freely available at our fingertips. Therefore, you have the freedom to surf and obtain information on whatever you want.

It is time you take control of your life. Stop blaming others or circumstances for your inability to succeed. Opportunities are there for you; recognize and take them. Even where there are no opportunities, create them. Look around you; there are numerous things you can do to generate wealth. You cannot continue to look up to others to provide you with opportunities to start up something or change your career or job. No one is standing in your way as you believe hitherto. You are your own obstacle. Purge yourself of all negative thoughts and replace them with positive ones. As I said in chapter 17,

"Realistic Thinking for Positive Change," to experience positive change, *you need to change the way you think—think positive, not negative.*

I want to ask you three fundamental questions. Your answers will tell you where you are in life.

- *What makes you think that your lack of progress is caused by someone?*

- *If family, friends, and society have failed you, and your prayers to God have not changed anything for you, is it not time you stand up and believe more in yourself?*

- *How many failed ventures have you embarked upon, and why did they fail?*

Chapter 6

Confront Your Fears

One of the monsters most people face in life is fear. Fear comes in different forms—fear of making relevant and necessary changes in life; fear of venturing into the unknown; fear of speaking our minds; fear of confronting the truth about others and ourselves; fear of failure; fear of defying the ethics of our individual society; fear of being different; fear of being the first person to do something out of character; and so on. In fact, we experience fear of the *unknown* at one stage or another in our lives. This is one of the reasons why many fall short in achieving their set life goals. In other words, non–risk takers will never embrace meaningful success in life. On the other hand, only risk takers are able to experience meaningful breakthrough in their chosen careers and therefore attract huge difference to their lives. Many people feel more comfortable residing in their *comfort zone*—to just be satisfied with what they have and wait for God's time for change to come.

I often wonder why there are not many people from developing countries who are known world-class scientists, explorers, inventors, and discoverers. This is not because we are very backward in academics. After all, there are many people of African origin occupying high-profile positions in the world who happen to be black people. We have produced a head of state of the most powerful country in the whole world in the person of President Barack Obama. We have produced a secretary-general to the United Nations in the person of Kofi Annan of Ghana. The late Nelson Mandela became president of South Africa after spending twenty-seven years in prison—defying all odds. Apart from these few examples, we have black people in other powerful and influential positions throughout the world. However, these people are only flourishing in political and administrative capacities. So the question is, why are we not able to excel in other areas of human endeavors such as discovery, invention, and science? Simply, it is because we are never comfortable delving into those areas of high risk taking and extreme challenge. We are scared of being different, so much so that we are afraid of doing anything that will change our position because we fear we will fail. We see such challenges as something foreign to us. Being a skydiver is for white people, not for black people. Going under water to discover life under the sea is sheer madness, therefore not for a black man. To spend years or decades discovering how an object (airplane) can fly not suspended by any other object is white man's witchcraft—not for us.

To effect desired and meaningful change to your life, first you must conquer your fears. Nothing will change unless you force the change to occur. As you all know, nothing good ever comes easy. Therefore, if you want to enjoy the good things in life, you need to sacrifice and work hard for them. For example, if you want to enjoy good food, you must either learn how to cook or have the money to dine at upscale and expensive restaurants. Either way, sacrifice has to be made. This is the point I am trying to make writing this book: *You alone are responsible for whom or what you turn out to be in life.* Therefore, you must confront and defeat your various fears in life. You must be prepared to go the extra mile in whatever you do to effect meaningful change in your life. Furthermore, you need to acknowledge your capabilities, your deficiencies, and the resources available to you. Above all, you must remain focused and determined to successfully push down all barriers and obstacles on your way to success.

Nothing is impossible to achieve if you put your mind and soul into it. However, to begin to plod new areas of endeavors such as science, invention, discovery, and so forth, you must first change the way you think. Every product, invention, or scientific discovery you see or feel around you began with a thought. Therefore, you must remodel your thinking pattern. As you go through life, millions of thoughts are processed through your brain. You must discount those thoughts that tend to undermine your abilities and capabilities. Focus on those that exude and reinforce confidence and self-belief in you. For your thought pattern to change from negative to positive, you need to start seeing all things in a positive way. You must find a new approach to the way you view things. Instead of finding reason or creating one to prevent you doing new things, you must focus on reason and purpose to do them. I want you to know this: negative thought will not give you a positive life.

As I said in chapter 13, "Tradition, Culture, and Development," there are many factors that are derived from our upbringing, particularly as Africans that tend to drive unnecessary fears into us while we try to do something new and different. There is the parental teaching factor to which many can relate. As an African myself, I fully understand the influence my parents had on my development as a child. We were taught to respect the family name—that is, to not do anything that will bring the name of the family into disrepute. We were taught not to do things outside the confinements of the *ethics of our society*—whatever that means. Our parents dictated to us what to study at school and university. Subsequently, we were dictated to the career and profession to pursue as adults. In other words, right from the moment you were born, your life is mapped out for you, and you are obliged to adhere to it, otherwise you are branded a disobedient child or black sheep. Our society does not forgive anyone who disobeys his or her parents in the family. Therefore, we conform so we are seen as "good children."

However, the trend is changing. More and more young people are now choosing and doing what they want. In contrast to what happened in earlier years when parents were unrelenting in mounting pressure on their children to pursue specific careers chosen by them, young people are now defying their parents. They are now focused and courageous enough to push for what they want and are pursuing their careers in sports and entertainment, to mention a few. These are areas previously deemed as taboos by most African parents. Modern African parents are beginning to show understanding that for a child to fully achieve his or her potential he or she must be allowed to pursue their own objectives. The results are there for everyone to see. The most influential and wealthy people in the world today are pop stars, actors and actresses, sportsmen and sportswomen, designers, and technologists. Do not get me wrong: I am not in the least saying that other traditional professions such as doctors, nurses, lawyers, accountants, engineers, and so forth, are failed professions— far from it. What I am saying is that people achieve more in life when they explore and utilize their natural talents. Therefore, for you to maximize your reward and be successful in life, you must do what you love and are gifted to do.

Finally, I would like to emphasize that I do not condemn African tradition, culture, and way of life. However, I do not subscribe to any aspect of it that tends to oppress and repress individuals' choices. When you deny someone his or her right to choose what he or she wants and where he or she wants to be in life, you may have robbed him or her of the opportunity to develop his or her full potential. That singular act of denial may result in underdevelopment of self and consequently underachievement in life.

Chapter 7

Creating and Identifying Opportunity

A common economic statement suggests "you speculate to accumulate." For you to grow in wealth, you must be prepared to invest and wisely, too. Investing is taking a chance as you never know whether your investment will yield any dividend or occasion complete loss. This is like taking a plunge from the top of a cliff into a deep blue sea or river, hoping the water is deep enough, and there are no rocks, crocodiles, sharks, or other objects that might harm you. Usually, the higher the risk, the greater the profit you make, bearing in mind, of course, that you could also lose everything. However, as an investor, you take your chance when opportunity presents itself. Do not forget: *only risk takers can be successful.*

As a clever investor, you also do not wait for opportunity to present itself all the time. You sometimes have to actually create opportunity for yourself. It is no secret that those who do not see opportunities are those who do not look hard enough or lack the ability to recognize openings. Also, those who do not elevate themselves from their current position are those who shy away from risk and confine themselves in what I refer to as the "comfort zone," in other words, playing safe, not taking any risks, feeling contented with where you are, and not taking chances in case things go wrong. Well, no wonder many people remain unsuccessful in life. It is not because some evil person, bad spirit, or generational curse (as preached by unscrupulous pastors) prevents them from doing so. It is simply the individual's sheer naïveté, lack of vision, lack of drive, and lack of belief in himself or herself that prevents him or her from developing and achieving great heights in life.

When I was a little boy growing up in a small village in Nigeria, there was this man who had a small corner shop near the market square.

He ran his business with the support of his young wife. They both toiled hard to grow the business. As I remember it, the man would ride on his bicycle to a neighboring town to purchase goods for resale in his shop. Whenever he was away, his wife ran the shop. Soon, the family business began to grow. He began to invest in other areas of business. He cultivated a large farm from which farm produce were sold after harvesting. He then sold his farm produce in the local market to those who do not have enough to feed their families from their own farms. As the little village grew, development also began to take place. People started to build new houses using local building materials with zinc (corrugated iron sheeting) roofing.

In our little village, there was an abundance of timber. Timber is very valuable tree from which solid wood for the manufacture of furniture and building planks are derived. As people began to build new homes using sticks, mud, cement, and zinc, this was seen as a new innovation in building construction in the village. It was a complete improvement and diversion from the traditional mud-and-rafter huts we were used to. The trader saw an opportunity in the new way people were building houses. He saw an opening for a new venture to expand his business— *sawmill.*

First, he sought to know of any legal implications of sourcing his raw materials from the village forest from the local authority. He applied for a license from the Department of Forestry in the local authority to enable him cut down trees and processed them into planks for building and furniture making in his new sawmill. The sawmill business took off and grew like wild fire. Soon, people began to come from afar to purchase wood from his sawmill for their building and furniture. As purchases increased, he acquired more machines and workmen to run the mill. Then another opportunity presented itself—*transportation.* He saw the difficulty in customers carrying home their purchases and thought he could also help them by arranging delivery for them. From the profits he made, he branched out to haulage. He started delivering to customers planks purchased from his sawmills.

This attracted huge financial benefit for his business.

His business experienced a big boom and in a very short time. He became a multi-investor and his empire grew beyond his own imagination. As the businesses grew, his children became involved and supported their parents in running it. Soon, the one-time small-village petty trader and his wife became big-business tycoons and very rich, creating a huge business empire for his family. They both retired when they came of age. However, their children who have been involved in the business took over the management of the empire. The couple eventually died, leaving behind a business empire of international repute. From a very humble beginning, a local petty trader in a small village, with sharp business acumen succeeded in creating a multinational concern. The business now has branches in several big towns and cities in a number of African countries servicing both local consumption and international export in wood products.

As you can see from the story, a village petty trader rose from obscurity to an internationally acclaimed business magnate. Anyone can do anything as long as he or she is positive in his or her thinking, work hard on his or her ideas, and make them work for him or her. As I said in other chapters, positive thinking sets you on the winning path in whatever you choose to do. Conversely, negative thinking, self-doubt, and relying on God's miracle will only leave you with shattered dreams. So what is it going to be? Are you now ready to pick yourself up, go out there, and face your challenges with the conviction of a champion and conquer your fears, or sit back and wait for God's time? I will say to you, do the first, and I can assure you that you will succeed in attaining the success that had eluded you all these years.

Another very important factor that negates against individuals trying to develop themselves in most African communities is the lack of mentors. As has been proven in most developed countries (Europe, the Americas, and Asia), a mentor is vital in the development of individuals within industry and commerce. Young people need to learn from successful businessmen and women how businesses are created, nurtured, and sustained in their environment. A typical example is *The Apprentice*, a television program in the United Kingdom created by an investor and a multimillionaire (Sir Alan Sugar). This program has created many young entrepreneurs, who in turn have become successful in their chosen industries through the guidance of experts and funds provided to them.

Africa and other developing countries should emulate this practice. The process should be incorporated into secondary, college, and university curricula so that young people are availed the opportunity to develop their business acumen while studying. Each country's government must create conducive environment and financial support for those venturing into self-employment to make the system work. This will contribute immensely to the growth of not only the individuals involved but their countries as well. Instead of chasing jobs that are not readily available, some of the new graduates will have the choice of going into businesses of their own, thereby creating their own wealth and providing job opportunities for others.

You are designed to succeed. Locate your key to the door of your success.

Chapter 8

Success and Risk Taking

To be successful, you have to take risks. Only risk takers are successful. We often wonder why many people who work so hard in life are still unsuccessful in real terms. To be successful, one needs not only work hard, but one must also do extraordinary things. Those things include but are not limited to taking extreme risks. Many people are scared of the unknown and therefore will do everything to avoid venturing into things with which they are not familiar. People would rather hold on to what they have or are doing rather than delve into areas or activities that are alien to them.

For those of you in employment, even though you are in dead-end job, you are scared to change jobs or profession. You chose to remain where you are and continue to moan about poor condition and remuneration. If you are not enjoying what you are doing or your job is no longer financially rewarding, do something about it. There are a number of things you can do to change your situation. First, you have to identify a career path that you want to follow, then seek information about it for clearer understanding. Second, you must identify additional educational or technical training required to enhance your knowledge and ability to work in your new chosen career. Lastly, you must go out there and knock on doors for opportunities to open up for you. Even when it appears there are no opportunities, you must create one. Unless you do these things, change will never happen for you. There is no magic or miracle about change. You simply have to do things differently. As discussed in chapter 17, "Realistic Thinking for Positive Change," for you to experience change in whatever you are doing, *you need to change the way you think—think positive!*

For those aspiring to or are already in self-employment, (trading, manufacturing, or services), the same process applies to you. You need to understand your line of business so that you can make it work for you. If you do not understand the intricacies of the business in which you are involved, you will likely be making losses and eventually close down. However, if you take time to study your business and the environment in which you operate, you are guaranteed success. You have to know what your customers need so that you can serve their purpose. Furthermore, for your business to prosper, you need to invest in infrastructure that will enhance your trade. Infrastructures such as adequate communication system, transportation, and service personnel to enhance your products or services should be priority. As a general economic saying suggests, "you have to speculate to accumulate."

Finally, there is one vital aspect and ingredient that many venturing into self-employment lack: mentorship. To mentor someone is a very important process in developing people. Unfortunately, many aspiring businessmen and women, particularly in developing countries, do not have the privilege of having someone in their chosen career to mentor them. This is very scarce particularly within African communities in diaspora. When you compare the situation with the Indian, Chinese, or Greek communities, you can see a clear difference in lifestyle. While African and Caribbean communities strive to educate themselves for the sole purpose of gaining general employment, their counterparts from Chinese, Indian, or Greek communities are more diverse. The situation needs to be addressed.

Africans must therefore be prepared to change their approach to individual development. We must embrace a broader way of thinking about careers and professions to include commerce, public service (politics), manufacture, craft, sports, entertainment, and so forth. As for those in business, they must develop an inclusive approach to involve our younger generation in commerce. In time, a new ideology will begin to emerge in the continent, and our educational system, too, will change to accommodate our new way of thinking.

Chapter 9

Building on a Wrong Foundation

Hard work guarantees success in life. This is what we are told from a very tender age. However, it was never explained to us that we have to *work hard doing the right thing,* not *the wrong thing.* Many people go through life working hard but doing the wrong thing. Even though you work as hard as humanly possible, you record little or no success; this is because you have been doing the wrong things. For you to fully achieve your potentials in life, you need to identify your natural abilities and capabilities. You must also focus on your dream and desire in life. It will amount to nothing if you just keep working hard at things that you are not entirely happy with or doing something that you are not very comfortable doing. Doing so, no matter how persistent you may be, will amount to no success or fulfillment. It will be like fitting a square peg into a round hole. Many spend a long time in this situation in life. Some come to the realization late that one needs to do what he or she loves to be successful, but most never do. This is one of the many reasons why so many people, irrespective of their acquired education and training, are still unable to lead a successful life.

Everyone dreams of success in life. From when you were a child, you dream of becoming rich, successful, and influential in your society. You dream of being like the rich man or woman on your street or town. You imitate them in aspects of your child's play—driving a toy car like the rich people do; speaking like they do; and generally acting out how they live their lives. You look at their families and dream of having a family like that when you grow up. Now you are grown up, and none of the dreams you had as a child seems to be materializing. You are unable to hold down a good job. Your trade is not developing, and everything you try appears to bite the dust before it even takes off. You run from pillar to post in search of answers to your lack of success; you run to people in the same field of business or career, seeking their opinion as to what to do to improve your situation. You listen to anyone and everyone offering you all kinds of advice and suggestions, but nothing seems to work. The problem is not your level of commitment or hard work; it is simply that you are in the wrong field of work or career. Therefore, you need to reassess yourself, retrace your dream, and reevaluate your approach so as to ascertain you are still doing the right thing. This is the most difficult thing most people have to do but are afraid to even attempt it. This is the reason why many remain in dead-end jobs that do not give them any satisfaction or financial independence. In other words, many will rather stay in their unproductive ventures or careers than find an alternative route. This is where the danger lies—*staying in the comfort zone.*

Working hard doing the wrong thing and expecting success that never comes is simply an incentive to give up trying. You decide to just stick with what you have—a job, career, or a relationship that is going nowhere. You resign to your fate believing you are never going to make it beyond where you are. You have done everything and every job under the sun, yet you have nothing to show for it; you simply accept that success was not meant to be. You start believing that there may be evil forces behind your failure and lack of achievement. You may even become very weary of your friends, family, spouse, or even your parents, suspecting some or all of them to be responsible for your misfortunes in life. This is the point where drive, confidence, and motivation divorce you, and the spirit of failure takes over. What do you have left? Oh yes, God Almighty through Jesus the Lord, Allah, native doctors (herbalists), or fortune tellers from whom solutions can be sought or bought. When you get to this point in your life or if you are there now, you need to snap out of it **RIGHT NOW**. You need to discover who you truly are, including your strengths, weaknesses, and desires. No one is interfering with your life. It is simply the fact that you have not been able to identify your strengths and weaknesses. Simply put, you have been fishing in the dead sea—***Working hard doing the wrong thing!***

Chapter 10

Everyone Is a Gambler

Everyone is a gambler in every sense of the word. We all gamble one way or the other every day and every time. When we wake up in the morning, we decide whether we want to get out of bed or remain in bed that day. Whatever decision we make at that point in time will have a significant effect on the entire day. When we decide to remain in bed because we feel tired or uninspired, then whatever business or activity that needed our attention that day will not be attended to. On the other hand, when we decide to get out of bed and do what is necessary, our action will enhance whatever it is that we do. That singular action of whether we get out of bed in the morning has multiplying effects on the entire day, week, month, year, or lifetime.

Every action or inaction encompasses an element of gambling. For example, when a grocer decides not to open his or her shop for business early in the morning on a specific day, he or she risks losing income that day. Customers shopping for items for their breakfast will not come to his or her shop. However, if he or she decides to open early for business, people will come into the shop and buy whatever they need, and his or her business will make good sales that day. The same process applies to everything we do in life. When we make a decision or take action to do something, we hope for a good reward. However, when we fail to take action or delay in acting, there is also a consequence.

We all bemoan our misfortunes in life but never stop to think if we are actually responsible for the unpleasant situation in which we find ourselves. As children, our parents engage us in diverse activities to shape our upbringing— education, training, sports, and other activities. Some respond to instructions and guidance positively while others do not. In hindsight, we all can see that the result of what we did or did not do in our formative years is traceable to what we are today.

It is time for you to ditch the sentiment of what could have been. Take charge of your life and do what is necessary to effect change in your life. You are now a full-grown person, still unaware or undecided on what to do to change your situation. You cannot continue to do the same thing the same way over and over again expecting different results. You should seek advice or guidance and stop jumping to the conclusion that you are not cut out to be successful. Stop believing that you are cursed or bewitched by your enemies who often are members of your immediate family. You have enough trouble as it is struggling with a hard life. You do not want more heartache by creating friction among your family, friends, and yourself. Like most people in utter confusion, you have gone ahead to commit the biggest mistake of your life—*turning to God for solution.* You may think I do not believe in God, but I do. I just do not subscribe to the belief that prayers and fasting will change things that are not working in my life. My belief is that only concerted efforts can do it for you because that is what did it for me.

All Christians say, "Jesus is the answer," but they never tell us what the questions are. A friend of mine once said, "Only a weak man or woman runs to God for help." Initially, I did not understand what he meant. He was patient to explain it to me. He said, "As a successful businessman, I understand my business and know what my customers want. Therefore, I am able to run my business providing the products and services desired by my numerous customers and service users." He further explained, "Whenever any aspect of my business is faltering, I survey the market to affirm people's needs, fine-tune my approach of dispensing my services, and increase my dedication and commitment." That is what people who want to succeed in business or other aspects of human endeavor should do, not run to a pastor or other religious leaders to intercede with God on their behalf. That is wrong. After all, there is a statement in the Bible that says, "God helps those who help themselves."

If you truly want a change in your life, you need to do something about it. You need to reassess and reevaluate what you are doing. If you aspire to change your employment for a better and more rewarding job, then you need to perhaps get more training and specialize in an area you wish to seek employment. On the other hand, if you own your business and you wish to make it more successful, show more commitment, understand what you are doing and engage those who know the business better to assist you. You need to stop doing the same thing that has not worked for you, day after day, year after year, expecting miracles to happen. Things do not work that way.

Many are stuck in career wilderness, those in employment and are not progressing. It is either they do not know what to do or are too scared to do something about it. The same applies to those who choose to be sitting on the fence waiting for "something to happen." Well, let me tell you, nothing will happen unless you make it happen. You need to make a decision as to where you want your career to go. You need to have a clear vision about what you want to do. If you are not sure, seek professional advice; it does not hurt to ask questions and clarifications about something you are not sure about. Sometimes, you need to pay for sound advice. Be bold and take the necessary steps toward the realization of your dream. Be professional in every aspect of what you choose to do. This is one factor that usually spells doom in people's lives. We attend to our businesses in a casual and unprofessional manner and expect things to turn out well. I have another news flash for you—you and your business will fail. The key to your success is to boldly follow your dream and desire and remain focused on your target—success.

Make a move. Nothing will happen unless you make it happen.

Chapter 11

Pursuit of Greener Pastures

At some point in our lives, we feel and believe that the environment and locality in which we reside is no longer conducive for us to achieve our goals or maximize our potentials. All sorts of negative ideas start popping into our heads. Our thoughts are filled with negativities. We start to search for reasons as to why things are not going our way. We begin to audit our catalog of friends, family, associates, and indeed anyone close to us for possible hints to confirm our suspicion that they may be diabolically responsible for our state of unhappiness. Funnily enough, people often tend to find unproven reasons to believe that their ill-luck or general lack of progress in life is attributable to the fact that their "enemies" have cursed them. The curse, or in other instances, the witchcraft, perpetrated by the common enemy is causing them to lose their job and suffer poor health, barrenness, sudden death, and abject poverty. This negativity is all in your head. No one is causing you to suffer ill-health, poor economic achievement, and other vices plaguing your life.

Now that you have convinced yourself that people close to you and the town or city in which you reside are cursed, the only escape route is to avoid suspected family members and friends, and to migrate to another town, city, or country. You conclude unequivocally that migrating is the only solution available to you to turn things around. You are so wrong. While you seek to find solutions to your problems of underachievement and other matters, and conclude that your enemies are responsible for all the bad things happening to you, you never stop to examine yourself to see if you are doing the right thing to change your misfortunes. You run from one place to another, changing jobs and trade, thinking that the environment and people around you have something to do with your situation. This situation has caused many to resign from their job, sell off their business and any properties, and head to another town, city, or foreign country. Well, know this for a fact that your decision to relocate (or rather, run away) will not solve your problems because it is based on a wrong premise. *You can run away from your home, town, city, country, and indeed people close to you, but you cannot run away from yourself.*

In the past two decades, a very high number of people from Africa and indeed other developing countries have embarked on economic and educational migration to Europe and the Americas. A good number of migrants only travel abroad for economic reasons. While it is true that, a great number travel abroad to enhance their education, most never return to their original countries at the end of their course. Many of them now suffer even worse conditions than what they had left behind in their respective countries. This is so because they failed to think things through before making that one important decision to relocate. It never crossed their minds that living, working, or studying in a foreign country requires you to abide by the laws and regulations of your host country. To study, your fees and maintenance money must be provided either by yourself or by your sponsor. On the other hand, for you to be eligible to work, you need to have your visa status changed. If you are a student or just visiting, you have to apply to the immigration department of your host country to remove the control on your visa (i.e., either to issue you with a work permit or give you indefinite leave to remain, which would allow you to trade or work). These are some of the facts that those migrating to other countries never bothered to find out or are interested to know.

In the United Kingdom where I reside, you find many highly qualified professionals doing all kinds of menial jobs such as cleaning offices, public restrooms, train coaches, train stations, railway tracks, and restaurant kitchens (washing plates and serving food). Others do jobs that may be fairly described as better jobs. These may be classified as upper level to those mentioned above but still not in line with the academic or technical qualifications they possess. Such jobs include but are not limited to housing officers, bus or train drivers, taxi cab operatives, club bouncers, health-care and support workers (working with people with mental or physical disability), and so on. As demeaning as some of these jobs may appear, doctors, accountants, lawyers, pharmacists, and so forth, without resident status or work permit do them with pleasure. Why? Because they have no choice! The only other choice they have is to leave the country or starve to death.

This is not to say that foreigners are not employed in high-profile jobs. There are foreign doctors employed by many hospitals in the United Kingdom. I am sure it is the same in other European countries and the Americas. There are also many foreigners plying their professional trades as lawyers, pharmacists, accountants, economists, and many other professions. Of course there is also the big foreign employer in most foreign countries—soccer and other sports. However, the percentage of those in respectable jobs is so low compared to those working in the black labor market in spite of their qualifications and experience.

Talking about choices, migrants are stock in the system. They run around like headless chickens and live substandard lives. They cannot afford decent accommodations. They are unable to afford decent food and any health care. In a nutshell, life can be unbearable if you are illegal in a foreign country. By the time most realize what mistake they have made by migrating to a foreign country, much has already gone wrong. They have lost everything back in their home country, and their own and their family's expectations have also gone with the wind. A few wise ones start to think of a way out of their predicament. Living in a foreign country sometimes not only changes your way of life, but it also changes your character and generally who you are. You start behaving like most people around you and trying to fit in so as to be accepted. Your criteria for choosing friends and the type of people you associate change to accommodate your present situation. This can be really disturbing as you are no longer yourself but can't help the situation.

In an attempt to remedy the situation, many brave illegal immigrants resort to all kinds of legal and sometimes illegal processes to regularize their stay in the country. The Foreign Office provides guidelines for those wishing to regularize their residence in the United Kingdom (same with other countries in Europe, the Americas, and Asia). There are many ways illegal immigrants can regularize their immigration status. However, there are two very popular options, namely, getting married to a British citizen or seek asylum (political or others). These processes are not only acrimonious, but they are also exceedingly difficult and expensive to actualize. Furthermore, by making any of the applications, the illegal immigrant is now on the radar of the immigration department. If the application to change their status (i.e., remain indefinitely in the country) fails, the authorities are quick to pick you up and deport you to your country of origin.

Many illegal immigrants who choose not to regularize their status or cannot afford the legal costs disappear into the system without trace. Consequently, they are unable to travel out of the country they reside to visit their home country. When this happens, many illegal immigrants cease to use their original names and personal details to avoid detection by the immigration department. They suddenly become men and women without faces. In this situation, they suffer untold hardship. Many work without being able to enjoy the money they earn as they are forced to use other people's (friends or families) bank accounts for payment of their wages or salaries. There have been cases where money paid into these accounts are seized by the account holders, and the affected illegal immigrants could not ask for their money or go to the police to seek redress for fear of reprisal. This is double tragedy for illegal immigrants.

So, before you make that very important decision to leave your town, city, or country to seek greener pastures, think again. Examine yourself to ascertain that you are not the problem. Some of you are in the wrong job, while many are not putting in a day's work in your chosen careers. Much will change for you if you alter the way you think. All the negative vibes around you stem from the negative thoughts you have over many things. For meaningful change to take place in your life, start thinking positively. Believe more in yourself and in what you are doing. When you succeed in doing this, **failure will be alien to you.**

Chapter 12

Do Not Believe in Miracles

There is nothing miraculous about success. Success is a reward for those who work hard. Hard work per se does not guarantee success. This may sound confusing to you. Yes, for hard work to be rewarding, you must do the right thing. This is the difficult part many face. Everyone wants to be successful. However, only a few know what to do to achieve that feat. Many of us begin life after our education or training by working for others as employees. Employees working for salary or wage believe working hard means doing extra shifts or taking up extra part-time work to augment their meagre income. There is absolutely nothing wrong with that, not at all.

However, I would like to say that earning a good wage or salary will not guarantee you the level of success many of us dream about. Of course a good wage or salary will enable you to provide your family with basic standards of life only to the extent that you are able to pay your bills, educate your children, and offer shelter. You will not become a millionaire being on a wage or salary no matter how decent your pay may be. I know everyone cannot be a millionaire, but why should it be you who will be among those who are not? Our personal attitude is responsible for who we turn out to be. You have been an employee since eternity, yet you have little or nothing to show for the salary or wage you have collected over the years. The reason is simply that it is never enough. Salary or wage paid by an employer is just a little guarantee that an employer needs to ensure the employee continues to be loyal to the company. The employee will always need money to cater for his or her needs and that of their family. The salary or wage he or she receives as an employee will never make him or her rich and comfortable to the point where he or she decides not to work for the employer. This is the reason why many work for so many years doing all kinds of jobs, then retire and still have to depend on the meagre pension as the only income. This may not apply to the privileged few who happen to have high-flying city jobs or political appointments in government. On the other hand, some may have wealth bestowed upon them by virtue of inheritance from family or the odd chance of winning the lottery.

It may be true that not everyone is born with a silver spoon in their mouth. I do appreciate the fact that many of us have to start from the basics, picking up employment and doing odd jobs. However, you must identify where you want to be in life. In other words, you must have a dream as to what and where you want to be in the future. To make this happen, you have to start putting money aside and planning toward implementing your plan. This will take a number of years to achieve, but as long as you remain focused, it will happen. Prior to your set target time for implementing your plan, you must carry out extensive research into the workability of your intended project, product, or service. You will require training and seminars to enhance your knowledge and understanding of whatever it is you intend to do. The better the understanding you have of your plan, the better your chances for success.

For those of you who still clamber in churches and other places of spiritual connection, you need to think again. How long have you been attending church where the pastor propagates miracles that turn "disappointment into blessing; healing the sick and raising the dead"? It is incredible what you hear in some of the modern churches (particularly Pentecostal). There was a time when I was a regular church attendant in London. I even rose to the position of deputy leader in the drama department of the church. As an entertainer myself, I felt it was right to worship God with my given talent. Anyway, that was as far as it went. During service, there was always time for testimonies. That is, time for those whom God touched in a special way to come forward and share their testimonies. You would be bewildered by some of these stories. I am sure even God would be angry with these people for telling lies about Him. Some tales are so ridiculous that you wonder if these people have been paid by the pastor to say the things they claim God has done for them. Such miracles include "I have been unemployed for five or more years. Suddenly, I received a job offer for a position I did not even apply for." What utter nonsense. How can a job be offered to a ghost (you) without applying for it? Well, the congregation believe it. On such occasions, you have to marvel at the general chorus of "Hallelujah, the Lord is good!" Listen to more: "I have been married for ten years with no child. I am now pregnant." Wait a minute. Even those who do not go to church get pregnant after several years of trying. You will also find those who are very ill, some on wheelchair, all coming to the church for miracle healing for their ailments. It is surprising to see many of them pretending they have received healing. The truth is that they are deceiving themselves as they can be seen limping back to their seats, still unable to walk properly. How can people be so naïve and gullible? If indeed these churches and their pastors possess the healing powers of God as Jesus Christ is said to possess in the Bible, their healings should be perfect and total. The Bible never tells of any one healed halfway. According to the Bible, when Jesus healed the cripple, He told him, "Rise and walk," and the man got up and ran. The Bible never said he limped away.

Know that the only process that can guarantee you success is working hard doing the right thing. Also, when you are unwell or are seeking to start a family but your wife is not conceiving after trying for a while, seek medical assistance and deal with the situation. You need to remind yourself of facts around you. When Muslims are ill or late in having children, they seek medical assistance, and they get over their problems. China, the most populous nation in the world, does not particularly encourage Christianity. Delayed pregnancy or barrenness is a medical and biological issue that can sometimes be corrected through a doctor's intervention or body change. Delayed pregnancy or barrenness may also be associated with incompatibility of the couple involved. Also, you must know that not every man or woman has the biological composition to bear children. You need to wake up from your slumber. If you have to go to church, do so by all means, but stop believing that God through His chosen pastor will change your misfortunes into abundant blessings. You have been told time and time again that you need to have unquestionable faith in God for a miracle to happen to you. You have parted with your hard-earned cash paying your tithe and have also given away your valuables as offerings to the church. Still, no meaningful change has occurred in your life. Apart from the significant amount of money you have lost through paying of tithe and offerings, you have also wasted your money by "sowing." Sowing in Christian terms is when you give money to the church as a means of challenging God to do wonders for you. In my understanding, that is nothing short of gambling. You give a sum of money to God through the church in hopes that God will in return multiply your lots million fold. *That is betting—a mug's game.*

The pastors through their overt and covert preaching styles blackmail you psychologically when they constantly recite passages from the Holy Bible that deal with those who fail to pay their tithe. They conclude by saying that when you fail to pay your tithe, you are stealing from God. The punishment for stealing from God is that "you will rot in burning hell." That will strike you at the center of your nervous system, and suddenly, you become hysterical. "Oh no, I cannot steal from God." So you continue to pay, and your lots continue to dwindle. You need to ask yourself what currency is used in heaven and why God would need your money to support His existence. After all, it is written in the Holy Bible, "Come to me, all ye that labor and are heavy laden and I will give you rest" (Matthew 11:28). God does not need your money; the pastor does. You better wise up.

If you want to continue to believe this mumbo-jumbo, it is entirely up to you, and you are free to continue to do so at your own peril. Your great-grandparents, your grandparents, and your parents have been attending the same church as you for aeons *(eternity),* believing the same message of miracle and deliverance. Their lives did not change for the better. You need to ask yourself this question: *If they have not experienced God's miracle (success) without working for it, how can I continue to believe it will happen to me?*

Be wise and get serious with your life. I did, and that decision changed my life for the better. That is the experience I am sharing with you as you read this book.

Locate your unique key to the door of your life success.

Chapter 13

Tradition, Culture, and Development

Culture and development are correlated. I am an African, and my development to a great extent is influenced by my culture and belief. My socioeconomic development has been affected by my culture, way of life, and unparalleled economic and political dispensation in my environment. As a child, I was controlled by many factors emanating from my parents, siblings, and indeed extended family members who happen to be part and parcel of a typical African family setting. Nothing much is wrong with the African family setting. It is built around respect for your parents, elders, your community, and cultural heritage. These values are vigorously enshrined into the lives of African children. How we develop, approach, and see life in general stem from this foundation. This basis in effect influences our vision, understanding, adaptation, and generally how we live our lives. I was in this bondage until I liberated myself from this ideological imprisonment.

I have attained sound education and emancipated myself from the shackles of illiteracy and lack of knowledge that permeate the minds of many Africans. There is absolutely nothing wrong with embracing one's culture and way of life, but unquestioning adherence to them sometimes hinders development of self and consequently full realization of inherent potentials. It must be understood that some of our cultural beliefs are repressive and antidevelopment. Therefore, they must be rejected.

As a child, I was raised with grave fear in my mind. I grew up not allowed to ask questions about things I did not understand and was never allowed to ask for explanations as to why I had to do things in a particular way. It was a golden rule to never talk back at your parents or anyone older than you, or challenge anything said or done to you or you were asked to do. I was taught to just obey unequivocally. I am not alone in this regimental way of bringing up a child in Africa. It is normal. Many generations before mine went through it, and generations after my time are still going through this system of upbringing. However, things are beginning to show signs of change in the modern generation of Africans due to exploits of many through traveling, formal education, and generally relating to diverse people from other developed countries outside Africa. Still, this change has been painfully slow and sporadic.

As a result of my upbringing, I was unable to experience meaningful development as I subconsciously restricted myself from such activities that would have changed my fortune. My mind-set was such that I limited myself to activities that were not very challenging or daring in terms of exploration or cultivation of ideas that are considered too far into the unknown. I remained in my comfort zone, with no daredevil ideas of taking up challenges that undoubtedly would have had dramatic and life-changing effects on me. Again, I am not alone in this syndrome of playing safe to protect my existing position, especially if I am the breadwinner in a family. Everyone does the same thing.

Our education and training remain orthodox. Few privileged families were happy to have their children educated so that they are able to secure one of the normal jobs or careers such as doctor, engineer, lawyer, accountant, and administrator. Others solely engaged in trading and farming on a small scale. The majority of families and their offspring just wallowed in hard labor doing varied manual work throughout their lives serving others. Things are now beginning to change. Africans are excelling in the fields of science, technology, and medicine throughout the world. This shows that we are perfectly capable of doing more to change our economic and political destinies.

However, there is a big clog in the wheel of progress preventing a large number of Africans, educated or otherwise, from achieving success in their chosen professions or careers.

Africans work conscientiously, but many do not challenge or push the barriers hard enough. Since embracing Christianity and other forms of spiritual relationships with God, many Africans have grown weak. As a people, our blind but strong belief in God for miracles, signs, and wonders are causing many to fall by the wayside. While Jesus has been turned into a commodity, God has become the sole solution finder for all our problems. We are no longer able to exercise our God-given abilities to resolve problems. Even simple matters frighten many. Africans now package all their problems with little or no thought or imagination and run to God for solutions. The church and other spiritual places of worship have become shrines where solutions to all problems are solved through God. Members of various faiths ranging from orthodox churches to new-generation Pentecostal and African garment churches are flooded with members seeking spiritual solutions to common physical, psychological, and ideological problems. *It has never worked and will never work.*

Bishops, pastors, and other spiritual heads in these houses of worship are busy diagnosing problems, interpreting dreams, prophesying, and prescribing doses of prayers and tracts of fasting to cast away the demons and banish the devil and his works in the lives of worshippers. No misfortune is spared—death, sickness, barrenness, joblessness, failed business, migration and immigration, divorce, poverty, singledom and troubled marriage, and so on, are all tackled in the house of God. Instead of seeking information and professional advice concerning their business, career, jobs, health problems and general well-being, worshippers expend valuable time praying, fasting, and obeying the wills and commands of men of God. As they search for better life through God's intervention, their problems continue to multiply.

There is another group that does not fall into the above category. This group, some of whom are Christians and others non-Christians, have a completely different approach. They do not believe or rely on God coming to their rescue. Instead, they seek the help of other human beings believed to possess the powers to change their misfortunes. They are popularly known as native or witch doctors. Their activities involve plenty of diabolical exercises and processes. Some are said to involve sacrifices using human beings or their body parts. Even though no one can really prove this, it is a belief that permeates most African countries. As a Nigerian, I grew up with the notion that people can become rich if they carry out certain rituals. For example, in Nigeria there is an association known as the Ogboni cult (secret cult). It is widely believed that their members possess powers to do whatever they choose. It is also floated that they get their powers from diabolical processes of initiation and practice that guarantee their members affluence and prominence in society. Furthermore, as a result of the life-changing success of members, it is claimed that they pledge a token obligation or indebtedness to the cult. It is widely believed that some members choose to die early while others may sacrifice their manhood (impotence) for success sustenance and longevity. It is further alleged that other members of the Ogboni cult sacrifice their wife, first son, or mother to enhance fortune-changing process. None of these claims are confirmed to be true; they are merely claims and speculations.

The irony of this is that the so-called native or witch doctors with their inherent powers to change people's misfortunes also boast of the powers to cast spells on those who offend or fail to honor their pledge to them. By the same token, it is believed that within the Ogboni cult, erring members suffer punishments such as sudden death, loss of affluence and influence, and debilitating diseases. There is no truth in these claims. At best, they are mere speculations or superstition, not realities. These ideologies and beliefs have existed in most African countries for centuries and therefore have become engrossed in people's way of life. It is no surprise that many fail to attain their full potentials, thus falling short in economic and social development.

You do not have to live your life this way. God has given you the ability to achieve your goals in life. You have all that you need to make it great in life. Therefore, you do not need the help of a pastor or other spiritual persons to do it. For you to fully embrace meaningful growth, you need to have a new approach. First and foremost, you need to understand how things really work in the real world. You need to purge your mind of the wrong belief you presently hold—that is, God is the only answer to all your problems. These problems include poverty, disease, deprivation, and the biggest one of them all, corruption and political instability in Africa. Start applying the knowledge you have acquired through formal education or training to problem solving, and stop hoping that your lots will change so long as you have Jesus or whatever else you pin your belief on. It did not work for believers before you. Therefore, you are deluded if you continue to believe it will work for you. It has not and will never work for you. Your world will not develop through God's miracles, signs, and wonders. Development can only take place through your concerted efforts to develop yourself, your country, and your continent by doing the right physical things, not the spiritual mumbo jumbo.

Change your thought process to change your life for the better.

Chapter 14

Time Forgives No One

Whatever you plan to do in life, get up from your backside and do it the moment you are sure it is what you want to do. As the saying goes, "Time waits for nobody." Many ask themselves questions such as, "Am I doing the right thing?"; "What if things do not work out as I expect?"; "Is the time right for me to do this or do that?"; "How do I get the money or support to implement my plan?"; "Do I have enough knowledge or experience to do this or do that?"; "If the business venture fails, how do I cope with the failure, consequently the shame, and so on?" Well, I have got news for you. As long as you are burdened by all the above questions and self-doubt, you will never do anything to change your life situation. Many people spend eternity thinking, planning, consulting, procrastinating, and waiting for the right time. You are not alone in this situation.

During the course of writing this book, I interviewed many people across the ages of twenty to fifty years old. The result of the survey was staggering to say the least. Many of the interviewees do not know what they need to do to change their situation, whereas others are just satisfied with what they have (normal day jobs). So, you see, you are never alone. Now is the time for you to change the way you think. Change your negative, self-doubt approach and replace it with a positive, can-do approach. Remember, as I said in chapter 17, *"Realistic Thinking for Positive Change,"* you need to change the way you think to enable positive change to occur in your life.

As we go through life, we meet different people. The process of developing ourselves takes us through elementary to secondary school, then through university. For those who may not be academically privileged or inclined, you meet people from other walks of life such as trade, entertainment, business, and so forth. Those we come across have the capacity to influence our lives negatively or positively, depending on your perspective. When we come in contact with a successful person from a field or career path, whether or not it is the same as us, we wish we could be as successful as they are. We wish this upon ourselves even though we are not sure we can do what he or she does as a professional. This is very normal. However, for many, that is where it ends. If only everyone can pursue their thought of becoming successful as the other successful person, no one would be a failure in life.

Everyone has the ability to be successful. It is not bestowed upon a selected few as we often think or are made to believe. Those who are successful are not created differently from you by God. They do not enjoy a different relationship with God by way of serious prayers, dry or wet fasting, or unequaled knowledge of the Holy Bible. It is needless to remind practicing Christians that it is written in the Bible that "we are all equal before God." That is to say, you are equal to the next person and possess equal abilities. However, the difference in people (successful or failure) is dependent upon individual application of God-given abilities. It is not difficult. All you have to do is tap into the positive energy in you, focus on what you want, and go ahead and do it. Of course, it will be difficult, if not impossible, if you do not believe in yourself. The first and most important step to succeed in life is, believe in yourself.

Time does not forgive anybody for wasting it. If you waste your time in making up your mind about what you need to do to enjoy success, time will not forgive you. Every minute, day, and year you lose procrastinating or feeling unsure of what you want to do, you will be punished. Lost time can never be regained. Often, you find people doing something they ought to have done when they were young, and they say they are catching up with time. Nonsense! You can never catch up with time lost. True-life time is not like a television program you record, rewind, and play back. There is this old adage, "Make haste while the sun shines." However, it is never too late to start something. It is better to be late than never.

For those who are still young, decide today on what you want to do with your life. Seek information, advice, and support to enhance your success in whatever you choose to do. Apply yourself diligently, and you will succeed. You will liberate yourself from the burden of facing life not sure of who you are or where you belong. It is not an option to be passive in life. Be active and be part of the progressive elites. You are a special being, and when you start believing it, much will start to change for you. Life starts at forty (as it is often said), therefore, if you are one of the over-forties out there, do not despair. It is never too late to start. Start afresh; it does not matter how many times you have failed in the past. Your past failures may have been a result of your lack of belief in yourself or your being ill-equipped for the ventures. Now that you realize how powerful you can be, get yourself together and start on your journey to success today. Yes, now—not tomorrow.

Everyone deserves to be happy in life. It does not matter who you are, what your race is, or where you come from. If you do the right thing in your career or profession, you will be successful. Stop listening to negative statements that you hear every now and again about yourself, and stop feeling inadequate about yourself. Remember, everything you see around you today that have been created began with a *thought* by somebody. Therefore, start to think and plan positively today. I assure you that your level of success will even surprise you. If you continue to procrastinate and ignore this golden advice, time will not forgive you.

Think positive for realistic change.

Chapter 15

Superstition and Blame Culture

A great number of people across all ages and educational background are superstitious. This tendency can easily be traced to fundamental cultural and traditional beliefs most people hold. Irrespective of whether you are educated, your culture and way of life influence your thinking and reasoning when it comes to matters of poverty or success. Superstition and blame culture prevent people from having a positive view on matters of development and wealth, especially when things are not going so well. This is very common among religious people who believe that only God is able to make good things happen. On the other hand, the devil is responsible for all the bad things that happen to us. This belief is prevalent among Africans and those from developing countries. We are in the twenty-first century, yet many, particularly Africans, still believe that their failure to be successful in life is attributable to bad luck or misfortune caused by their enemies, usually within the family.

Apart from witchcraft spells, there is also the issue of generational curse. To many readers of this book, this may sound strange and confusing. Do not despair too much as I will endeavor to explain it. Many Africans, particularly those who are religious, are often told by their pastors and spiritual leaders that their poverty, ill-health, barrenness, sudden death, and so on are caused by a certain curse that has been placed upon their past generations (ancestors) that they have inherited. In another instance, they claim that generational curse could also be a result of indebtedness to the gods for a pledge our ancestors made in the past. These are speculations without proof, yet many still believe them. Instead of dealing with issues that confront them, such as poor health, unemployment, premature death, or failed business, in a logical way, many resort to endless prayers, fasting, and exorcism.

In recent times, there have been reported cases in Nigeria, Uganda, and the Congo of children and young adults tortured and killed because they have been condemned by pastors as witches and wizards. The question that begs for an answer is: After these children were tortured and killed by fake pastors or spiritual leaders, did the problems facing these families subside or completely disappear? The answer is emphatically no! I have only cited these few examples to buttress the fact that none of these are true. They are unfounded and are mere superstition. They are speculations born out of sheer ignorance and backwardness. The saddest thing about it all is that even educated people in our society are equally guilty of this calamity.

This problem grew out of our blame culture. People always look for someone to blame when things go wrong. Rather than search for real answers to their problems, they look for a scapegoat, be it their mother, father, husband, wife, brother, sister, uncle, aunt, neighbor, or coworker. Some people have gone as far as accusing their own children for their misfortunes. Whenever things go wrong, it has to be caused by someone who does not want their progress. As ridiculous as this may sound, many don't find it funny. They will go to any length to find out who among their family members is responsible. In doing so, they play into the hands of unscrupulous pastors and spiritual healers who take full advantage of their stupidity and grave ignorance.

This madness has to stop. As a people, you cannot afford to remain oblivious to the facts of life if you are to elevate yourselves. You have to start today to focus on what really matters to your existence. If you are a professional seeking employment, the first thing you do is make sure you are qualified and have the experience for the position for which you are applying. The second step is to make sure that you complete the application form as detailed as possible. If you are consequently selected for interview, prepare adequately to ensure you answer questions correctly and in detail during the interview. If you accomplish these preparations, you would have put yourself in good stead to do well in the interview—bearing in mind, of course, that there might be other candidates who are more brilliant and experienced than you.

This process applies to whatever profession or career path you may be pursuing in life. As a businessman or woman, you need to understand your business. Furthermore, you need to understand your product and your target market. With the understanding, you are able to manage your product development and marketing so that you can compete in the volatile marketplace. If you get your sums right, there is no reason why your business will not succeed. Furthermore, as an entrepreneur, apart from your products, the most important factor to your success is manpower. You need to engage the right people for the right jobs. Above all, there is a great need to treat them right as valued employees. Consequently, they will guarantee you good service for the growth and sustenance of your products and/or services.

This process applies to almost everything we do in life. As a student, if you want to pass your examinations and graduate with flying colors, you just have to study hard. You must complete all your assignments, essays, research, and assessments thoroughly. You cannot spend your precious time clubbing, partying, and spending romantic weekends away from campus and expect good results at the end of your course. For those of you who believe in signs and wonders, you will be disappointed when you receive your result and discover that you have failed your course. Instead of studying hard to make sure you make your grades, you have expended valuable time praying and fasting, hoping that the Holy Spirit will intervene in your case.

It cannot be emphasized enough that hard work and diligence will always be rewarded with success. On the other hand, failure is the product of laziness, lack of focus, or inconsistency. If you have failed in the past, stop looking at the dark corners of your life seeking someone to blame for your failure. It is never too late to start again.

Begin a new chapter in your life with renewed vigor and devotion, focus of your plan, and execute it with all sincerity of purpose. If, however, you are just starting off in life, purge yourself of all the negativities in your mind and hold on to all the positive thoughts concerning your product or idea. Success will be the name at the end.

It is said that as individuals, we often know where we went wrong in the past or when we are going wrong in whatever we are doing that is not coming off right. You only have to sincerely and boldly confront your fears and do the right thing, no matter how difficult the choice(s) may be. If you apply the same principle to everything you do in life, failure will be alien to you. But if you continue to resist the truth about yourself concerning your failures and shortfalls, change will never occur in your life. There is nothing spiritual (evil or good) about it. It is simple. I strongly believe that *"Life is like a bank account—what you put in is what you take out."*

If you learn to save, you will have a healthy bank balance. But if you keep spending all your earnings without saving, your account will always be in the red.

Learn to separate fiction from reality in everything you do; this way, you will be assured good results.

Chapter 16

Success: Reality against Fiction

In life, many dream of being rich, successful, and affluent. Most importantly, we dream of leaving our footprint in the history of time. However, not many realize this dream during their lifetime. For some, this dream comes true, but for others, it remains a fallacy and just a dream. The reality of it is that while we all dream of becoming someone successful and important during our time, many of us continue to dream while others wake up and go about setting up and pursuing factors that will enable the realization or actualization of our dreams. When we look around us, we are overwhelmed by examples of why some people succeed in life while others in the same environment fail. There are reasons for this, and I will try to examine some of them.

Before going further, I would like to look at the definition of success, what many describe as success, the different types of success, and perhaps what success means to different people. A simple dictionary definition of success may be, "The achievement of something desired, planned, or attempted." This is a very simple and concise meaning of success. However, success means different things to different people; therefore, it can be described in numerous ways. Many see success as the acquisition of a good portion of wealth: money and property. To others, success may mean creating something unique, special, and beneficial to humankind. This category of success could mean someone's success in designing a product, system, or ideology aimed at enhancing our environment or creating a direct impact on people's lives. It is therefore safe to say that success means different things to different people, depending on what in your opinion and understanding constitutes success.

To further examine the matter, I would like to invoke philosophy and morality in the debate and description of success. From a religious point of view—that is, for those who believe in a specific faith and religion—success may mean the level of one's relationship with God or indeed whatever is sacred to his or her religion and faith. This category of people will pursue their faith with every vigor, humility, and determination to succeed. Their ultimate goal and indeed success in life is to enter the kingdom of God or whatever represents eternity for them. That is the ultimate and absolute object or desire to the fulfillment of their lives. It does not matter to them if they have money, a house of their own, properties, cars, or other items that would make their lives more comfortable and enjoyable. It does not matter as long as they remain faithful to their religion and are assured to inherit eternity—that is, a good life after death. Morality and faithfulness to God rank very high in their priority. On the other end of the spectrum, there are other forms of success that people pursue. Some devote their entire life pursuing money and other materials that will make their lives and that of their family or generation after them very comfortable. Some in this group will do anything to get rich. It does not matter what it is, as long as the result means more money and wealth. This category of people may include drug dealers, fraudsters, hackers, and indeed all those who do evil, cause pain and discomfort to others, and profit from the action. That explains the notion that *there is no morality in business—everything goes as long as profit is guaranteed.*

To another group, legitimate business, general endeavors in enterprise, good education, training, planning, genuine desire and hard work to achieve, creating designs, and investing in products and services bring success. In this circumstance, the person(s) responsible can well be described as successful, rich, and wealthy, and they are therefore recognized, respected, and acknowledged by society. A final chapter to these descriptions is one segment of society who inherits wealth either as birth right imposed upon them or reborn into wealth by way of marriage, or dropped into it by way of winning the lottery. Either way, people in this category also treat wealth in different ways, and wealth means different things to them, too.

Now, having described and defined what constitutes success and what it means to different people, let us now look at the variety of factors or actions that bring us success or lack thereof.

Successful people dream big. So, for you to succeed in life, you must dream big. You must be clear in your mind what it is you want in life. You must be focused and above all, be 100 percent committed to whatever it is you choose to do to make your dream come true. As highlighted in a number of chapters in this book, what many lack is a clear-cut path they want their career or profession to take. To choose a career or profession suitable for you, first you must appreciate your personal qualities. By this I mean your individual characteristics. You need to acknowledge your strengths and weaknesses in order to determine what it is you are good at doing. Once you do this, you are then able to say to yourself, "I want to be an artist, engineer, pilot, doctor, furniture maker, etc."

After deciding on what it is you want to do, you then set out by seeking information and advice to adequately equip yourself. This aspect of the process is vital. Many plans fail because people do not know much about what they do and are unwilling to seek help and advice. You must, as a matter of necessity, make extra effort to research whatever academic pursuit, products, or services in which you venture. It is not only necessary, but it is also absolutely vital to do this if you want to succeed.

The reason why the above process is necessary is not farfetched. It is not enough to want to pursue a particular career or profession. You must understand and appreciate what is required to successfully go through the process of qualification to be a true professional in your chosen field. Failing to acknowledge this simple, yet vital, factor will spell doom for your dream to be successful.

On the other hand, many dream of success and great achievement but are not sure exactly what they need to do to achieve it. To this group of people, life is nothing short of fiction. That may sound a bit harsh, but it is true. It is not enough to wish to be successful; you have to want it so badly that you can smell it every time.

Unfortunately, unsuccessful people only wish success upon themselves; they never actually pursue it. If all you do is hope for fortune to locate you, then you must accept that it will never happen. It is now commonplace to find people trooping in and out of various churches and other spiritual places where they commune with God. A sizable number of them have a common goal—God's blessing. This does not necessarily mean feeling at peace with oneself. Oh no. It means abundant blessings (financial and material) from God. If you are one of them, you are still dreaming, and you need to wake up and face reality.

You continue to blame your personal circumstances and negative environmental influences for you failure. You need to look at yourself again. Ask yourself a few basic questions to ascertain that you are not to blame for your misfortune and failure.

- Am I good at what I do?
- What are my strengths and weaknesses?
- Am I 100 percent devoted to what I do?

- Do I manage my time well?
- Do I know enough about my chosen career path?
- Is help and further information available, and how can I source them?

The fact remains that in the same environment and place where you fail, many are recording success. Therefore, you must be doing something wrong. You need to examine yourself: what you do and how you do it. It is not necessarily the fact that individual circumstances or negative environmental influences are to blame for your failure. It must be something you are not doing right. Unless you accept this fact and commit yourself to change your approach, success will be alien to you.

You must alter the way you think. Replace your negative thoughts with positive thoughts so that you can see things for what they truly are. This will enable you to apply true solutions to whatever problems you may have.

Remember this key phrase: *Positive thinking for realistic change.*

Chapter 17

Realistic Thinking for Positive Change

Realistic thinking creates positive change. *True change cannot happen unless we change the way we think.* Being realistic about situations we are in, our environment, who we are, what we do, and with whom we associate, all play a part in how we feel, react, see, or do things. In other words, our environment, including those we relate to, help shape who we are. If that is true, it is incumbent upon us as individuals to recognize this fact when making efforts to change any unfavorable circumstance in which we may find ourselves, be it economic, educational, or social.

Many people are unhappy with their lives. Unhappiness may be a result of economic failure, educational inadequacy, or poor health. Often, people think they are not working hard enough, have been bewitched by their enemies, or are suffering from the sins of their ancestors (otherwise known as generational curse). This belief does not only compound their problems but also render them dysfunctional. Once in this state of mind, they focus all efforts on finding out what they should do to remove the so called curse or seek spiritual help to counter the evil spirit preventing their success. This quest takes them on diverse routes. While some resort to seeking spiritual solutions through shamans (African native doctors), others turn to modern churches (particularly Pentecostal and other African garment churches).

Being poor and underachieving makes one vulnerable. Some of these shamans and modern-church pastors target defenseless people in our society. Because of their desperate situation, these vulnerable people are willing to do anything to change their misfortune. Consequently, they are subjected to all kinds of rigorous and sometimes dehumanizing activities. In the process, people's minds are reprogrammed in line with the thoughts of those pretending to help them. They become an army of followers without thoughts of their own. Their ability to think and reason rationally has been taken away, and their minds are filled with the design thoughts of their new masters. One might think this is only peculiar to illiterates or primitive people. It is not true. Highly educated people are also fooled and deceived by these unscrupulous "men and women of God," as they are often called.

I have been through some tough times in my life, so I understand why many resort to all sorts of things to get out of their unfortunate economic and social predicaments. For many years, I struggled to find success. Every concerted effort I made was met with failure. At one point, I, too, believed that some "people" were against me. I thought I was not good enough at whatever I did. However, when I confronted the truth, I liberated myself. The truth is that I realized my emotions were ruling my thoughts. I let people—pastors, friends, family, and even professional colleagues—tell me what I should and should not do. The solution was simple. I took just one single step: *I simply changed the way I thought. I replaced my negative thoughts with positive thoughts.* That is what I did, and everything changed for me.

As an educated person, you are knowledgeable enough to know that the sins of your parents or grandparents have no bearing on your poor health or underachievement in life. Nothing in the spirit world is equally capable to define your success or lack thereof. Simply put, that is utter nonsense! Whether you acquire formal education or not, God created you with adequate powers and abilities to do things that will define your life. All you need to do is have a clear vision about your life and where you want to be. Then you go about achieving your goals by doing the right things.

This can only happen when you change the way you think. You need to be realistic about yourself and things around you. You need to start seeing things for what they truly are and not what they seem. To achieve this, you must first purge yourself of all superstitious and spiritual misconceptions about things happening in your life. You need to look at yourself and assess your abilities and capabilities to adequately identify your potentials. This will lead you to direct actions that will guarantee that success in anything you choose to do. It does not matter whether it is picking up employment or engaging in a trade or business. Whatever choice you make, you are able to put in all your effort because you understand what you are doing, and you believe in yourself. I have no doubt whatsoever that when you identify your goals, your given strengths and abilities when applied judiciously, will assure you success.

People's belief that their hardship and misfortune will change after denying themselves food in the form of fasting and spending endless time in the church or other places of worship offering sacrifices and supplication to God is a cause for worry and is highly questionable. I am not in any way discounting people's religious beliefs—far from it. However, I am concerned about the reverence people pursue their faith when it comes to doing the right thing about their lives. I was once a staunch member of a progressive Pentecostal church in London where I was a deputy leader in the drama department. That position drew me very close to the hierarchy within the church. Also, I was highly spiritual to a great extent, carrying out all stipulated and prescribed prayers and fasting exercises as indication of my commitment and belief. At the time, I was going through hard times economically and health-wise. Despite the length of fasting and volume of prayers, my lot never changed. I only encountered breakthrough when I changed the way I think. Now that I have shared this experience with you, I hope that you will do the same so that you, too, can experience economic and social liberation.

Change the way you think. Think positive for realistic change!

Printed in Great Britain
by Amazon

Human Reason and Its Enemies

A Rigorous Critique of Postmodernism

Human Reason and Its Enemies
A Rigorous Critique of Postmodernism

Sheryar Ookerjee

PROMILLA & CO., PUBLISHERS
in association with
BIBLIOPHILE SOUTH ASIA
NEW DELHI & CHICAGO

Published by
PROMILLA & CO., PUBLISHERS
in association with
BIBLIOPHILE SOUTH ASIA
URL: www.biblioasia.com

C-127, Sarvodaya Enclave
New Delhi 110 017, India

First published in 2009

ISBN: 978-81-85002-94-1

Typeset in AGaramond
Layout by Suresh Sharma

Printed and bound in India by Bibliophile South Asia (Printing Division), New Delhi

Contents

Prelude • The Mischievous Mirror   9

1 • Reason: There's the Enemy   11

2 • The Pedigree   18

3 • Philosophy: Search for the Non-Existent Black Cats   22

4 • Poor Descartes   26

Interlude • Wittgenstein's Parrots   32

5 • Assault on Saraswati   36

6 • Contextuality, Truth and Absurdity   57

7 • Is Ratiocination Dead?   82

8 • The Golem   130

9 • Cultural Monadology   152

10 • The Ghostly Point   183

11 • Can Dinosaurs and Dragons Be Tamed?   201

12 • The Roar of the Paper Tiger   234

13 • The Wonderworld of Feminism   294

Postlude • Vanitas Vanitatum   359

Bibliography   363

Index   366

Dedicated to
J.C.P. d'Andrade
who taught us
what philosophy is

Acknowledgements

I thank the Indian Council of Philosophical Research and its then Chairman, Shri Kireet Joshi, for awarding me the Council's National Fellowship for two years (2004–2006), which made it possible for me to write this book.

I am grateful to Dr. Aspi Billimoria, Professor Persis Kothawalla, Professor Shirin Kudchedkar, Mr. Yogesh Kamdar, and Professor John Lyle for reading the manuscript, making corrections and giving suggestions.

I express my appreciation to (Mrs.) Freny Mehta and (Mrs.) Hutoxi Panthaki for typing out the final version of the manuscript.

Prelude

The Mischievous Mirror

In 1979, Richard Rorty produced *Philosophy and the Mirror of Nature*, in which he argued that philosophy does not mirror nature or anything else. Now imagine you are looking into a mirror. Instead of your face you see the back of your head, and yet it looks like your face; you are seen standing on your head, and yet your feet are firmly on the ground; your nose has curled round your neck, throttling you, and yet you are smiling happily; you feel that you are bodily in the mirror and your mirror-image is leering at you from outside. Postmodernism, or whatever you may call it, is this mirror.

If you pick up a book whose title suggests it is a book on philosophy, if you look at the index for the usual philosophical topics, if you start reading the pages indicated, and if you get a rather strange feeling, a kind of weightlessness and disorientation, then you have begun reading a book on postmodernism.

The purpose of this essay is – to change the metaphor – to pin down this slippery, wriggling, amorphous creature and examine it.

The task is extremely difficult, for the creature constantly changes whatever shape it has, shrugging off one of its skins (of which it has a good supply) and slipping it on as required. If you think you have got it, it turns itself inside out, laughs in your face, declaring that it was only teasing you and you should not have taken it seriously. In this teasing mood it calls itself 'ironism'. The puzzle is that it has been taken seriously not only by its buddies, but also even by fairly decent philosophers. My attempt is to treat it seriously and show that it should not be taken seriously. If this strikes you as a paradox, postmodernism thrives on 'paradox and style'.

The reader will probably feel irritated at finding my writing too liberally strewn with quotations, hampering the flow of the narrative. I have done it in order to show that I am not conjuring up spooks and then exorcising them, but dealing with real people and their real work.

Chapter 1

Reason: There's the Enemy

'Here, where men sit and hear each other groan.'
John Keats, *Ode to a Nightingale*

Postmodernism sometimes regards itself as philosophy, at other times it regards philosophy as its enemy, and sometimes it assumes both attitudes simultaneously. In its pontifical stance, it is philosophy, but when it is critically assessed, it turns into a 'theoretical and representational "mood"', which has emerged out of 'purely *aesthetic* concerns'.

Writes Giles Deleuze, a postmodern master:

> Discussion is a narcissistic exercise, where ... no one knows what they are talking about ...
> How does discussion take place if there is no common set of problems, and why should discussion occur if there is one? ... But discussion is in no way part of philosophical work.[1]

This passage, says Bouveresse, is 'quite representative of the methods used by many great thinkers of contemporary philosophy' who make their refusal to discuss appear in the guise of a theory implying that 'discussion in philosophy is futile'. The benefit of this stance is that one is 'once and for all immune to the objections other philosophers might be inclined to make'.[2]

According to postmodernism, says C. Norris, 'we have moved into a new (and yet unthinkable) stage of postmodern evolution' where 'we had best help the process along by not putting up any kind of misguided theoretical resistance'.[3]

So, while postmodernism has a theory about the futility of philosophy, it also believes a theoretical resistance to its own theories to be misguided. Paradox (or shall we say, contradiction?) is the heart of postmodernism.

Apart from theory itself, postmodernism has many other phobias. The Enlightenment is one of them.

According to Kant, 'Enlightenment is man's release from his self-incurred tutelage', which is 'man's inability to make use of his understanding without direction from another, and the cause lies not in lack of understanding but in lack of resolution and courage to use it'. 'Laziness and cowardice are the reasons why so great a portion of mankind ... remain under lifelong tutelage', for 'I have a book which understands for me, a pastor who has a conscience for me ... I need not trouble myself. I need not think'.[4]

It is clear that, for Kant, the refusal to think is due to a defect of will; no fault is felt with the understanding or reason. Michel Foucault disagrees. For him, 'enlightened reason ... has placed us in the iron grip of forms of oppression ... more insidiously powerful than postmodern forms of control' (such as physical force and torture); it is the 'ideological arm of the rationalizing and dehumanizing logic of industrial capital's drive towards an efficiency which is its own (ultimately irrational) end'.[5] This, says Waugh, has consistently been Foucault's position, though later he 'somewhat modifies his earlier position and commends Enlightenment's critical perspective ... and emphasis on autonomy'.[6] For Kant, autonomy is the ground on which reason can perform.

Foucault's hostility to reason is not because he finds any defect in reason itself, nor does he find anything wrong in the Enlightenment as such. It is based on his belief that capitalism uses reason to rationalize its drive towards its irrational ends. Whether that be so or not, the very mention of 'rationalizing' pejoratively and of 'irrational' with disapproval, implies that there is, or at least could be, a rational, non-rationalizing use of reason and that there can be rational, as opposed to irrational, ends.

Alasdair MacIntyre summarizes the Enlightenment aspiration thus:[7] 'to provide ... standards and methods of rational justification' by 'appeal to principles undeniable by any rational person and therefore independent of ... social and cultural particularities'. This is fair, but one wonders from where he got his next point: that 'rational justification could be nothing other than what the thinkers of the Enlightenment had said that it was came to be accepted' by the 'vast majority of educated people'. Even if that were so, it does not, of course, mean that the standards and methods provided by the Enlightenment could not be corrected or improved on as long as you subscribed to the Enlightenment idea of reason and its autonomy.

MacIntyre very confidently asserts that we 'already have the best of reasons for supposing that' the standards of the

Enlightenment 'cannot be met'. Perhaps they can at least be approximated and used with profit. Foucault's anger against Enlightenment reason knows no bounds. The world that reason has set up 'in its own terms' is a 'manifestation of a will to power which secures itself through an insidious exclusion of all that it identifies as non-rational: desire, feeling, sexuality, femininity, art, madness, criminality, non-Caucasian races, particular ethnicities'. Reason is 'seen as part of the impulse to control and subjugate which is the logic of capitalism … colonialism, racism, sexism', and even the 'destruction of the environment'.[8] Against such rage, reason and argument are helpless.

Feminists claim to have exposed 'the most entrenched and disguised contradictions and limitations of Enlightenment thought', which claims universality as one of its features but in which 'this "universal" principle is contradicted'. How so? Because it makes a 'split of public/private', consigning women to the 'private' realm of 'feeling and domesticity' different from 'a public realm of Reason as masculine'. In this at least, says Patricia Waugh, 'feminism can be seen as an intrinsically "postmodern" discourse'.[9] And in this, also, we see an example of postmodern distortion.

'By the public use of one's reason, I understand the use which a person makes of it as a scholar before the reading public,' writes Kant. 'Private use I call that which one may make of it in a particular civil post or office', where 'one must obey orders'.[10] This is certainly a strange use of 'public' and 'private' on Kant's part, but stranger still it is to see it made to coincide with masculine and feminine, respectively. Surely, feminists do not think that in Kant's time, civil posts and offices were filled by women and that even if they were, they were realms of feeling and domesticity.

It also turns out that the contradictions that feminists see in the Enlightenment are really in feminism itself, for, writes Waugh, feminist theory recognizes 'a central contradiction in its attempts to define an epistemology: that women seek equality ... which has been constructed through the very culture ... which feminism seeks to challenge and dismantle... Awareness of such contradictions' (so there are others too?) emerged 'as early as 1971', says Waugh;[11] that is, among feminists themselves; others saw them much earlier.

The belief in inherent human rationality is the core of Enlightenment thought. Postmodernism's assault on the Enlightenment is an assault on reason. According to Lyotard, enlightenment values 'are totally obsolete', having produced 'nothing more than a lamentable series of failed or miscarried political projects'.[12] Postmoderns can never leave politics alone.

Those who stand by reason believe that it transcends personal situations and prejudice and reaches a point 'which would apply to all rational beings', but the 'most radical mode of postmodern thought is that which rejects Kantian reason and autonomy', 'even as an ideal'.[13] It celebrates the 'collapse of the grand narratives of history, justice, equality, founded on the concept of universal reason', whose basic features have always been thought to be objectivity, impartiality and universality. Philosophy, so far understood (even if criticized) as an attempt to understand the universe, has to give place to hermeneutics, the technique of interpretation, which, according to MacIntyre, is somehow to repair the fragmentation caused by the Enlightenment. Truth is to be abandoned, because 'knowledge always arises out of embodiment, cultural and biological'.

'Postmodernism tends to claim an abandonment of all metanarratives which could legitimate foundations for truth', for 'we neither need them, nor are they any longer desirable', though, it seems, once upon a time they were. The same goes for truth itself. The collapse of the grand narratives 'was famously proclaimed by Lyotard … but was already familiar in the thought of Nietzsche, Wittgenstein and Foucault'. But, adds Waugh, 'There is often an alternative foundationalism lurking in many postmodern arguments.'

Leave alone truth, even meaning is claimed to have been 'shown to be radically indeterminate', enmeshed in 'an endless intertextuality', with 'no space outside of text, no origin or source of meaning', no ' "foundationalism": the idea that knowledge is the reflection of truth' with a stable foundation in Reason. All this was shown by Derrida, Lacan and Barthes.

The implication of this, says Waugh, 'is that "truth" cannot be distinguished from "fiction"', nor, I would say Descartes and Kant from Derrida and Foucault, nor anybody from anybody. All are indeterminate. Indeed, all so-branded foundationalisms of reason, all '"totalities" of Enlightenment universalism', are equated by Lyotard with 'totalitarianism and terror'. Recent history has had a crippling effect on the postmodern mind.

There is a cozy smugness coupled with a gloomy prophetic or 'apocalyptic' strain among postmoderns. The Enlightenment may, they believe, 'be coming to an end, strangled by its own logic'. What is that logic? Anything even remotely connected with 'information technology, consumerism and global economics, which erode the stability of concepts such as nation, state, or essential human nature'. But these are concepts which postmodernism rejects! Arnold Toynbee believes that 'the postmodern age would be the ... final phase of Western history and one dominated by anxiety, irrationalism and helplessness', where 'consciousness is adrift, unable to anchor itself to any universal ground of justice, truth or reason'.

In the last five paragraphs I have quoted rather generously from Waugh's *Postmodernism* (pp. 4-6) to give the reader a vivid and true picture of postmodernism in the words of the postmoderns themselves, a picture which will form the basis of my critical assessment of this 'philosophy'.

References

1. Deleuze, G., quoted by J. Bouveresse, 'Reading Rorty', in Brandom, R. (Ed.), 2001, p. 142.
2. Bouveresse, J., op. cit., p. 142.
3. Norris, C., 1990, p. 165.
4. Waugh, P., 1992, *Postmodernism*, pp. 90-91.
   The passage from Kant is a modified version of a translation by L. W. Beck, *Kant on History* (1963).
5. Ibid., p. 88.
6. Ibid., p. 88.
7. MacIntyre, A., 1988, pp. 6-7.
8. Waugh, P., 1992, *Practising Postmodernism*, p. 74.
9. Ibid., p. 119.
10. Waugh, P., 1992, *Postmodernism*, p. 92.
11. Waugh, P., 1992, *Practising Postmodernism*, p. 119.
12. Norris, C., 1990, p. 7.
13. Waugh, P., 1992, *Practising Postmodernism*, pp. 67-68.

Chapter 2

The Pedigree

'Irrevocably dark, total eclipse
Without all hope of day.'
John Milton, *Samson Agonistes*

Friedrich Nietzsche occupies, in the postmodern world, a position akin to that occupied by Old Major in Orwell's *Animal Farm*. He is the patriarch (matriarch, our feminists would insist) who spawned a brood of anti-rational, anti-philosophical views. Perhaps we could go further back in the genealogy of postmodernism to the Greek Sophists, but let it be.

Nietzsche writes:

> The deeper one looks, the more our valuations disappear
> – meaningless approaches! We have *created* the world that
> possesses value! Knowing this, we know, too, that
> reverence for truth is already the consequence of an
> illusion.
>
> (*The Will to Power*, p. 602)

Shirley Jethmalani, sympathetic to Old Major, tells us there are 'no facts in Nietzsche's view, therefore there are no truths but only interpretations from different perspectives'.[1] While

Kant held that the empirical world is interpreted by our perspective, it is the 'only one possible perspective', the human perspective, 'universal' for the species. But Nietzsche believes, and believes it to be true, that there are 'an indefinitely large number of historically and biologically permissible perspectives'. Who has permitted them? None of these 'can be regarded as constituting genuine knowledge'. 'Nietzsche is a relativist.' Surprisingly, he is said to make a 'most significant contribution to philosophy', which is 'that all our central conceptions are errors'. He also 'found the culture of his own time and country completely suffocating'.[2] He managed for sixty-five years, though!

The postmodern hobby-horse connecting reasoning with seeking power is to be found in Nietzsche. 'Scientists "seek the truth whatever the consequences", hence, their discoveries are so often used for destructive purposes', and 'secular crusaders for truth and justice fight for world domination', the 'drive to knowledge', along with the sex drive, being, in Nietzsche's words, 'both signs of vulgarity'.[3] It is clear that for Nietzsche, the difference between the politicians who crave world domination and the scientists is too insignificant to matter.

Nietzsche rejects the logical laws of identity and non-contradiction as 'fictions', the former being inapplicable to reality because it is always in flux. He believes that the human tendency to behave as if logical principles were true, is an 'advantage in the struggle for existence, but might not always be useful in the future'.[4] Like steroids, they must be used rarely and selectively. They may have helped before Nietzsche's time, but after the birth of the messiah of anti-reason, such laws would only be a nuisance.

Engaging in argument with Socrates would be, for Nietzsche, a 'subjection to the tyranny of reason', points out MacIntyre. 'Socrates is not to be argued with; he is to be mocked for his ugliness and his bad manners.' Nietzsche speaks, instead, in aphorisms; an 'aphorism is not an argument', says MacIntyre; it is, says Deleuze, 'a play of forces'.[5]

Nietzsche, who regarded himself as the 'first perfect nihilist of Europe' (*The Will to Power,* p. 3), is, at the same time a prophet – of doom, naturally – and *The Will to Power* has, says Jethmalani, a 'biblical ring', for he saw that 'the cultural forces … would inevitably land nineteenth-century Europe in a predicament of having to go without any meaning or purpose'.[6]

Teichman thinks Nietzsche's nihilism can be answered by confronting him with the dilemmas and contradictions of his own utterances. But this would be the Socratic way, which Nietzsche looks down his nose at. He cannot be hoist with his own petard, for dilemmas and contradictions are, for him, fictions (and so is the petard). Our author sighs in despair: 'Nietzsche himself sometimes says one thing and sometimes says another', and solemnly Teichman informs us, 'He is not a consistent thinker and it is not much use to turn him into one.'[7] Then why not just throw him overboard?

It is clear that postmoderns have learned all their tricks from the grandmaster. A lesser master is Jean Paul Sartre, a founding father of existentialism. He holds that there are no objective moral laws, morality itself being a kind of fiction. MacIntyre comments on Nietzsche and Sartre: 'Both saw their own task as in part that of founding a new morality, but in the writings of both it is at this point that their rhetoric … becomes cloudy and opaque, and metaphorical assertions replace argument.' The Superman (*Ubermensch*) of Nietzsche and the 'Sartrian Existentialist-cum-Marxist belong in the pages of a philosophical bestiary rather than a serious discussion'.[8] (A bestiary is a moralizing treatise on animals.) And MacIntyre is sympathetic to postmodernism! Or is he?

References

1. Jethmalani, S., 1993, p. 5.
2. Teichman, J., 'Friedrich Nietzsche' in Teichman, J. & G. White (Eds.), 1995, pp. 77-78, 85.
3. Ibid., pp. 77-78.
4. Ibid., pp. 85-86.
5. MacIntyre, A., 1988, p. 368.
6. Jethmalani, S., 1993, p. 89.
7. Teichman, J., op. cit., p. 86.
8. MacIntyre, A., 1985, p. 22.

Chapter 3

Philosophy: Search for the Non-Existent Black Cats

'I maintain that one should always talk philosophy with a smile.'

J. Renan

MacIntyre says that 'philosophy as an ... autonomous enquiry to be conducted by professionalized specialists is in the end barren' and the 'attempted professionalization of serious and systematic thinking has had a disastrous effect upon our culture'.[1] We are told that post-modernism and feminism 'have offered deep and far-reaching criticism of the institution of philosophy' and 'have sought to develop new paradigms of social criticism which do not rely on traditional philosophical epistemologies'.[2]

Jane Flax lists beliefs which, though still prevalent, are derived from the Enlightenment and which 'postmodern philosophers seek to throw into radical doubt'.[3] Some of the tougher black cats are:

1. The 'existence of a stable, coherent self' whose properties include 'a form of reason capable of privileged insight into its own processes and into the "laws of nature"'.

2. That 'Reason and its "science" – philosophy – can provide objective, reliable, and universal foundations for knowledge'.

3. That 'the knowledge acquired from the right use of reason will be "true" … will represent something real and unchanging (universal) about our minds and the structure of the natural world'.

4. That 'reason itself has transcendental and universal qualities' and that its 'bodily, historical, and social experiences do not affect reason's structure and its capacity to produce atemporal knowledge'.

5. That 'all claims to truth and rightful authority are to be submitted to the tribunal of reason' and that 'the rules that are right for me … will necessarily be right for all other such beings'.

6. That 'science, as the exemplar of the right use of reason, is also the paradigm for all true knowledge'.

7. That 'language is in some sense transparent'.

Some of these beliefs of traditional philosophy are stated a little too vaguely, ambiguously and inaccurately, but the list gives a fair idea as to what postmodernism is opposed to.

What 'continues to unify philosophy in English is a determination that philosophical discussion and debate are to be conducted through the critical construction and discussion of … arguments', says Thomas Baldwin. 'Yet, surprisingly, there is currently an influential opinion which holds that this optimism is altogether misguided' and that philosophy is a 'largely futile and anachronistic cultural relic'; 'we must prepare ourselves for "post-philosophical modes of discussion"'.[4]

These, however, are not modes of discussion at all; they are, according to Richard Rorty, 'satires, parodies, aphorisms'. Baldwin tells us that postmoderns like Foucault and Derrida do not despise discussion altogether; it is Rorty, he says, for whom there is no longer any merit in discussing issues like truth, knowledge and meaning. Rorty's view is based on his conception of Descartes' conception of mind as a 'mirror of nature', and Rorty pontificates that such a conception 'has been definitely overthrown' by Dewey, Heidegger, Sellars, Quine and Davidson, and of course, himself. [6]

Rorty admits that these mind-busters have no '*alternative* "theories of knowledge" or "philosophies of mind"', for they do not "argue against"' Descartes and company: they only 'set aside' their theories and set aside epistemology and metaphysics as possible disciplines; they are not concerned in 'discovering false propositions or bad arguments', for they hold the vocabulary of traditional philosophy just 'pointless'. But is not Rorty himself making a philosophical point and arguing? 'Although I discuss "solutions"', he retorts, 'this is not in order to propose one but to illustrate' that there is no problem. His work, like that of his philosophical role models, is 'therapeutic rather than constructive'. [7] Philosophy as therapy is at least not pointless, and its tools are, like all philosophy, propositions and arguments.

Continental thinkers, strongly influenced by Nietzsche, Heidegger and Sartre, either subscribe to, or are sympathetic to, postmodernism. Jurgen Habermas is critical of it, seems to have got out of it, and yet cannot quite tear himself away from it. He has tried to 'relegitimate the tradition of Western philosophy that one associates with the Enlightenment', and not as *Western* but 'on a universalistic basis', which means stressing the universalistic character of reason. This characteristic, he believes, makes communication possible between humans, however far they may be separated in space and time. It also separates humans from non-humans.[8]

References

1. MacIntyre, A., 1988, p. x.
2. Fraser, N. & L. J. Nicholson, 'Social Criticism without Philosophy' in Nicholson, L. J. (Ed.), 1990, p. 26.
3. Flax, J., 'Postmodern and Gender Relations in Feminist Theory' in Nicholson, L. J. (Ed.), 1990.
4. Baldwin, T., 2001, pp. 268-69.
5. Rorty, R., 1983, p. 369.
6. Baldwin, T., 2001, p. 270.
7. Rorty, R., 1983, pp. 6-7.
8. Strong, T. B. & F. A. Sposito, 'Habermas's Significant Other' in White, S. K. (Ed.), 1955, p. 264.

Chapter 4

Poor Descartes

Epistemology: Magic Eye or Blind Spot?

Epistemology (the study of knowledge) has always been regarded as an arm of philosophy, the other arms being ontology and axiology, with both of which it has important connections. Postmodernism is hostile to epistemology, partly due to confusion and partly to error.

Charles Taylor points out that postmoderns are unfairly hostile to epistemology, because epistemology is only the name of a 'problem area', the area of human knowledge. The nature, capacity and extent of knowledge have always been thought to be open to philosophical enquiry. As such, as a discipline, epistemology is uncommitted to any particular doctrine. Nevertheless, Taylor thinks that epistemology deserves the bad name it has got, because a certain epistemological doctrine to which Descartes gave articulation has given epistemology a pride of place it should not have. The doctrine is that we must first 'somehow come to grips with the problem of knowledge', find out what knowledge is like, and only then determine what we can know about the world, human life and God. This somehow gets the postmoderns' goat. This 'terrible and fateful illusion', declares Taylor, has wreaked 'havoc throughout the intellectual culture of modernity'! So 'epistemology' for postmoderns is any theory or view about knowledge that they don't like.

Rorty attacks a particular kind of epistemology – that which is practised in 'the Cartesian and British empiricist tradition'. 'He has no time for a different, and perhaps useful, kind of reflection.'[2]

Does Descartes mean that unless you first understand the human mind and the nature of knowledge, you cannot raise other issues? Even if you interpret him to mean this, it is still a question whether he means that the nature and function of the mind are to be understood psychologically or otherwise, that is, epistemologically. If psychologically, then epistemology will be 'naturalized' and will become one of the sciences.

The two principal arguments forming the basis of the Cartesian philosophy – the *cogito* and the ontological argument – are far from being psychological; they are not even epistemological. Therefore the charge of holding that unless we first understand knowledge we cannot raise other issues cannot be laid at least at Descartes' door.

Descartes' epistemology, says Taylor, 'assumes, wrongly, that we can get to the bottom of what knowledge is, without drawing on our … understanding of human life and experience'. This criticism, whether true of Descartes or not, needs to be examined. It is too imprecise. How much of life and experience are needed to be able to understand the nature of knowledge? Certainly, we must have some first-hand acquaintance with knowledge-seeking before we can start investigating its nature, just as without some experience of morality you cannot do moral philosophy. But, surely, it is not necessary to consider human life in general or those aspects of human experience, like swimming and eating, which are not directly cases of knowing, in order to understand knowledge.

'The heart of the old epistemology was the belief in a *foundational* enterprise,' writes Taylor, which means that the credentials of all the truth claims of the positive sciences must be checked by this 'rigorous discipline' called epistemology, which 'would ultimately make clear just what made knowledge claims valid'. Such 'foundationalism' has to be abandoned, which means the overcoming of epistemology.[4]

I do not know if there is anything to support this view of the old epistemology. Such a 'foundational' claim is preposterous. If at all there is a discipline that can check the validity of scientific claims, it would be formal logic, though, even so, it would be silly to suggest that scientists must run to logicians or epistemologists to have the validity of their theories tested. To understand, philosophically, the nature of knowledge is not to possess a magic eye that can expose all scientific errors.

Jean-Francois Lyotard, committed to the 'anti-epistemological strand of postmodernist thought', also seems to labour under the misapprehension that epistemology is somehow concerned with norms of thinking. Thinking, for him, is playing a 'language game' and its rules are strictly 'local'. There are no 'trans-local norms of rationality and justification' and to try and impose such on thought would be 'an act of "terror"'.[5] The 'rules defining a game and the "moves" playable within it *must* be local … agreed on by its players and subject to … cancellation', writes Lyotard.

Lyotard's locality is not even the locality of a culture or even a social group. It is the locality of 'a fleeting agreement by "present players", something closer to a single conversation', comments Fricker, very far removed from an 'entrenched and historically stable discursive practice' such as most postmoderns believe thinking to be. Fricker calls Lyotard's a 'bizarrely voluntaristic brand of relativism'.[7] According to it, each conversation between parties is considered to be correct or incorrect according to specific, unique rules fixed (in advance or, maybe, as they go along) by the parties themselves. Imagine the following scenario:

At a social gathering, Friedrich, Dick and Jean have formed a group and agreed on rules 'a', 'b', and 'c', according to which they could converse. Genevieve, Donna and Sandra have formed another group and agreed to converse according to rules 'l', 'm', and 'n', which they have jointly formulated. After some conversations, Dick who gets easily bored, is bored with the conversation of his cronies and moves over to join the other group. But he has not agreed to rules 'l', 'm', and 'n', so he doesn't know what on earth they are talking about or whether they are even talking sense. Now, though Genevieve and her friends are willing to allow Dick to play their language game, they are at a loss to explain to him what the rules are, for they cannot do it according to rules 'a', 'b', and 'c', for those are not the rules of their language game, and they cannot do it according to rules 'l', 'm', and 'n', because Dick hasn't yet agreed to them and therefore cannot understand them. Either poor Dick will be left high and dry or Genevieve, Donna, Sandra and Dick will have to invent another game and formulate new rules by which to play the game.

In the meanwhile, Friedrich and Jean have their own problems. Friedrich accuses Jean of not playing the game according to the rules they have agreed on, for he (Jean) insists on saying that p is self-contradictory and so he cannot accept it, while Friedrich, very angry, reminds him that according to rule 'b', which they have agreed on, there is nothing wrong about self-contradictions and therefore he should accept p. This is a conversational deadlock. Will they now have to appeal to some trans-local norms to resolve the dispute? That would be blasphemy. Like a certain Indian thinker, they would be reduced simply to wagging a finger. But why even that?

If we were to take Lyotard really seriously, each person would have to formulate his own rules, local to himself alone, and then, too, not once and forever but different rules from moment to moment – locality *in excelsis*. In fact, one would not be able to hold a conversation even with oneself; in other words, think.

'The insistence on the localness of all norms of judgement renders postmodernism incapable of sustaining ordinary critical judgements, such as … that some beliefs are plain false. The question whether any particular critical judgement is reasonable cannot depend on the "agreement" of those who happen to be one's interlocutors.' But, why only critical judgements? Surely this would be true of all judgements. Fricker adds that 'not all forms of postmodernism need imitate Lyotard's rhetorical extremes'.[8] However, the relativism of norms is an essential feature of postmodernism and Lyotard's extremes are the logical culmination, a *reductio ad absurdum* of that relativism. If you go the whole hog, that's where you will land, but, of course, postmodernism being skeptical of logic, will stop short of going the whole hog.

Rorty, as one would expect, dismisses epistemology altogether. He does not 'substitute one sort of account of human knowledge for another', but wants to 'get away from the notion of "an account of human knowledge"'.[9] However, his writings, as critics have pointed out, 'articulate a number of claims which obviously add up to a substantial (if controversial) account of knowledge'. In spite of this, for Rorty, the subject matter of epistemology is 'illusory and does not exist'. '*Knowledge* is first of all a word, not a thing-in-itself about which we should expect an interesting theory.'[10] Rorty finds most things uninteresting and, like a peevish child, throws them out of the window.

References

1. Taylor, C., 1997, p. vii.
2. McDowell, J., 'Towards Rehabilitating Objectivity' in Brandom, R. B. (Ed.), 2001, p. 109.
3. Taylor, C., 1997, pp. vii-viii.
4. Ibid., p. 2.
5. Fricker, M., 'Feminism in Epistemology' in Fricker, M. & J. Hornsby (Eds.), 2000, p. 149.
6. Lyotard quoted by Fricker, op. cit., p. 149.
7. Fricker, M., op. cit., p. 149.
8. Ibid., pp. 149-50.
9. Rorty, R., 1983, p. 180.
10. Barry, A., 'What is Epistemology' in Brandom, R. B. (Ed.), 2001, pp. 220-21.

Interlude
Wittgenstein's Parrots
Language Games and Other Baubles

Whenever a great master makes a discovery and proclaims it to the world, lesser mortals bandy it about and use it to make some point of their own and impress others. This has happened with Wittgenstein's concept of language games. In matters of truth and knowledge, it is used to throw you off the scent in pursuing a consistent and rigorous argument. Theories, particularly scientific theories, are said to be language games, and when science moves from one theory, like the Ptolemaic, to another, like the Copernican, it is described as a change from one game to another. This sort of talk is so glib and paraded with such a show of obviousness that we should look at it more closely.

1. It is conveniently concealed that 'language' here does not literally mean language in the ordinary sense, the sense in which we speak of English or Hindi or even a signalling code or musical notation. 'Language' here means a theory, a view, a manner of understanding. When, sometimes,

we say in exasperation to an opponent, 'we don't seem to be speaking the same language,' we don't mean that I am speaking English and you are speaking German; we mean that we are not able to understand each other's views. When Rorty, for example, keeps talking of language, it is a clever strategy to evade problems about truth. He is actually talking about a change in beliefs; beliefs have to be true or false, but languages can't be either.

2. Further, (intentionally produced) confusion is occasioned by speaking of theories as 'games', and that, too, 'language games'. Sophistical use is made of the fact that languages and games have something in common – the fact that they have rules – rules made by people or evolved through use, which have to be followed if we want to use a particular language or play a particular game. This does not mean that languages (in the common, garden sense) are games or that games are languages (the fallacy of the undistributed middle). Confusion is multiplied when, from language understood literally as language, we now jump to language in the sense of theory. Theories are also formed according to certain rules, the rules of scientific investigation and formulation of theory, but they are very different from the rules of games and languages, for they are concerned with truth and validity. Theories propound laws, which may look like rules but they are discovered and not made or decided like the rules of languages and games. You can switch from English to Gujarati (Parsis do it all the time, even within the same sentence) or from playing badminton to playing tennis as the fancy takes

you, but you cannot skip from one theory to another just because you are, as Rorty suggests, fed up with the earlier one.

3. Trading on the equivocation of language (language in the ordinary sense and language as theory), postmodernism tries to wriggle out of the question of truth. If we ask whether a theory (language game) is true or not, we are told it is just a language, and a language, as such, is neither true nor false, because it is just a tool, which, being a tool, can be useful or useless for a particular task (as a drill, say, is useful to drive a hole in the wall), or, as Rorty says, 'obsolete and clumsy', but not true or false. The sophistry is smart but transparent.

Since language (in the literal sense) obviously helps us to achieve something, it is a tool; but it is a special kind of tool, its *differentia* being that, very unlike other tools, it is used to express judgements that claim truth. Other tools do not claim truth though some of them, like stethoscopes and spectacles, are used to get at truth. Hence, language (now in the sense of theory) can be 'obsolete and clumsy' in a way in which other tools cannot be, that is, by being false and/or invalid, and *therefore* discarded.

That you cannot change a language or language game (meaning a theory or an argument as a piece of reasoning) at your sweet (or sour) will, is recognized by Rorty, who regretfully complains that the 'trouble with arguments against the use of a familiar and time-honoured vocabulary is that they are expected to be phrased in that very vocabulary', which means that those who stand by the time-honoured rules of reasoning demand that those who attack them must also, in mounting that attack, respect those very same rules, particularly the rule about consistency. 'Any argument to the effect that our familiar use of a familiar term is incoherent, or empty, or confused, or vague, or "merely metaphorical" is bound to be inconclusive and question-begging' (which is itself a time-honoured concept to trip the neo-vocabularists). This is rather awkward, for how can the fly get out of the fly bottle? By persuading itself and by trying to persuade others (but how?) that the fly bottle is an illusion or that indulging in argument in the old familiar way is boring. 'Interesting philosophy is rarely an examination of the pros and cons of a thesis', the 'entrenched vocabulary' that keeps on harping on consistency and other old-fashioned logical constraints, 'has become a nuisance', like our traffic signals, and we will simply have to jump them by using a 'new vocabulary which ... promises great things'.[1]

Enough for the present about language games. We will hear more about them in the chapter specially devoted to Rorty.

Reference

1. Rorty, R., 1989, pp. 8-9.

Chapter 5

Assault on Saraswati

'Hovering and blazing with delusive light,
Misleads the amazed night-wanderer from his way
To bogs and mires, and oft through pond and pool,
There swallowed up and lost...'

John Milton, *Paradise Lost*

Much against their will and their grain, postmoderns and their camp followers, feminists, talk quite a lot about knowledge. Indeed, the very core of postmodernism is the thesis of the cultural relativism of knowledge. Their belief in the disappearance of knowledge is the logical consequence of their belief in the relativism of knowledge. However, they don't seem to see this, for while on the one hand, they don't believe in knowledge, on the other, they hold that there are many knowledges, each valid according to its own culture, and each incommensurable with any other.

Let us just make sure what, in the name of knowledge, we are exactly talking about so that we can avoid later possible misunderstandings. With people who do not have much respect for familiar vocabularies, the danger of (often intentional) misunderstanding is a real one.

The first question is whether knowledge should be considered to be properly and exclusively human knowledge. We may agree that knowledge is made up of truths and that we should be able to produce some sort of reasons, however minimal, for those truths. To make statements which turn out to be true, but for which I can only say 'I feel it is so,' or 'I have a hunch that,' or which, as Klein says, 'come out of the blue' or for the wrong reasons, cannot count as knowledge. Even *true* astrological, numerological and tarot predictions are not knowledge. Further, to constitute knowledge, the truths should be more than a mere collection; they must form an interconnected system. This requires reasoning. The degree to which the system is rigorous and tight varies according to the subject matter and purpose at hand.

Animals are often said to know things. Animal lovers are sure of this. 'Dogs scratch at doors, knowing, in some sense, that they will be opened; but dogs do not have reasons,' and even humans 'know that it is cold without having reasons'.[1] But the two cases are different. The dog may have, due to psychological association, images of the door being opened; the human is simply conscious of feeling cold. If he says, 'I am cold,' he is simply reporting his feeling cold, but if he says, 'It is cold,' he may be contradicted by someone, and then he would give his reason for saying that he is feeling cold.

Peter Klein pursues the question further.[2] 'Mr. Truetemp has a thermometer-cum-temperature-belief-generator in his head, so that ... he has perfectly reliable temperature beliefs.' Does he *know* the temperature? Klein replies, correctly, that he doesn't, but adds that Mr. Truetemp 'knows' the temperature in 'the same way in which the dog can "recognize" his owner's voice or in which a thermometer "knows" the room temperature'. Surely, the two cases are different, for the dog is conscious and may have *something* like a belief in embryo (who knows?), but the thermometer does not know in any sense, for the top of the mercury column seen against the temperature markings, which *we* interpret as the temperature, is a physical effect of a physical cause, the heating of the mercury. And both the cases are quite different from a man feeling cold and realizing it. Klein quotes Ernest Sosa:

> And there is an immense variety of animal knowledge … which, facilitates survival … Human knowledge is on a higher plane of sophistication, however, precisely because of its enhanced coherence and comprehensiveness and its capacity to satisfy self-reflective curiosity…

Here 'higher plane of sophistication' suggests merely that the difference between human and animal knowledge is a matter of degree, but the reference to 'coherence and comprehensiveness' shows, correctly, that the difference is one of kind, for animals presumably know nothing about coherence and self-reflective curiosity, that is, not merely the curiosity to find something (like a dog digging to find a bone) but to find reasons and arguments for what one believes.

What is called 'radical reliabilism – the view that claims that having reasons is never necessary for having knowledge – fails to capture what is distinctive about adult human knowledge'.[3]

The term 'knowledge' in connection with animal behaviour, however complex that behaviour may be, may be used 'colloquially, carrying little … theoretical commitment' to the 'existence of genuine intentional states'. Thus we might say that an electrical gadget 'knows' that someone is coming or that 'lowly creatures' like plovers 'know' things about their environment. Hilary Kornblith says that even if animals have (something like) intentional states, 'How big a step is it … from attributions of belief to attributions of knowledge?' Of course, very big. In ethology (study of animal behaviour) the idea of knowledge is mainly used as a working hypothesis to understand the conditions required by the animal to function.[4]

Kornblith, like Klein, goes on to say that humans 'have reflective powers to a degree which is not found elsewhere in the animal world', a 'degree of conceptual sophistication which is unrivalled by other animals', and that 'our ability to integrate and revise our corpus of beliefs is substantially more sophisticated'. In fact, all the human capacities mentioned here are peculiarly human, animals cannot properly be said to have them at all, and, therefore, to talk in terms of 'degree' is quite out of place. What Kornblith proceeds to say suggests the correct position:

> What piping plovers know today is not much different from what piping plovers knew one hundred, one thousand or ten thousand years ago. The same may be said of the most sophisticated non-human animals. But human knowledge is not like that. Much of what we know today about the world around us was undreamt of a few hundred years ago. Our scientific knowledge … is of recent vintage, and in particular, is not the product of some evolutionary change from the period which preceded it; the scientific revolution is far too recent to have been the product of evolutionary changes.

Kornblith is clearly telling us that the difference between animal and human cognition is not only one of degree (which, of course, is the case) but of kind. Where the jump occurred need not worry us here.[5]

Kornblith continues the discussion further.[6] He admits that some philosophers, such as L. BonJour, define knowledge 'in terms of characteristics widely believed to be the exclusive property of human beings' and talk of a human belief being one only if it is justified as being 'the product of reflection upon the extent to which it coheres with a believer's entire corpus of beliefs'. Of course there is no evidence, grants Kornblith, that this sort of thing exists anywhere among animals, but what BonJour requires is 'rarely if ever satisfied even by human beings' and 'the vast majority of human belief is surely arrived at unreflectively'. We may certainly add, without the least attempt to see that it coheres with the whole corpus of beliefs, even if such a prodigious feat were possible.

Kornblith is right so far, but concludes that the arguments which attempt to show that human knowledge is distinct from the kind that ethologists study, fail. 'Human knowledge is not different in kind from knowledge which other animals enjoy. Knowledge seems to be a single natural kind.'

But this conclusion does not follow even if we reject BonJour's stringent requirements for knowledge. One may soften his demands by suggesting that a knowledge-belief need not be the product of an explicit act of reflection to see how far the belief coheres with the entire corpus of one's beliefs. What might be required is that, if doubted or challenged, a belief should be justifiable by being shown to cohere, not with the entire corpus of beliefs, but with a certain segment or sub-system of beliefs, more or less immediately relevant, to validate the particular belief under consideration. To judge, for example, the validity of a legal claim, a lawyer does not, cannot, pull out from the recesses of his mind his entire legal knowledge; but his expertise makes him resurrect only that which is relevant for the claim in hand. The relevance which he claims, and on which he bases his judgement, may be challenged by the opposing counsel, in which case he would have to give further reasons to show that he was right in what he did or he might have to dig further into the recesses of his legal knowledge. When a belief is shown to cohere with a system of beliefs that all concerned parties accept, the belief is justified. Of course, doubts may, in turn, be raised about that system itself. It would then have to be justified by a similar process.

I have said that knowledge about any subject is made up of truths – truths arranged and organized in a system. This is the work of reason and this is where logic enters the picture. Postmodern conventionalism holds that the principles of logic are conventions or stipulations decided by logicians and not, in any way, necessitated by reality, physical, mental or of any other kind. Every logician, or for that matter, anyone, says Carnap, 'is at liberty to build up his own logic, i.e. his own form of language, as he wishes', but 'if he wishes to discuss it, he must … give syntactical rules'. The influence of the idea of games is clear.

These rules would also be his own, as he wishes. But whatever rules he makes, however eccentric they may be, and so however many different and even conflicting systems of logic or logico-syntax there may come to be, internal consistency 'seems to be a required feature of all systems', says O'Grady. Why 'seems'? If the principle that whatever be your rule, you must apply it consistently within the same 'game', is itself a rule which you have formulated because you just wished it, then one could even wish to, and formulate, the opposite rule – never apply the rules consistently. That you are bound to apply the consequences that follow from the application of your rules, cannot itself be a rule, which you may or may not adopt. The notion of 'consequence' is the thorn in the side of conventionalism. Logic, whose core principle is the law of consistency or non-contradiction, is, writes O'Grady, 'so basic to our conceptual system, to our whole way of dealing with the world, that conventionalism relies on it, and not vice versa'.[8] Without the basic notion of consequence – that you must go where the argument leads – conventionalism or any other 'ism' cannot even start.

The laws of logic may be said to be 'analytical' as A. J. Ayer calls them, but they are not as he thinks, 'truths by definition alone',[9] as if they are a matter of stipulation, taste, arbitrary choice or dictated by pragmatic considerations. They are analytical in the sense that they are not the result of empirical inquiry and they 'tell us nothing about the actual world', that is, about factual details regarding what exists or happens, about whether, for example, yetis exist or there were weapons of mass destruction in Iraq. But logical laws do express the general structure of reality, which is such that, if, in your thinking, you were to violate these laws, your thinking will not be valid and will not accord with reality. 'We aren't really free to make up logic as we like,' says O'Grady, for if we did, it 'would destroy the whole point of logic, which is to preserve truth in inferential moves'. Carnap, while allowing different systems of logic, still 'does envisage practical constraints'. What does this mean except that if you don't observe these restraints, the restraints of not thinking in violation of logical laws, your thinking would go haywire? Systems of logic 'that allowed wholesale contradiction would be spectacularly useless'.[10]

Postmoderns are fond of talking in terms of 'frameworks'. They maintain that propositions can be judged true or false only within specified frameworks. O'Grady maintains that logical laws or principles of rationality 'constitute a core conception of rationality' which allows us to have at least 'a minimal theory of universal rationality that forms a universal framework – a universal precondition for all other frameworks'. This will provide 'sufficient leverage to allow reasoned disagreement', yet allows 'a great deal of legitimate diversity', but blocks 'an "anything goes" relativism'.[11]

A framework is a system, a set, wide or narrow in varying degrees, of presuppositions, postulates, assumptions or views, explicitly or implicitly held in different degrees, in the clear foreground or in a hazy background, against which the truth-value of our beliefs is ultimately assessed. 'The chief task of philosophy,' says O'Grady, 'is to render explicit such presuppositions and to judge them.' It is not only the task of philosophy and O'Grady soon corrects himself. However, first, he stresses that philosophy does not, in Wittgensteinian fashion, leave everything as it is, but 'actively tinkers with the framework, attempting to correct perceived problems and create new models – new ways of conceptualizing the world. In this', O'Grady corrects his earlier statement, 'it shares common cause with natural science; it just differs in scope and also asks more fundamental questions'. It is not possible to decide or determine in general, to what extent this tinkering with, and judging of, frameworks is the legitimate job of science and where philosophy has to pick up the task. Frameworks or viewpoints 'are keyed to purposes or ends', the most fundamental of them being the acquisition of truth.[12] More about frameworks will be considered later.

Postmoderns are also, as we shall see again, prone to recommend hermeneutics in place of philosophy. Charles Taylor, greatly interested in hermeneutics, says that knowledge is the way in which engaged, embodied humans 'encounter the world cognitively'. Being 'self-interpreting animals' (something like being reflecting creatures unlike animals), we interpret what we encounter. All knowledge is interpretative or, as is often put, theory-laden. As hermeneutics sees it, it is not 'necessarily conscious or articulate'; 'interpretations can be tacit and pre-reflective', forming 'part of the taken-for-granted background of knowledge', a background formed of ideas once perhaps actively considered and which have then become familiar and lapsed into the background.[13] This account is acceptable, but 'Taylor repeatedly emphasizes,' writes Ruth Abbey, that 'the background cannot be turned into an object of reflection' because 'for some things to be studied and examined, others must remain in place'.[14] 'The background is a transcendental condition of knowledge' and so 'cannot be completely objectified', since any knowledge about it 'must itself have a "background" presupposition'. The 'transcendental level of reflection, therefore, exposes limits to the objectifiable, representable world'. This negates 'the widely held presumptions about the in-principle limitlessness of objective enquiry'.[15]

Taylor's view is an example of the linear conception of knowledge; knowledge as made up of a superstructure built on an unshakeable foundation. It is foundationalism, which, in fact, is opposed by postmoderns, who seem to subscribe to a different concept of knowledge, that of a coherent system of mutually supporting elements.

Taylor says that our sense of reality and our knowledge of the world, natural and human, are 'bound up with our being in the world'. We have a kind of 'pre-objective sense of reality', which the natural sciences 'refine' by 'depicting nature from a subject-neutral point of view', but he thinks 'this strategy is unsuitable for deepening our knowledge or understanding of the human world.[16]

Science's boasted neutrality or what is called 'God's-eye view of the world' has been a target of postmodernism. Taylor at least admits neutrality in the study of non-human nature, but in the social sciences he thinks this approach unsuitable, for 'meaning-content and subject-relatedness are integral to the very notion of human activity'. The meaning of this rather vague statement is clarified by the next: 'Human activity is by its very nature directed by desires and purposes … and interpreting these desires and purposes is an essential part of reaching an understanding or explanation of the activity.' The task of anthropology, for instance, 'is to advance the prevailing understandings of the purposes expressed in a particular culture'.[17]

This description of the nature of human activity and the need of the human sciences to take account of the desires and purposes operating in a culture is unexceptionable. But Taylor's remark against neutrality in the human sciences is an amazing blunder. The neutrality which is a requirement for objectivity in science is the neutrality on the part of the investigating scientist, *his* not being swayed by private and personal desires and purposes in conducting the inquiry; it has nothing to do with the desires and purposes operating among the members of the activity or culture he is studying. The meaning of scientific neutrality is that, apart from the one desire and one purpose of understanding his object, he or, more particularly she, should not have any other desires or purposes that might distort and compromise the impartial nature of the research. Incidentally, God's eye view and 'view from nowhere' has nothing to do with scientific neutrality as I have explained it. The social sciences do not 'have an "interpretative logic" that departs in key ways from the logic of the natural sciences', as hermeneutics mistakenly claims; at least certainly not with regard to the matter of neutrality; the logic of the scientific procedure is the same in all the sciences, natural and human.

Taylor claims: 'In our everyday coping experience we sense that we are in contact with a nature with a structure of its own which supports our coping.' This everyday coping is surely more systematically extended by science. And do we only 'sense' that we are in contact with a real nature? Do we not believe it also, and believe it reasonably? Hubert Dreyfus thinks that, in order to 'understand Taylor's robust realism', we must extend Taylor's claim 'to the stronger claim that it makes sense to think that we can correctly describe that structure and that, indeed, there is evidence that our current science may well be progressively getting it right about (at least some aspects of) the universe'.[18] (The 'at least some aspects of' has a point, which will be discussed later. It must be noted that 'we sense' is different from 'it makes sense to think'.)

Taylor believes that 'some understandings of the world are truer than others' and also that in our coping with the world, 'we develop a sense that there is a deeper reality that does not depend solely on the meanings we accord to it' (so much for conventionalism) and that this reality 'sets limits or boundary conditions on the ways in which we can cope with it' (which includes, of course, our thinking about it). All this means that 'it is not a case that anything goes or thinking makes it so'. 'There are structural realities to which we accommodate ourselves, not vice versa.' And 'the more responsive to these realities we are, the better able are we to cope with the universe.'[19] I suppose the boundary conditions referred to are the ones set by those elements in our experience that are 'given' and by the principles of reasoning or logic.

Things become more complicated. According to Dreyfus, Taylor would claim that 'it makes sense to think of science as attempting to describe the universe as it is in itself'. But Dreyfus adds, 'He does not have to hold that our current science is getting it right about the universe or that any science will ever get it right.' Or: 'That we could ever know for sure whether the current science is in fact on the right track.' Dreyfus is walking on a sharp knife-edge. What he means is that to say that 'science is describing the universe' is a meaningful statement and not gibberish, but we can't be sure if it is a true statement. He goes on to say that Taylor 'argues *convincingly* that, given our science's supersession claims, it makes sense to hold that our science is in fact zeroing in on (one aspect of) the physical universe', but this is so only given the supersession claim, which is that 'we may well be learning more' about the universe (italics mine). But this is only what science claims; we can't say whether to admit the claim or reject it.[20]

This scepticism about 'our current science' is, among postmoderns, coupled with open-mindedness about alternative 'sciences'. We now enter upon an involved discussion on this point.[21] Heidegger, quoted by Dreyfus, writes: 'The statements of physics are correct. By means of them, science represents something real.' But 'science always encounters only what *its* kind of representation has admitted beforehand as an object possible for science'. This looks upon 'our science' as a kind of club whose members play a certain language game according to certain rules, but there can be other clubs where members play the games according to other rules, and all these clubs are equally respectable. It means that, for some undisclosed, esoteric, mysterious reason, 'our science' chooses or decides what kind of objects *it* will study and in what way it will proceed to do so, but some other kind of 'understanding' is free to decide to study some other kinds of objects and also in its own way. In fact, it may create its own objects. 'On this view,' writes Dreyfus, 'the Egyptians' understanding of the essential property of gold, if true, would also … reveal an aspect' of gold, the property in question being something that was 'sacred and so shone with divine radiance'. It is not clear if Dreyfus endorses this position. The words 'if true' are crucial, for the entire debate is about whether the Egyptian understanding or any understanding other than that of 'our science' makes sense and whether there can be a kind of truth other than what 'our science' accepts.

The mention about the Egyptians refers to Kripke's example. Kripke thinks that by examining this shiny substance we call gold, we find that its essence is to have the atomic weight 79. It is that property, which explains all the other properties of gold. Taylor, 'with his openness to other cultures having an understanding of nature different from ours', would reject Kripke's position, because it would imply that the views of the other cultures that are different from ours must be considered false.

By what method did the Ancient Egyptians discover that gold has this 'sacred' property and in what way does it explain the ductility, conductivity and other qualities of gold? Without caring to answer such questions, questions which always arise, Dreyfus goes on to put forward some weird notions. *Our* scientific understanding, he says, 'would be true in the world of the Egyptians even though they couldn't understand it'. Correct. This is so because it is the truth, and the only truth, in the one world inhabited by them and us, the common empirical world; but if Dreyfus means that *our* understanding would be true even in *their* 'world' of belief (such as it was), he is quite wrong, because not only would it not be true, it would not even be meaningful. Dreyfus himself says that other 'cultures do not ask about the universe … in the sense of modern Western science'. Next, Dreyfus says that what they meant by gold would not be 'determined by our science'. May be. So what? So much the worse for them, not us. People believe all sorts of things even in *our* culture which are not determined by our science, but that shouldn't push us to think that some aspect of the world is revealed to them that is not accessible to science. Referring to the Homeric Greeks and Native American tribes, Dreyfus writes, 'They presumably sensed that they neither discovered nor invented their classification of things … but drew on their form of life to reveal nature … from their own perspective.' So, things are revealed but it does not amount to a discovery! Of course they did not discover because there was nothing like that to discover. Of course they did invent things, but without realizing they were inventing them and believing, mistakenly, that things were revealed to them. And what exactly is this enigmatic drawing 'on their form of life'? Heidegger explains it all by telling us of 'different kinds of seeing and questioning natural events'. There are also different kinds of bunkum.

Taylor takes a more sensible line. He would claim, writes Dreyfus, 'that we could, at least, in principle, have taught the Ancient Egyptians our science'. Yes, because they also had minds like ours and accepted (though unreflectively) the same common principles of reasoning. But now Taylor flies off at a tangent; or is it Dreyfus who does? For Dreyfus's next sentence reads: 'They could then see both that gold is a natural kind in our sense with its atomic number of 79, and that our disenchanted understanding ... overlooks the fact that nature is sacred,' which 'our science can't see', and, further, that ours 'is only one limited way of disclosing' things. Is it not likely that the Ancient Egyptians, being perhaps more intelligent than Dreyfus gives them credit for, might, on learning our science, see things quite differently and realize that *their* way of drawing on their form of life and *their* way of seeing things was quite wrong, and so discard it?

It is extremely unlikely that they could, even in principle, teach us their science. How could they *teach* us what we knew to be mistaken? Modern science can understand what the ancient people believed – understand without believing it – because it can see where they went wrong (due to drawing on their form of life instead of observing nature more carefully) and how and to what extent their beliefs were inadequate, and how they could be corrected. If, *per impossibile*, they were able to correct our scientific beliefs, they would then be doing our science.

In fact, there is nothing like *our* science and *their* science, as postmoderns are fond of suggesting. Modern Western science did not, miraculously, erupt one day from some god's head and it does not, never did, require a 'view from nowhere'. All this is postmodern mythology. The roots of science lay in the earliest of human beliefs about the world, the one common real world. These beliefs, by a long, arduous and gradual process over more than two millennia, have developed, along a more or less steady line of progress (that is, barring a number of wrong turnings and eccentricities, which were discovered and corrected) and reached the present state of science. The whole process is one of 'refining', which, as Heidegger correctly sees, 'is characteristic of physics' and, in fact, of all science. Whatever, in the beliefs of the ancients or of any culture other than modern Western scientific culture, can stand critical, rational inspection and criticism, can and must be accepted and absorbed by modern science. Whatever cannot be is not different but false and must be rejected. 'The more the merrier' is not a principle of science. It is also extremely unlikely that even those of the ancient beliefs which are accepted, could be accepted unmodified.

Let us grill Dreyfus a little further. He writes that just as gold's physical properties are '*causally* explained in terms of universal laws by our science', gold's sacred property 'may only be accessible to Egyptian religious practices' and the 'aspect such practices revealed might have causal properties that could only be activated by those specific practices, and so would not be discoverable by a disenchanted science with a view from nowhere'.

How could one respond to such claims? Our scientists, suspending beliefs, could perform these religious practices and see whether there is any evidence of the sacred property and its causal efficacy. Such an experiment would, in the first place, depend on our knowledge of such practices; if we don't know anything about them, our Egyptologist friends have another piece of ignorance on their hands, which they will, of course, make a virtue of. If our scientists were to report that they have found no sacred property and its causal activity, Dreyfus would have a ready answer – that the Ancient Egyptians had a special kind of vision that could detect such things. This would be an *ad hoc* hypothesis to get over a hurdle without having any basis other than supporting a fantastic claim. We have to conclude that the Ancient Egyptians would be, thus, unable to demonstrate to us the alleged sacred property and the cryptic causation.

Dreyfus rises to the occasion. What 'might seem a mystery or even an impossibility from the standpoint of our science might have a causal explanation' that would 'reveal another type of causality'. We are now gifted a new but unfathomable hypothetical concept – another type of causality, take it or lump it.

So, while any demonstration to our scientists by the Ancient Egyptians of their esoteric claims is, in principle, ruled out, if the Ancient Egyptians were to desire to understand *our* science, it could, in principle, be demonstrated to them, provided they had, as we presume they must have had, sense organs like ours and the same kind of rational capacities which most ordinary mortals, including non-postmodern scientists, have. Dreyfus might go to the extent of hypothesizing that the Ancient Egyptians might have had quite different kinds of sense organs from us, if indeed, they had anything like sense organs at all, also very different kinds of rational or quasi-rational faculties and, naturally, a very, very different kind of logic. In the world of make-believe anything is possible. We have seen that, all along the line, Dreyfus has to stage a succession of strategic retreats in order to hold on to fictitious sacred properties and imaginary causality.

Dreyfus has not yet had his full say. 'In the most extreme conceivable case, these culturally activated causal properties might even override the causal properties discovered by our science.'

For this to happen, the properties or, at least, their causal functioning, should be observable by us. How else would we know they have overridden the causal properties of our science? (Perhaps Dreyfus means that the Egyptians knew this but we don't!) A contact with *our* science would have to be made at some point. 'If confirmed,' writes Dreyfus, 'repeatable levitation would be such a case and, our physics would then have to be revised to take account of such a phenomenon.'

What does this mean? 'Confirmed' by principles and methods of *our* science or by those of the Ancient Egyptians? If by the latter – whatever be the nature of that 'confirmation' – it would leave us cold and the so-called phenomenon would, as far as we are concerned, remain unconfirmed. Surely, in a case like this, it is we who have to be satisfied, not the Egyptians, and whether they agree to our methods and principles or not, is beside the point. Repeatability, which Dreyfus cites, is a principle relied on by our science; the Ancient Egyptians might well argue (if they can argue with us at all) that for them *un*repeatability is the criterion of confirmation; they might believe neither in confirmation nor in criteria. It should by now be clear that Dreyfus's entire case is bogus.

Forget the Ancient Egyptians. If a case, even a single case, of alleged levitation observed under stringent scientifically controlled conditions did happen to be confirmed, of course our physics would have to take account of it and either throw the law of gravitation on the scrap-heap of scientific fictions or suitably reformulate it to find a place for this phenomenon. This is because it is a logical principle that our science respects that a genuine exception 'proves' (i.e. tests) the rule or law.

Dreyfus, a paragon of modesty, says that 'there is much we don't understand', but that doesn't allow us to jump to believing that the Ancient Egyptians may have understood the world in a way not only different from, but contrary to, the way in which modern science, which has a history of steady rational development, understands it. A crucial question is, if and when we did come to, or attempted to, understand what we do not understand at present, would we have proceeded according to the known and success-yielding methods and principles of *our* science or would we have looked for some unknown but purely fanciful ones for the success or even existence of which there is not a shred of evidence?

Dreyfus cites acupuncture as having 'so far resisted all attempts to understand it in terms of Western medicine'. If its success is indeed a fact confirmed by strict scientific tests, it would mean that modern science still does not know enough about the human system, just as till 500 years ago Western medicine did not know about the circulation of blood in the human body. It *does not follow* that 'we may simply have to accept two accounts of the body', one according to Western medical science and another in terms of a kind of 'energy that can't be understood in terms of our current physics'.

I have spent so many pages on Hubert Dreyfus because he, like many others, represents a species of thinking and a 'style' of arguing which is common among postmoderns, a style 'blazing with delusive light'.

References

1. Klein, P. D., 'Human Knowledge and the Infinite Regress of Reasons' in Tomberlin, J. E. (Ed.), 1999, p. 301.
2. Ibid., p. 302.
3. Ibid., p. 302.
4. Kornblith, H., ' Knowledge in Humans and Other Animals' in Tomberlin, J. E. (Ed.), 1999, pp. 328-29.
5. Ibid., p. 334.
6. Ibid., pp. 334-35, 337.
7. Carnap, R., 1937, p. 52.
8. O'Grady, P. O., 2002, p. 123.
9. Ibid., p. 122.
10. Ibid., p. 123.
11. Ibid., p. 128.
12. Ibid., pp. 127-28.
13. Abbey, R. (Ed.), 2004, p. 3.
14. Ibid., pp. 3-4.
15. Smith, N. H., 'Taylor and the Hermeneutic Tradition' in Abbey, R. (Ed.), 2004, pp. 34-35.
16. Ibid., p. 35.
17. Ibid., p. 35.

18. Dreyfus, H. L., 'Taylor's (Anti-) Epistemology' in Abbey, R. (Ed.), 2004, pp. 68-69.
19. Abbey, R. (Ed.), 2004, p. 7.
20. Dreyfus, H. L., op. cit., pp. 74-75.
21. Ibid., pp. 76-79.

Chapter 6
Contextuality, Truth and Absurdity

'Sport that wrinkled Care derides
And laughter holding both his sides.'

John Milton, *L'Allegro*

As in other matters, post-modernism has an ambivalent attitude to truth and understanding – straight massacre or torture and mutilation.

Knowledge involves truth, and reason is used for understanding anything. All these cause postmoderns acute discomfort.

W. V. Quine, a thinker very sympathetic to postmodern ideas and one whom postmoderns admire, a pragmatist in the line of John Dewey, 'thought of knowledge instrumentally: knowledge is a tool we use to deal with the world'.[1] Remarks similar to those I had made in the Interlude, about language being regarded as a tool, can also apply to Quine's view about knowledge. Knowledge is certainly used by us in order to do things and get things that we want, but this is not its essence, which is our understanding of the world or anything in the world. An important feature of knowledge, which distinguishes it from all other tools, is that it is true and not just useful, and it is useful *because* it is true. Pragmatists always, and postmoderns often, suffer from a disease which we may call the cart-horse flip.

There is something sinister about stressing the utility attribute of knowledge, for it can be mischievously used to denigrate traditional philosophy, which, as they say, bakes no bread, and also epistemology, as understood by postmoderns, both of which are valuable but not directly useful disciplines.

The existence of different communities and cultures over space and time fascinates postmoderns. They somehow find it self-evident that truth and reasoning (like certain manners and certain kinds of dress) must be peculiar to each different community and culture. The fact that people belonging to widely different cultures can communicate with each other, can understand each other and assess, by common principles, the truth-value of what they say to each other – all these cause postmoderns painful *angst*.

Truth is said to be contextual or culture-relative.[2] One speaker says 'S knows P' and another says, about the same 'S' and 'P', 'S does not know P'. Cohen says that 'both speakers can be speaking the truth'. This is contextualism, which holds that 'ascriptions of knowledge are context-sensitive – the truth-values of sentences containing the words "know", and its cognates, depend on contextually determined standards'. This, in simple English, means that 'know' has different senses in different situations. Therefore, each of these two statements instanced above 'have different truth-values in different contexts' – that is (I think he is trying to say), 'S knows P' and 'S does not know P' in the *same* context could not both be true, because they contradict each other (otherwise what is the law of non-contradiction all about?), but 'S knows P' in context A could mean something quite different in context B, so that a speaker in context A could say 'S knows P' and another (or even he himself, why not?) in context B could say 'S does not know P', and both could say this without contradicting each other and so both truly. After so much effort a very small mouse has thus far been produced and has actually made no contribution to the culture-relatedness of truth.

The truth-value 'of a sentence containing the knowledge predicate' (why only the knowledge predicate?) depends on 'things like the purposes, intentions, expectations, presuppositions, etc. of the speakers'. We could add 'places, times and circumstances' to the list. This is true. But once the purposes, etc. have been made explicit and clarified, two propositions, which exactly contradict each other, cannot both be true; it is when they are vague that they often appear to defy the law of non-contradiction.

Now into the fray:[3] Mary and John ask Smith if he knows whether their flight stops at Chicago. Smith, looking up the itinerary says, 'I know it does.' Mary and John (this devoted couple always speak with one voice) say that Smith does not *know* what he claims to know, because the itinerary might be unreliable. (If only Smith had said, 'It says so in the itinerary,' there would have been no further discussion.) Cohen wants us to believe that this little incident shows that both 'S knows P' and 'S does not know P' (about the same 'S' and the same 'P') are true. Hence, contradictory propositions can both be true together! Cohen's intellectual naiveté is greater than that of a ten-year-old. The two propositions can, of course, both be true together for the obvious reason that they are not contradictories. The two parties differ on the question of evidence. Cohen himself says, 'Mary and John seem to be using a stricter standard than Smith.'

If we were to write out the propositions in full, they would read: 'Smith, relying on the itinerary, which is unreliable but which Smith seems to trust, says that he knows that the flight stops at Chicago.' And: 'Mary and John, skeptical about the itinerary, think that Smith does not know that the flight stops at Chicago.' The contradiction has vanished and there is no damage to traditional logic either. The two statements, the statement about 'S knowing P' and the statement about 'S not knowing P', are not made by the same party; hence they are not contradictories. The trick (if meant to be so) is too transparent to fool any non-postmodern. Is Cohen fooling himself?

Cohen now raises a different point. He says, 'If we deny that Smith knows, then we have to deny that we know in many of the everyday cases in which we claim to know' and that 'even Mary and John's standard does not seem strict enough', for they only checked with the airline agent, who could very well be mistaken. Cohen is quite right. A relation of mine prefaced any statement of his with: 'Subject to correction.' How much and what sort of evidence we are prepared to accept as warranting a claim and how far we are prepared to take a risk in believing the statement, depends on several factors, among them the purpose for which we trust the statement and (like my relation) our inherent sense of caution. But granting that 'know' is used strongly and weakly in varying degrees and, perhaps, never indubitably strongly, nothing that Cohen has so far said is able to defend his thesis that 'ascriptions of knowledge are context-sensitive', understood in the sense that two contradictory, exactly contradictory, propositions can both be true.

Cohen himself sees that a similar 'problem' will arise in the case of predicates that, like 'knowledge', admit of degrees: 'flat', 'bald', 'rich'. Both the context, as Cohen realizes, and the joint stipulation by the disputants will determine how the predicate will be understood.

Just as two *apparently* contradictory propositions can both be true (as we have seen), two different theories put forward to explain the same fact could both be true.

Quine is one of those who has popularized the idea of 'conceptual scheme'. The word 'framework' is also used, and I have made some remarks about frameworks in Chapter 5. According to Quine, every inquiry is pursued with a conceptual scheme or a 'posit', which is 'culturally constructed'. Different sciences have different posits. For example, economics and psychology, though both deal with human concerns, have different posits. What happens in one posit may affect what happens in another. Financial setbacks may lead a person to drink. Even within a posit, there could be and most probably would be many sub-posits dealing with different areas and perspectives. Quine believes that science is a refinement of the conceptual schemes within which common sense works. All of us think within conceptual schemes. (I am seeing Quine through O'Grady's eyes.[4])

So far I have no disagreement with Quine. Doubt begins when he accepts 'other ways of talking about the world', that is, about the empirical world and in the way science talks about it. And he is not referring to philosophy. The way of science and these other ways 'are conflicting accounts of reality'. Remembering Wittgenstein, 'Quine says there are other kinds of language use, such as fiction and poetry.' So far we can still be with him. We can use language to 'talk' to our pet dog and also to abuse our enemy. But when we are told that these different uses of language 'present imaginary worlds, alternative takes on this world, new ways of seeing', this is rather a mixed bag and we are heading for trouble.

Presenting imaginary worlds which we consider to be imaginary and alternative takes on this our real space-time world are very different things, and 'new ways of seeing' takes us back to Dreyfus and Heidegger's 'different kinds of seeing'. 'There are resources in Quine's philosophy' that defend literally 'radically different factual accounts of reality to the standard ones we have', that is, those which modern Western science gives us. Quine holds that this standard account and Homer's account of the gods are really 'conflicting accounts of reality'. Both are posits, epistemologically on par; only 'the physics posit has better evidence'. According to O'Grady, Quine has the following reasons for his view: firstly, our 'beliefs' and 'our conceptual scheme' are revisable and secondly, 'alternative possible theories' are 'compatible with the same basic evidence'. It is interesting to note that Quine admits that even our conceptual scheme is revisable, because this is not in line with postmodern notions, according to which truth-value, correction and reversability operate only with regard to beliefs within a scheme and do not touch the scheme itself. In fact, it is the very core of postmodernism that schemes just are what they are, cannot be reasoned about, are merely different and are incommensurable because there is no neutral position from which they could be compared and assessed. Quine also seems to deny a neutral position, and yet he holds that schemes are revisable, which suggests that this neutrality idea is a bogeyman specially created by postmodernism.

The two contentions mentioned above in support of Quine's view about 'conflicting accounts of reality' are both true, but neither of them can really support that view. Regarding the first case, it is a basic idea of science that schemes – such as the Ptolemaic system and the Copernican system – and beliefs within a system are revisable and are, in fact, continuously undergoing major or minor revisions as science progresses. But from this it does not remotely follow that mythological, poetical or any other fictional schemes are on par with scientific ones as claiming to describe the real world. In these, anything goes. What would make us revise the Homeric account about the gods? You may give another account out of your imagination but it would not amount to a revision of Homer's account, just as I might have dreamed two nights ago that I went to England and I might dream tonight that I did not, but it would be absurd to suggest that tonight's dream revises the earlier one. Fictional schemes may appear to contradict each other, but they really don't and can, therefore, merrily exist together. This is precisely what contradictory scientific schemes cannot do.

Regarding the second case, the fact that alternative theories are sometimes compatible with the same evidence means only that, at a particular stage of inquiry, the available evidence is not sufficient to rule out at least one of the two rival theories, which are still considered to be hypotheses. To rule one of them out is the purpose of running a 'crucial' experiment. None of this shows that 'theory is under-determined by evidence'.

If the Homeric and modern scientific accounts of reality conflict and the latter 'has better evidence for it', then they are *not* two incommensurable but equally respectable alternative conceptual schemes, each with its own kind of seeing and own exclusive kind of truth-value. If one hypothesis has better evidence for it, it is the one provisionally accepted, and if the other hypothesis has weak evidence for it, it is rejected or kept in animated suspension till further investigation decides its fate. For the account of Homeric gods what evidence is there anyway, except that Homer tells us about them or, perhaps, that this was what was part of Greek mythology and popular belief? Indeed, what evidence could there possibly be about the doings of the gods?

The Homeric account is included in modern knowledge, not in the way Newton's theory is included in Einstein's, but in the sense that, in the universe which is studied by modern science and can only be so studied, the Homeric account about the gods exists as a poetic myth. One cannot figure out what to make of the statement: 'Now it is clear that Quine thinks of science, and specially physics, as having the most inclusive conceptual scheme. It covers everything that exists;' it is 'the best one we have'. It is equally clear that Quine thinks there are or can be other schemes, maybe not as good (true?) and covering less ground, but to be taken as seriously as we take science.

Thomas Kuhn's notion of paradigms is similar to Quine's of conceptual schemes. Kuhn is one of the two scientific experts on the postmodern panel, the other being Paul Feyerabend. It seems that Kuhn would not include myths, fiction and poetry in his talk about paradigms. Kuhn's paradigm is (in O'Grady's words), 'specifically in relation to scientific inquiry ... the assumptions, training methods, standards, goals, methods and expectations that characterize the scientific community at a stable stage of scientific development'. The essential point about both Quine's and Kuhn's schemes and paradigms is that they are incommensurable with each other, because reason can operate only within, and peculiarly to, each. 'It may well be impossible even to understand paradigms different from one's own,' writes O'Grady, and 'leads to a very strong form of relativism', having 'currency in many parts of contemporary culture'.[5]

Rorty speaks of two approaches to past philosophers: firstly the 'past-centred', understanding philosophers 'in their own terms, in relation to their own agenda', and secondly, the 'present-centred', 'as colleagues with whom' one 'can engage in philosophical debate'. We can do both; we can understand how Galileo, in keeping with the beliefs of his times, tackled the, now abandoned, project of turning iron into gold. And we can understand his work on the planets, which, though limited and even at points mistaken, is continuous with ours. We can understand how we are different from our philosophical ancestors but also show that there is steady, almost unbroken 'rational progress' along the line and that we differ from them 'on grounds which our ancestors could be led to accept'.[6]

This account, taken from an article by Genevieve Lloyd, a passionate feminist and staunch relativist, clearly and surprisingly, controverts the incommensurability thesis. Although Galileo's thinking arose out of a conceptual scheme which, due to historical circumstances, was quite different from ours and, in this sense, was context-related, it is admitted that he could have been made to see the problem as we see it and was actually trying to solve it, be it inadequately and even mistakenly (as we, too, could very well be doing), and solve it by the same tools of reasoning as used by us. In this sense, Galileo's work was context-transcendent.

Thus, at least regarding work on the planets and related matters, sixteenth to seventeenth century intellectual culture and twentieth century culture can measure themselves against each other and are *not* incommensurable. It is also important to notice that Galileo's attempt even in alchemy, now of historical interest only, was, in principle, no different from his work in astronomy, for though he was, let us say, mistaken in believing that iron could become gold, he was still using a scientific method, unlike, perhaps, some Ancient Peoples who might have tried the same thing by sacrificing a goat to the gods or doing a ritual fire dance. We can show that, by using the same scientific methods but now greatly refined, the thing can't be done and so the project should be abandoned. Both we and Galileo (if he were now with us) could distinguish 'what is necessary' from 'what is the product merely of our own contingent arrangements' (Q. Skinner's words). Even Rorty says, 'We need to think that … the mighty mistaken dead look down from heaven at our recent successes, and are happy to find that their mistakes have been corrected.'

Why talk only of Galileo? Surely even Ptolemy or Heraclitus or Thales could be made to see the difference between the necessary and the contingent and also how, what was really scientific in their thinking, is connected by a very, very long chain of links with what modern science accepts. If, as is now admitted by relativist stalwarts like Lloyd and Rorty, reasoning and science can bridge cultures across immense chunks of time, there is no reason why it can't be done across space between the Hopi tribes and modern Western culture. I hope that, in saying this, we are not going to run away, shouting, with the idea that Hopi 'science' is as good and true, or even, perhaps, better and truer than modern science. If it is, as I am insisting, connected with ours, it can't be better and truer or even as good as ours. All that I have said is that whatever is essential and scientific, however minimal, in Hopi culture, is one with our science though very distantly related to it, and whatever is not, is idiosyncratic and fictitious.

'To say that truth and knowledge can only be judged by the standards of the inquirers of our own day,' says Rorty, is 'to say that nothing counts as justification unless by reference to what we already accept'.[7] Rorty fondly thinks this is a pragmatist-relativist view. In the light of our recent discussion, this is perfectly correct and does not in the least harm a non-pragmatist-relativist position. The standards, which we now accept and by which we judge claims to truth and knowledge, are those which have been reached as the culmination of a continuous process of development and progress. The standards which modern science accepts are not new ones that have been dropped on us by the Great Pragmatist; they are the refined products of this long line of progress.

Of course we judge claims and justify our beliefs by reference to what we already accept and by the standards of our own day. How else can we do it and what other way would we find satisfactory? We couldn't perform the feat of judging and justifying by somebody else's standards or those of other cultures. That would be like tasting food with somebody else's tongue. But this is because standards are not the exclusive and private property of persons and cultures. Dick can throw a dinner with Genevieve's money, but he can't think (if he can think at all) with Genevieve's mind. As Rorty says, 'there is no way to get outside our beliefs', and, also, standards; but it is not even necessary. And not doing so does not mean that we are subscribing to pragmatic relativism. We of the present day, in judging a claim or justifying a position, believe, and justifiably and reasonably believe, that we are at a vantage point from which we may claim that we are right. This is not, though it may appear so, a conceited stance. Nor is it to say that we may not be wrong in what we believe, or that we are not aware that we may be wrong. But unless someone (maybe we ourselves) can show us that we are wrong, we need not be unnecessarily bashful and say we are wrong. The belief that we believe we are right till proved wrong and the belief that we may be wrong, are not incompatible. Coherence, as Rorty absolutely rightly says, is the test that will decide whether we are right or wrong in our judging and justifying. And there is no need to find some other test. Coherence is precisely what respects what we are and also takes us out of ourselves and connects us with others and other cultures. Two cheers for Rorty and for other postmoderns for recognizing coherence as the test, and the only ultimate test of truth. But do they quite understand what they are saying? We shall see; we shall hear more about coherence hereafter.

MacIntyre writes, 'It is not then that competing traditions do not share some standards. All the traditions with which we have been concerned agree in according a certain authority to logic… Were it not so, their adherents would be unable to disagree in the way in which they do.'[8] This is a very big admission for a relativist, but he has some hesitation in going the whole hog. He refers only to 'all the traditions with which we have been concerned'. Only these? Do not all traditions accord authority to logic? If not, how do they disagree with each other and with others? Or do they never disagree? Then 'some standards'; so which standards are shared and which not? Is it a free choice? Can a tradition declare, as against another, that in the following controversy, we will not share the law of non-contradiction with you, but we don't mind sharing excluded middle? On what principles will some standards not be shared? And, again, 'a certain authority to logic'. How much? We will be logical thus far, but no further – don't you dare! After this point (to be mutually or unilaterally decided?), it's free for all, anything goes.

MacIntyre goes on to say that that on which traditions agree (because, remember, of sharing some standards and according some authority to logic) 'is insufficient to resolve those disagreements'. Further, 'we can have no reason to decide' between 'the rival and competing claims of a number of traditions'. Is this unfortunate situation occasioned due to the insufficiency of logic, as he seems to be suggesting, or due to the fact that, with regard to the conflicting claims of two traditions or communities, the facts might be so thick and tangled and the assumptions on which each party argues might be so complex and so difficult to unravel or make explicit, that it is not easy to find one's way? For example, many years ago in a dispute between two states about the consumption of river water by the two states, it took several months of arguing in the court just to fix the exact issues and charges. This was not because the parties did not give full authority to logic or did not agree on some logical standards.

MacIntyre is talking about moral traditions and presumably about moral standards or norms. If the disagreement is about some relatively trivial matter to do with social manners or modes of dress, it could surely be sorted out with a little good will on either side. If it concerns more serious matters, like the freedom of speech or conflicting religious practices, the parties would have, so to speak, step further and further back to find some common moral principle or idea which both parties share, and then work downwards to see what implications it has on the current dispute. The immense difficulty, several times, of finding such a common point of agreement and of arguing consistently and convincingly from it, is not to be minimized. But this does not show that it is, in principle, impossible. Ultimately, I suppose, appeal would have to be made to some concept of human nature and the meaning and value of human life.

That's where we'll come up against a roadblock. I think MacIntyre would endorse Rorty's position: for 'the pragmatist in morals, the claim that the customs of a given society are "grounded in human nature" is not one which he knows how to argue about'.[9] Some clarification is required. The non-pragmatist does not have to hold that a society's customs are grounded in human nature in the sense that they have originated and been derived from some idea of human nature explicitly held by a society. The point is that if a doubt about the *moral* legitimacy of a particular custom arises, such as, say, the custom of not allowing the *Sudra* to drink from a common well or barring non-Parsis from entering a fire temple, the argument would ultimately have to get back to the question: is there any quality that, as human beings, the *Sudras* possess which would pollute the water in a well or a quality which non-Parsis lack which then makes them unfit to enter fire temples?

The pragmatist's, or his cousin, the relativist's way of seeing the matter is that there is no way in which one can argue how a custom can be critically assessed or whether it can be or should be changed or given up. This is in line with their general postulate that change, when it happens, just happens. Hence, the only thing one can do with a custom or a social belief is to turn away from ethics and fall back on psychology, sociology and history, for 'once we understand', says Rorty, 'when and why various beliefs have been adopted or discarded', there is nothing 'left over to be understood'.[10] This kind of move to evade a moral or philosophical issue is typical of postmodernism.

I turn to Hans-Georg Gadamer, as interpreted and discussed by G. Warnke.[11]

'To be a member of a specific culture at a specific time,' so goes Gadamer's thought, 'means that our attempts to understand ourselves and our world always proceed on the basis of an understanding that has developed through the historical experiences and traditions of understanding we have inherited from the history in which we are immersed'. These experiences, for example, include the slave trade. That our understanding is 'shaped by a certain history' and developed through historical experiences, cannot be doubted by anybody. That 'we already possess an orientation toward … that which we are trying to understand' is also acceptable. What does not follow and is not acceptable is that 'we are prejudiced' and that this 'orientation' binds us in such a way that we must approve or not even question what we understand and have experienced – for example, the slave trade. What does the use of the morally loaded word 'prejudiced' imply? If our possessing an orientation is simply a fact, we cannot be said to be prejudiced. Does it then imply that we are not free to approve or disapprove of what we understand?

Such freedom seems to be granted by Gadamer. 'For Gadamer, prejudices are simply prejudgements or projections of meaning that offer at least a provisional framework for understanding,' which 'allow us to project a preliminary account of the meaning of that which we are trying to understand'. This freedom to project only a preliminary account concerns not only what we are trying to understand but the *meaning* of what we are trying to understand. We may have a different meaning if we so wish or think fit. The use of 'prejudiced' should, therefore, be dropped as inappropriate.

Gadamer's 'effective historical consciousness' is not only an awareness that is historically situated, but 'an awareness of the effect of being historically situated', that is that we are conscious of being influenced by history. This means that we have already transcended historical situatedness. We are influenced by history, but we are not determined by it, and so are capable of throwing it off. It would make no sense to say, for instance, 'I know the slave trade is wrong, but I am determined to think it is all right, so what can I do?' We can 'understand the history that has made us who we are', but it does not stop us from being something else.

Warnke mentions 'a further consequence'. 'If we are conscious of our debt to the past, if we recognize that we are produced by a particular history and that our understanding of the world is constituted within a particular vocabulary and frame of reference' – all of which is granted – 'then we can no longer equate that understanding with objective knowledge.' It is not at all clear from the way Warnke writes, if this is Gadamer's view, which it must be if it is a consequence of Gadamer's idea of effective-historical consciousness, as it is said to be. Does Warnke agree with it? What can you make of the following?

> Consciousness of effective history is consciousness that any understanding we … possess is relative to a particular … vocabulary. … Consciousness of effective history is aware, then, that our knowledge is the product of particular prejudices. … But if we are conscious of being prejudiced and concede that our understanding always diverges from objective knowledge, then we can be open to revising it. We can be open to the possibility that we might change our ways of thinking about the world, our situation, and ourselves.

This is extremely confusing. Firstly, 'prejudices' and 'prejudiced' seem to be used ambiguously, in the Gadamerian strange sense and in its standard sense. Secondly, up to the words 'product of particular prejudices' we seem to be doomed and imprisoned within a relative vocabulary and framework, but from the words, 'But if we are…', there seems a clear possibility of escape. Thirdly, why should we 'concede that our understanding always diverges from objective knowledge?' Even if we accept what Gadamer holds under his peculiar concept of 'prejudice', it doesn't follow that we cannot get objective knowledge. Fourthly, since Warnke says, quite rightly, that we can revise our knowledge, it means 'objective knowledge' not only makes sense, but, because it makes sense, we do have objective knowledge. Therefore, fifthly, we do not concede 'our understanding always diverges from objective knowledge', though sometimes it may do so.

Gadamer shows amazing perspicacity for a postmodern. According to him, one can emerge 'from particular points of view by encountering alien practices, other cultures', one can immerse oneself 'in that which is other', 'integrate that otherness into oneself' and 'get out of oneself'. This is the mark of being 'cultivated'. This emerging is called '*Bildung*', and achieving this 'standpoint of possible others' is 'the universal or humanity'. (We are dangerously near 'human nature', which so frightens postmoderns.) Though one is 'historically embedded' (a favourite postmodern expression), Gadamer at least seems to grant that 'one can begin the process of cultivation'.[12]

However, emancipation seems to have gone too far. Shades of the prison house are always threatening. Hermeneutics, which is the practice of interpreting cultures in different ways, and multiculturalism seem to be interested in 'preserving cultures for their own sake' (even the cultures of the Third Reich and Nietzschean nihilism?), assuming that 'all cultures are worth preserving', needing only to be interpreted, and that they 'need not be engaged in ... cultural *Bildung*'. This worries even Rorty. 'Once we recognize that our own account of what our country', tradition or culture is, is only one among many possible interpretations, that is, once truth and objectivity are banished from the debates, then they 'are not debates in which we can prove each other wrong but rather debates in which we try to show the significance of some feature of our history or society that we think the alternative interpretation overlooks or to which it gives insufficient importance'.[13] In short, they are not then debates at all but exhibitions advertising our wares. But why are we worried that these features are overlooked or given insufficient importance? Importance for what? We flounder in a sea of 'hermeneutic conversation', sometimes going under and sometimes bobbing up again. The conversation 'offers no guarantees'.[14]

Jurgen Habermas is an interesting case. He struggles hard to break away from relativism; some of his contentions are very sensible, but something keeps pulling him back.[15]

Habermas, along with others, was 'profoundly indebted to the Enlightenment conviction' that humans are endowed with 'the power to reason clearly'. 'Any invocation of the authority of tradition … cuts at the modernist, future-oriented roots of Habermas' outlook.' And yet we are immediately told that 'Habermas and Gadamer both agree that there are no truths or validating grounds which stand outside socio-historical circumstance'. Our 'cognitive perspectives' are 'formed by our "throwness", that is, by our being placed in a specific cultural-linguistic situation' (or "horizon").

However, we hear immediately after, that the 'inherited parameters of our cultural placement do not so much determine what we do, as serve as the enabling conditions of our enterprises.' The language of European philosophy is always rather flabby and obscure, but as long as we are sure that our 'throwness' does not *determine* what we do and, I suppose, how we think, the non-relativist should be satisfied. According to Habermas, 'Traditions can distort and limit any discussion of their own norms.' However, both Habermas and Gadamer 'assert the intrinsic rationality of historical and cultural discourses', which presumably means that reason can still somehow overcome those distortions and limitations. But then we are told that Gadamer (and, perhaps, Habermas too) is concerned that 'the aggrandisement of scientific rationality devalues both the historically transmitted insights of the humanities, and the ethical and legal foundations of our culture'. This, another kind of 'throwness', completely throws us off the track. Do these gentlemen think that 'scientific rationality' and 'technological reasoning' militate against the insights of our humanities and the ethico-legal foundations of our culture? That seems to be the drift, for Habermas is seen to be 'reasserting the presence of traditional wisdoms against the influence of technical rationality'.

More obscure and dubious views follow. Habermas 'insists that the claims of tradition be matched against a truth criterion', which apparently means that tradition's claims should not just be accepted without raising the question of their truth and, further, that the criterion of truth, whatever it be, is not supplied by tradition itself. This again means, that, by the application of this criterion, some traditional claims might turn out to be false and should therefore be rejected.

The extension of the same sentence makes us pause. The truth criterion 'once established', so we are told, 'will enable us to rationally endorse and extend the tradition'. This makes it appear that this truth criterion is simply a kind of official certification of the traditional claims and not, after all, a critique of them. It seems to be a foregone conclusion that the truth criterion *will* endorse and even extend the tradition; but may it not in fact do just the opposite?

While Gadamer insists that traditional truth claims 'cannot be externally legitimated' (which means that their truth somehow shines by its own light), Habermas 'is suspicious of historically transmitted material' and speaks, instead, "of a kind of truth which measures itself on an idealized consensus achieved in unlimited communication free from force". The words 'idealized', 'unlimited' and 'free from force' are indicative of the idea that reason works free of any actually limiting conditions or barriers; its only conditions are the principles of reasoning. Postmoderns and semi-postmoderns cannot dissociate themselves from the idea of consensus. Getting consensus is a secondary matter; truth can obtain even where all don't agree. Truth, for Habermas, is "unforced universal recognition". Once you bring in 'universal', you may bid farewell to relativism and postmodernism. Truth may not always be actually universally recognized, but it demands such recognition. (The words in double quotation marks are Habermas's.)

I shall end this chapter with some remarks on truth and warranted assertibility. The postmoderns' insistence on this distinction is motivated by their hostility to truth. The concept of truth is meaningless, postmoderns say, because we can never get to it; all we can get to is warranted assertibility. Rorty is the chief protagonist of this view.

Justification, according to Rorty, 'must be relative to some particular audience'. As usual, in Rorty's case, our reaction must be, yes and no. Yes, because, if I have got a truth, I would not then try to justify it to myself; I try to justify it because *you* seem to doubt it. No, because, to justify is to give reasons and arguments, and if these are good enough, they are good enough for *any* audience, though the manner of putting them might have to differ from audience to audience. We have, once again, the cart-horse flip. A claim is accepted by an audience because they consider it justified or 'rationally acceptable'; it is not justified because it is accepted. A thoroughly spurious claim may be accepted by a dumb audience. How else do charlatans flourish?

Rorty's point that a claim 'will always invite the question "to whom?"' is irrelevant. The right question, as McDowell shows, is 'in the light of what?' If we go along with Rorty, Galileo would have had hardly a warrant for his claims and, on Rorty's showing, they became warranted only when, centuries later, they were accepted – but not by all even till now![16]

Much depends on the quality of an audience. When a person makes what he believes to be a true proposition, the only correct answer to the question, 'to whom?' is 'to myself'. Thinking is a dialogue with oneself. The history of science and of mankind has plenty of instances of truth not having been accepted by communities, even scientific communities. After Galileo had recanted and declared that the earth does not go around the sun, legend has it that he whispered, 'But it does,' to himself.

Is there, then, a distinction between truth and warranted assertibility or justification? Again, yes and no. Yes, because of the following: The warrant depends on the facts known and the principles used at the time of making the claim. From the available evidence, a validly drawn conclusion would amount to complete justification and so accepted as true. Not to accept it would be perverse. There is, at the time, nothing like 'climbing outside our own minds', whatever that exactly means, as Rorty suggests. What our mind has brought to us, we must believe and believe to be true. It *is* true, as far as we can possibly be sure. But, of course, it is quite possible that new evidence may turn up and, also, that there may be a flaw in the reasoning and, therefore, what we took to be true, may be seen to be false. If and when it is seen to be false, we must take it that it was false even at the time when we (quite justifiably) took it to be true. There is, then, a distinction between warranted justification and truth, because a claim which is warranted might turn out to be false.

But the answer to our question is also, No. The truth cannot be got at by, in some way, bypassing the standard procedure of reasoning on available evidence. Even if a godman or prophet told us what later turned out to be true, we would not have been warranted in believing it to be true when it was told us. Knowledge and truth cannot be got on the cheap.

Thus, though there is a distinction between truth and warranted assertibility, its consequence is not a dismissal of truth. Indeed, it is precisely because there is truth that the distinction can be made. It is because a claim, which bore all the marks of truth, that is, it was warrantedly assertible, turned out not to be true, that we know what truth is and warranted assertibility is.

The problem of justification that worries postmoderns may be briefly stated.

According to epistemological relativism, a belief is justified relative to an evidential system, 'E', which is a 'bunch of rules for determining under what conditions one is to believe various things'. This is acceptable to a non-relativist. In fact, one must add that in addition to such rules, 'E' must also include a whole system of beliefs within which the belief in question would be assessed. For example, to justify a proposition in a criminal trial, the Evidence Act would be part of 'E' and regarding a claim about the movement of a planet, the whole theory regarding planetary movement would be 'E'. So far, no problem. The problem is, can rival, incompatible 'E's themselves be objectively or rationally evaluated? Can we say 'E^1's is a better or superior or more justified evidential system than 'E^2' absolutely or non-relatively?'[17]

Siegel, from whom the earlier quotation was taken, says that if we cannot thus compare rival beliefs, 'it is difficult to see how any belief, no matter how bizarre, can be ruled out or evaluated negatively', for it may fit into some equally bizarre system, 'E^1', and if 'E^1' cannot be rationally evaluated, one would have to accept the belief as true. This is exactly what postmoderns want us to believe. The most whimsical beliefs, they say, must be treated on par with those of modern Western science, which is just one evidential system among others.

There could be, in fact always are, hierarchies of systems. For example, the planetary system is a system within a larger system which includes suns and galaxies, so that a system itself can be evaluated by reference to a more inclusive system. Harré and Krausz point out that either there is an infinite regress of increasingly inclusive systems or there is a final system which is not included in a still more comprehensive system. They say, 'Neither horn suits the relativist book.'[18]

We must, I think, rest with the idea that science does not expect to reach a final system or, which is perhaps the same thing, one absolute Truth (the sort of thing Pilate, scoffingly, was asking for). Whatever, at the latest stage and in a particular field of inquiry, is seen as the most comprehensive system of beliefs, and the one least open to rational objections, has to be accepted as the truth, with always the proviso that it may be corrected, improved upon, made more comprehensive and logically tight, or scrapped. This is a necessary feature of any inquiry, narrowly 'scientific' or any other.

References

1. O'Grady, P.O., 2002, p. 17.

2. Cohen, S., 'Contextualism, Skepticism, and the Structure of Reason' in Tomberlin, J. E. (Ed.), 1999, p. 57.

3. Ibid., pp. 58-60.

4. O'Grady, P. O., 2002, pp. 17-18.

5. Ibid., p. 18.

6. Lloyd, G., 'Feminism in History and Philosophy' in Fricker, M. & J. Hornsby (Eds.), 2000, pp. 246-47.

7. Rorty, R., 1983, p. 178.

8. MacIntyre, A., 1988, p. 351.

9. Rorty, R., 1983, p. 178.

10. Ibid., p. 178.

11. Warnke, G., 'Rorty's Democratic Hermeneutics' in Guignon, C. & D. R. Hiley (Eds.), 2003, pp. 107-9.

12. Ibid., p. 110.

13. Ibid., p. 119.

14. Ibid., p. 121.

15. Teichman, J. & G. White (Eds.), 1995, pp. 150-51.

16. McDowell, J., op. cit., p. 117.

17. Harré, R. & M. Krausz, 1996, pp. 29-30.

18. Ibid., p. 30.

Chapter 7

Is Ratiocination Dead?

'Sir, I have given you an argument, but I am
not obliged to find you an understanding.'

Samuel Johnson

Deconstruction is 'a set of strategies' to 'expose and subvert the unarticulated presumptions of metaphysical thought' and to 'subvert logic rather than to support it'. It is 'a manifestation of postmodernity'. The tools and strategies used are rhetoric, metaphor, parody, the 'demonstration that truth is always a metaphor' and a 'reversal of binary oppositions', so that pain is preferred to pleasure, evil to good, retrogression to progress, lying to truthfulness, error to truth and, of course, female to male. It is not clear why logic should be subverted, nor why, indeed, it needs to be supported. Surely it can stand on its own.[1] One may say deconstruction is the militant wing of postmodernism.

Deconstructionist postmodernism denies the infamous Archimedean point and holds that even history and culture are only texts, not realities; they can be interpreted endlessly without ever making contact with anything real, if anything is real anyway.

Such interpretation is 'unstable'. (But why not stable?) In high metaphorical language we are told that 'metaphors of dance and movement have replaced the ontological fixed stare of the motionless spectator', and instead of the 'lust for finality', we have (in Derrida's phrase) 'incalculable choreographies'.[2] All is passing show and shifting sand; no rocks or land in sight.

One may mention some other strategies used by postmodernism: 'misappropriating ideas from the philosophy of science ... to support radical relativism', using 'scientific (or pseudo-scientific) terminology', 'shamelessly throwing around technical terms', 'intoxication with words, combined with a superb indifference to their meaning', the use of analogies 'to hide the weaknesses of the vaguer theory', 'obscure jargon'.[3]

Stephen Toulmin writes,[4] 'Eighty or ninety years ago, scholars and critics, as much as scientists, shared a common confidence in their established procedures... How little of that confidence remains today! One even hears it argued that the concept of rationality itself is no more than a by-product of Western or European ways of thinking' and 'the claims of rationality have been progressively challenged'. Toulmin believes, however, that since the 1960s (the very time when postmodernism sprouted!) the tide has turned due to the increased use of scientific technology in medical ethics, ecology and other such fields.

I am not so sure that the increasing prominence and astonishing developments of scientific technology are matched by a return to, and interest in, the philosophical concept of rationality. Postmoderns have to accept the fact of scientific technology, but they think they have a way of wriggling out of rationality.

I am also not at all sure that Toulmin would be the right choice for an advocate of rationality. He seems to be fascinated by the language of postmodernism.[5]

One of the top concerns of postmodernism is 'bias', concerning which their thought is terribly confused. 'In the human sciences,' writes Toulmin, 'the line between bias and detachment is very hard to draw… A judge may give every appearance of impartiality' and yet give 'disproportionate punishment' for racial reasons. How does this make it hard to draw the line mentioned above? If you detect an appearance, but not the reality, of impartiality, then you know very well what impartiality is. Do you then think that human nature is so chock-full of original sin that it can never achieve the real thing? Nobody has ever said impartiality or, the same thing, objectivity is easy to practise.

Toulmin proceeds, 'Yet the nature of "objectivity" in the human sciences can be clearly defined only if we keep our eyes open' to distortions. Absolutely right. But now he turns hostile against those (here the Frankfurt critics) who point out the liability of scientific views to distortion. The 'posture of such critics seems to imply that they alone can view the contemporary situation "objectively"', 'claim to cut through the fog and get to the truth', but, don't you see, Toulmin is saying, that they themselves run the risk of being misled in the same way as those they are criticizing? This *ad hominem* attack is a red herring. It is the old ploy of turning on your opponent with: 'Why do you think you are right? You also may be mistaken.' Judge not lest you be judged may be good moral advice, but with regard to an intellectual debate, it is silly and self-defeating, for the party to whom you say this could equally turn on you and point out that you too may be mistaken. This sort of argument gets us nowhere. Is

Toulmin suggesting that no one should point out cases of distortion or that even to refer to it is indecent? All that is necessary for the Frankfurt critics or any other critics to do is to take precautions against themselves causing the distortions that they are pointing out in others, and if they are (not 'may be') guilty of distorting things, it should of course be pointed out to them. In producing the red herring, Toulmin is proceeding in the manner that is standard practice for postmoderns.

In asking, 'Why do the critical philosophers think they are the only people having an impartial or unbiased position?' Toulmin has been carried far away from what he had begun talking about – the nature of bias and objectivity – but he has, unconsciously, admitted that some people, even if not the critical philosophers, can be impartial, unbiased and objective (all synonyms) or, at least, that these words stand for a meaningful concept and that the 'line between bias and detachment' is not really so hard to draw as he had supposed.

And now the Archimedean point. 'The pursuit of objectivity in the human sciences,' he writes (for, like Charles Taylor, in the physical sciences he admits objectivity), 'no longer depends on our ability to find a uniquely correct standpoint from which to arrive at proper judgements. No such unique viewpoint is to be found.' But neither the Frankfurt critics nor the critical philosophers have wanted to find such a viewpoint or needed one. How is that? Well, Toulmin himself now tells us. 'In the social sciences as elsewhere, the problem of achieving objectivity is that of learning to counter our own biases.' It was staring us in the face all the time! 'What fools these mortals be!' That he has just committed a *petitio* Toulmin hasn't realized. Anyway, objectivity can, then, be achieved, and that too, so simply. 'It requires us to make explicit, and to make allowances for, the interests and values that we ourselves bring to our research.' So, by subjecting ourselves to psychoanalysis, such of our interests and values, which (I take it) caused bias would, by their sheer exposure to light – the light of reason, perhaps? – wither and die. You see the 'space platform' was not required; the norms of 'bias, impartiality and objectivity' (of bias too!) are 'embedded in particular kinds of situations and cases'.

Poor Toulmin just doesn't know what he is saying, for now again he relapses into saying that in the human sciences 'attempts to maintain value-neutrality finally proved vain'.

Those who still have faith in the validity and objectivity of reason have to admit that it is logically impossible to convince, to his own satisfaction, the sceptic who sincerely and doggedly maintains an opposite stand. Let us listen to a dialogue between Miss Ratio, who is on the side of the angels, and Dr. Nihil, who is an anti-angel.

Miss Ratio: Reason is a faculty of ours by which we can understand something, examine it, criticize it, accept it as true or reject it as false. Reasoning works by means of arguments and counter-arguments either between different parties or even silently within oneself. Reason makes it possible for us to communicate with each other and understand each other's views. It makes it possible for us to argue and, if lucky, to reach some commonly acceptable conclusion.

Dr. Nihil: It seems that you think that there is something
             called Reason, which is common to all humans.
             I don't understand this at all and I don't agree
             with it. There is no such Reason with a capital
             'R'; there are only reasonings or reasonings
             within a particular culture, and the reasoning
             that operates in one culture is or may be quite
             different from that which operates in another.
             In other words, reasoning – like so many other
             things, like dress, eating habits, manners – is
             culture-dependent. Variety, my dear Miss Ratio,
             is the spice of life.

Ratio: Do you mean that if you and I belong to
             different cultures, you and I couldn't converse
             together or understand one another or argue with
             one another? That if you make a statement,
             I couldn't either agree with you or contradict
             you and try to show you that you are wrong?
             Do you mean we would not be able to discuss
             and thrash out our differences?

Nihil: Yes, that's what I believe.

Ratio: But in saying this don't you see that you are
             drawing conclusions from what you believe
             about reasoning? And drawing conclusions *is*
             reasoning.

Nihil: Yes, I am drawing conclusions, but that is
             according to my idea of reasoning, not yours.

Ratio: But *I* am accepting the conclusions *you* are

drawing from your premises – that is, that if reason is the kind of thing you say it is, *then* your conclusions follow, but they follow according to principles of reasoning which *I* am trying to convince you of and which, at this stage we are both of us using.

Nihil: I don't admit any of what you are saying, because it all depends on what you assume due to your idea of reasoning – that if we both agree, we are using the same principles of reasoning. But I don't accept your principles of reasoning and so I don't have to agree to all that you are trying to push down my throat. This is what Foucault would call tyranny and the reign of terror.

Ratio: But in trying so hard to explain all this to me, are you using your kind of reasoning or the kind of reasoning which, as I say, is common to both of us?

Nihil: My kind of reasoning, of course. How could I use your or any other kind of reasoning but mine? How could I, as Rorty would say, jump out of my own mind?

Ratio: But in that case, I remain unmoved, for can you hope to convince me by using a kind of reasoning, which I don't accept? You see, I can't jump out of my mind either.

Nihil: Exactly, you've got my point at last. I don't hope to be able to explain anything to you or convince you.

Ratio: Then what are you trying to do right now? Anyway, you think you can't convince me because you hold that your kind of reasoning is different from mine. I agree, but don't you see that in arguing that from your kind of reasoning you can't hope to convince me, you are using an argument, which you find satisfactory, and which you believe should also satisfy me and stop me from arguing further. But *you* have no right – logical right – to be so satisfied, because your satisfaction with your own argument is based on *my* kind of reasoning.

Nihil: You are quite right. I have no right to be satisfied because I was using your kind of reasoning in order to convince *you*. To convince myself I would use a different argument according to my kind of reasoning. You are trying to trap me by using your kind of argument, which I don't accept.

Ratio: This stand of yours is perfectly valid.

Nihil: No, no, you think it is valid according to your idea of validity, but that is not my idea of validity. In fact, I don't believe in validity and all that rubbish. So, you see, my argument, which you admit to be valid, is not really valid at all – not for me. It's quite elementary, really.

Ratio: But this last point of yours is itself...

This dialogue has the potential of going on and on till one of the parties dies of exhaustion. Although Miss Ratio can never convince Dr. Nihil that he is tying himself in a knot, that without using what he is arguing against he can't argue at all, it does not have to follow that those who are not of his way of thinking cannot see where he is mistaken and what is the truth about reasoning. Scepticism should not paralyse the non-sceptic and stop him from investigating the basis of scepticism. The point has been made long ago. Referring to Plato's *Republic and Gorgias*, McDowell writes:

> I think the moral, in both the dialogues, must be meant to be something on these lines: people who raise such questions are dangerous, and should be forced into silence, or acquiescence, by whatever means are available; people whose character is in good order will have confidence in right answers to the questions, a confidence that should not be threatened by the fact that questioners such as Callicles or Thrasymachus cannot be won over by persuasive argument.[6]

In this chapter I shall discuss a number of the salient features of reasoning. I use 'reasoning' and 'thinking' as synonyms, although in other discussions, 'thinking' may be taken to have a wider connotation.

It is generally agreed (as we have seen in Chapter 5) that reasoning is an activity peculiar to humans. Aristotle writes, '…in the brutes though we find imagination we never find belief. Further, every opinion is accompanied by belief, belief by conviction, and conviction by discourse of reason.'[7] (By 'imagination' he must be meaning 'having mental images'.) It seems correct to say that both animals and humans '*have* reasons for actions' because they both pursue goals consciously and their actions may be said to *be* reasonable to the extent that they are seen to be, in varying degrees, suitable for achieving those goals. Such behaviour is contrasted with other things that happen like the growth of plants, boulders rolling down the hillside in the monsoon or the functioning of machines, even highly sophisticated computers. Only humans are said to have 'the power of *reasoning*', which depends on 'powers that have a less fully actualized form in higher animals'.[8] This view is in line with the theory, fully argued by F. H. Bradley in *The Principles of Logic*, that thinking, which implies the use of universals, is or must be present, in embryonic form, throughout the animal kingdom. Whether this is so or not does not really concern us here; we are trying to understand reasoning as it occurs in humans.

In order to be justifiably called 'rational' or reasoning animals, humans do not have to be constantly and continuously reasoning or be 'always self-consciously logical'. They may be riding a bicycle, just enjoying a lilting melody or the fresh sea breeze, or engaged in looking at the sunset. L. S. Stebbing describes in detail the difference between the 'train of thoughts' (for want of a better word) passing through the head of a man lying on the seashore, daydreaming, and the way his mind works when he actively reasons. When daydreaming, thoughts unconnected with each other succeed each other, caused by what his eye happens to catch or by psychological association, as, when seeing a bird in flight, he recalls his first plane flight. All this is called 'unreflective thinking' by Stebbing. Now the man suddenly realizes that the tide has risen and he is in danger of being drowned. This begins a train of logically connected thoughts controlled by a desire to escape to safety. This Stebbing calls 'reflective thinking'; it is reasoning or thinking properly so-called. Such thinking can be initiated by a practical problem about, as in the above case, how to escape from the danger, or by a purely theoretical one. Our man on the shore might notice a wide opening in the rocky headland and he might wonder what it might be. His investigation, due to sheer human curiosity, into this theoretical problem could involve a vast amount of observation and reasoning.[9]

Can there be absolutely pure reverie without a tinge of reasoning in it, or, for that matter, in activities like enjoying music or the sea breeze, which are not generally classified as thinking? In cycling or having a stroll, some thinking is probably involved. For our discussion, such questions need not be further probed. I agree with Audi that humans have 'in some sense *internalized* rational standards which then guide them without the conscious thoughts one might cite in explicitly rationalizing their behaviour.' (What Audi means by 'rationalizing' seems to be 'reasoning in supporting their behaviour.') Audi further says that reasoning, that is, explicit reasoning, is not the only manifestation of our rationality nor a constant element in the formation of our beliefs.[10] Though we do not consciously and explicitly perform the act of reasoning, reasoning is always involved in all or most consciously performed activities.

Rationality can be attributed to actions and to beliefs, but, perhaps, to emotions too. A rational action is one where means are used to reach a goal. It might still be considered rational even if the goal is a mistaken one or the means not quite appropriate. For example: 'Given John's belief that he is Napoleon, it is quite rational for him to ... buy presents for Josephine,' says O'Grady. Don Quixote acted rationally when he charged the giants of his imagination. This is 'instrumental' rationality, rationally choosing appropriate means towards a chosen end. Can goals or aims be rational? Certainly, if a particular goal is a means towards a further end. If Bipasha buys a piano as a means towards learning how to play the piano, then the latter is a goal for which the former is a means, but learning how to play might itself be a rational goal if it is done as a means towards earning a living by concertising. But if Bipasha learns to play only because she wants to play, can that desire to play be rational? Most of our actions are done in order to go on living; can living be called a rational goal? If it can, O'Grady calls this 'a stronger sense of rationality than the instrumental one'. Are there 'universal criteria for evaluating goals which are not means to further goals?' And 'do they vary with culture and/or historical epoch?' Relativism would say, 'Yes,' they would vary and there are no absolutely universal criteria. O'Grady thinks there is 'a minimal set of such criteria'.[11]

In order to obviate future misunderstanding and misuse, it is necessary to point out that 'rational' is also used in another sense, that is, to mean 'a reasonable' belief or action, which means that the belief or action was sufficiently warranted. 'Rationality,' says O'Grady, 'is not keyed to truth.' We have seen that a belief that is false or turns out to be false may be completely and sufficiently warranted if based on facts then available. It would be called rational. But if 'rational' means (as we have argued) 'based on reasons', then, even if a belief is based on insufficient reasons or bad reasons, it would still be called 'rational', though, perhaps, called 'unreasonable'. Here purposes become relevant. If Mary and John were going to Chicago for a very important meeting and still made a casual inquiry of a fellow traveller if the flight stopped at Chicago, we would say they acted unreasonably and, *in that sense*, irrationally. If they made the inquiry merely out of idle curiosity, they did not act irrationally or unreasonably. Even in the case of something we are very concerned about, we would still not be charged with irrationality if we believed something without personally having sufficient evidence for it. In many important matters and where crucial decisions have to be made, it is often impossible, difficult, or inconvenient to gather sufficient evidence for believing something and acting upon it. The belief would not be irrational. It would be rational for a man to whom a surgical operation is advised by his physician, to take a second and even a third opinion, and if the opinions tallied, to undergo the surgery. If he is himself not a medical person, to go on seeking further opinions, or to study the problem on his own by consulting medical textbooks, would be irrational. We have, so often, to accept, almost 'blindly', the advice of a professional who is presumed to be an expert. This is entirely rational; not to do so would be irrational, even if the advice turned out, in the end, to be wrong.

Does this make rationality relative; relative to context or culture? The concept of rationality is not relative, for the criteria by which you judge the rationality of a belief or action are the same everywhere and at all times. As O'Grady says, it is not the context of the belief, but rather how one acquires the belief, how the belief fits in with the rest of one's beliefs ... that determines its rationality or not. So there are no intrinsically rational or irrational beliefs (apart from contradictions). So the *criteria* of rationality are absolute. But the rationality of particular beliefs is relative to a culture or to the stage which a science or any system of knowledge has reached. Even when a science has reached a stage from which an earlier belief is seen to be false, it is still possible to see why it was held and, by applying the above criteria, we can conclude whether vis-à-vis the time at which, and the circumstances under which, it was held, it should be called rational or irrational. At the time at which even the geocentric theory was not held, the belief of the ancients that every morning a new sun was born and during every sunset it was extinguished, was a rational belief. In this paragraph 'rational' is used as 'reasonable or well grounded'.

O'Grady gives 'two central components of rationality', a positive and a negative. The components are coherence and evidence.[12] 'Rationality is again used in the sense of 'reasonableness'.

Under coherence:

Principle 1: Non-contradiction. Even if different or 'paraconsistent logics are accepted in highly circumscribed contexts', these too are governed by the general criterion of non-contradiction. Though we do, not infrequently, commit contradictions, we cannot, if we want to think at all and argue correctly, take the position of not being sensitive to possible contradictions and of not wanting to resolve them. And wanting to or not wanting to think and think correctly are not open options. Even the decision not to think is a piece of thinking.

Principle 2: There are and must be inferential connections between the propositions that make up a piece of reasoning or argument. It has to be a coherent whole. Therefore one has to be on the watch for the fallacies of equivocation and amphiboly, which may ruin the wholeness of the argument.

Under evidence:

Principle 3: Seek as much evidence as possible and do not avoid contrary evidence. Evidence comes from many sources, principally perception, memory and testimony. O'Grady includes inference, but inference is what you do with evidence. One who ignores evidence and reaches a conclusion, false or true, has proceeded irrationally; one who considers all relevant evidence and still reaches a false conclusion has also acted irrationally, but his irrationality is logical.

Principle 4: Be intellectually honest. Do not cook results, deal fairly with counter-arguments and counter-evidence, and try hard not to be dogmatic and biased. These are as much ethical as intellectual requirements.

Thinking sometimes has a connotation wider than reasoning. What are you thinking of? 'My home in Mumbai', or 'I'm remembering my visit to New York'. Here there is no reasoning or inference, and it is debatable if there is even a judgement. On the other hand, there are judgements to which the term 'thinking' would not be applied even in its wider sense. According to 'the natural usage of a language', says John Cook Wilson, the term 'thinking' is not generally applied to 'every apprehension of the nature of an object' or to the 'apprehension of a feeling'. Here is a newspaper report:

> When they looked into the well, all they saw was a vague form and two glowing eyes. They deduced that an animal had fallen into the well.
>
> (*Mumbai Mirror*, 20 July 2006)

Does this sound a little odd? Did they deduce, or did they immediately realize that it was an animal? Was the fact of its having fallen into the well a piece of inference? If the whole animal were clearly visible, would there be a deduction? If I experience a certain kind of feeling in my leg, do I deduce that it is a pain or an itch? Wilson says there are 'activities' which 'would not be called thinking';[13] they would be cases of knowing without being cases of thinking.

Again, there are activities which certainly *involve* reasoning, but are not referred to as reasoning, like, for example, composing music or a poem or performing a surgical operation, and, perhaps, driving a car or conducting an orchestra.

There is another usage which often causes needless confusion. This is 'thinking' used to mean something less than knowledge. 'I think it will rain tonight, but it may not.' 'I think he is an ass, but I wouldn't be able to prove it.' 'I do not *think*, I *know* he is an ass', makes perfect sense, but 'I *know* that he is brilliant, but I don't think so,' doesn't.

'"Thinking" in its full sense, in its free and proper form, is explicit judgement or inference,' writes H. H. Joachim; it is 'a "discursive process"'. It is 'the activity of a finite intellect'; it is '(in one sense) "my own"', yet it is 'objective and impersonal, working in, and controlling, "my" mind' and 'I am in the grip, and under the governance, of a power … transcending … "my" intellect and "its" functioning.'[14]

It is, however, necessary to supplementally point out that the thinker also, according to his capacity and lights, controls the activity. It is not as if he is driven along by that power in the way he would be by a strong wind which he couldn't resist or made to act under hypnosis by a psychiatrist. He moves from idea to idea, premises to conclusion in keeping with logical principles and norms, as he understands them. He has a purpose in reaching a goal. Reasoning involves the 'ability to assess the evidence' and 'to discount, as far as may be, the effects of prejudice'.[15] 'As far as may be' refers to the thinker's own intellectual limitations, which can, in principle, be overcome, and not to any *external* compulsions forcing the activity in a particular direction as a railway track forces a train to take a certain course. Stebbing writes:

> To be thinking something out is to be in a questioning frame of mind. A necessary and sufficient condition of asking a question is being puzzled about something, i.e. about a topic… We should not be puzzled unless we already know something about the problem that sets us on thinking and are aware that there is more to be known about it.[16]

So far inference or reasoning has been seen as a mental process. This was good enough in order to mark some of its important features. This has now to be corrected in accordance with Bernard

Bosanquet's critical comments on F. H. Bradley's treatment of inference in *The Principles of Logic*.[17]

Bradley says that inference 'gives us something new'.[18] Bosanquet maintains that '*discovery* is an accident and not an essential of inference'.[19] There can be a discovery without any inference, as when Cortez (so says Keats) gazed on the Pacific, and there can be inference without a discovery, as when, after 399 BC, people knew Socrates was mortal without having to deduce it by means of a syllogism. An occurrence may be known as a fact without knowing why it happens. To find out why or how it happened is, for example, the detective's job. He uses both observation and inference. When the how and why are known, the occurrence is *understood*. This is, of course, new knowledge, but the occurrence as an occurrence was known already. 'Hey! This pool is much deeper than it looks; I nearly drowned!' 'That is because light coming from the floor of the pool bends where it leaves the water and … so it *must* look shallower than it is.' What was at first just a fact to the man who almost drowned has, through an inferential argument, been explained. Sometimes, even the 'facts' might turn out to be different from what they were thought to be, after the reasoning in the explanation is understood. An ignoramus might say, 'Every day the sun moves from east to west; I don't understand this.' Our small piece of astronomical reasoning would not only be an explanation of what the chap sees every day; even the 'fact' was not a fact – the sun doesn't move from east to west.

What Bosanquet wants to emphasize is that the *process* of combining the premises and drawing the conclusion is a psychological occurrence which takes time, has a beginning and an end; inference is the *insight* which springs into being the moment you grasp – it doesn't matter how long it takes – the connection between premise(s) and conclusion. Just as running takes time, but winning doesn't, thinking or reasoning takes time, but the inference or argument (as it is called) doesn't, because it is a logical entity and is grasped in a flash. 'Oh, I see', is a common expression that indicates this flash.

I shall deal rather rapidly with difficult questions that arise about perception, judgement and inference.

Judgement is, *prima facie*, distinguished from inference. The conclusion along with the premises is generally called the inference; the conclusion itself is a judgement. Wilson counters this. If 'we allow "judgement" the meaning necessary for the view under consideration, viz. the having any knowledge, belief, or opinion, the judgement called the conclusion is not anything apart from the process of inference, by which it is attained'.[20] (After listening to Bosanquet on inference, we should rather say, 'apart from the connection with the premises which make it necessary'.) Wilson's view is consonant with Bosanquet's that inference is judgement pulled out like a telescope.[21] The point is that a conclusion reached by invalid reasoning, or for the wrong reasons, or for no reasons at all, would not amount to knowledge because you have not really understood it. An inference can be looked upon as a judgement because it could be written out as a complex judgement, for example, 'Socrates is mortal because all men are mortal and he is a man.'

Is there any inference if, recognizing it, I say, 'That's the Qutab Minar?' It is, if I add that I know this because the guidebook says this is the tallest structure in this area, and I see that no building round about is taller. Suppose I say, 'This is a tower,' or suppose I just recognize it as a structure, or just an object; is there a lightning-quick inference in these cases?

Opinions differ greatly. Richard Sorabji thinks, 'Neither desire nor sense perception should be incorporated into reason, but should be recognized as distinct capacities', but 'all beliefs (*doxai*) should be incorporated into reason'.[22] But how far does one have to go to reach the point of distinction between belief and pure perception without a tinge of belief? If one trips over a stone, is there belief at that instant?

Sense perception is 'a form of "knowledge", a "cognizant experience", in which the mind thinks seriously', writes Joachim, 'but not thought free and explicit' which 'the percipient controls, or of which he is even aware *as* "thought". His mind instinctively interprets the *sensa*, "forms" or "constructs" them, analyses and (in analysing) synthesizes them'. 'And there is no "thought" in sense perception … which is not immersed in a *datum*' and there also is 'no *datum*, no sensuous material, which does not involve in its very constitution this interpretative … discursus'. In sense perception there *is* thought, but it is 'subdued' to the 'level of irreflective or perceptual cognizant experience.'[23] Nobody, adds Joachim, 'could maintain that "to perceive" is (or implies) *explicit* conception, judgement, or inference.'[24] In the interpretation of a *datum*, the percipient draws on a 'consciousness of a world', a background which 'forms the wider mental context which enfolds his "perceiving"' which is akin to 'judging (or inferring)'.[25] 'It is not possible,' writes Joachim, 'to "get below" the interpretative wrapping to a "primitive core" of sense perception unadulterated by "intellectual" activity;' there is 'not a "perception" *and* a "judgement about it"', these being 'complementary features' of the whole activity.[26]

Perception is, for Brand Blanshard, the simplest form of judgement, which is, 'by general admission', the 'simplest form of thought'. This simplest form of judgement, perception, is 'the simplest activity of mind that aims at truth directly', but it is 'the barest and vaguest apprehension of anything given in sense *as* anything'. 'Perception is that experience in which, on the warrant of something given in sensation at the time, we unreflectingly take some object to be before us' ('object', used widely, can include even the 'taste of a plum pudding'). What is given in sense is 'a cue' (which is not the 'object'). We have perception 'every hour of our waking lives'. Sensation by itself is 'below the perceptual level', 'perceiving proper' appears when we take something *as* something – say the colour blue as blue or even simply as colour. Explicit judgement is 'the upper limit' of perception; 'sensation is the nether limit of perception'. But it falls outside perception, doesn't it?[27]

Whatever way we find through this jungle, it is clear that perception is not a clear case of reasoning. The upshot of our tedious discussion seems to be that:

1. Even if there is actually a pre-perceptual stage of pure sensation, it cannot be a case of reasoning.

2. Perception, even at its most basic stage, should be thought of as a rudimentary, implicit piece of reasoning. This is, perhaps, a verbal matter.

3. Perception can be mistaken and the reasons for the mistake can be discussed. It is, therefore, to be distinguished from

cases of failure which are not regarded as errors by the party that experiences the failure. A dog that runs along a certain path looking for its master, doesn't find him and retraces its steps, probably feels frustrated and disappointed, but he doesn't know he is in error.

A piece of reasoning, we have seen, may be so called even if it is invalid or does not reach a true conclusion. This is because it is a consciously recognized connection between premise or premises, on the one hand, and the conclusion, on the other. And the connection, even if mistaken and so rendering the inference invalid, is a logical one. In this sense, as we have seen earlier, reasoning is unrelated to truth. And yet, in another sense, it is related to truth, because reasoning or thinking is motivated by the desire to reach a truth. One cannot reason aimlessly. Even a *reductio ad absurdum* seeks, in a backhanded way, to establish a truth.

The aim of truth-seeking in science is to build up a consistent body of knowledge. Some bodies of knowledge presuppose others and 'this, together with the instinct for simplicity and unification, encourages a further generalization which brings all partial bodies of knowledge together into the single body of unified knowledge.'[28] This, of course, is an ideal, a Cartesian dream, actually only approximated in various degrees. So, however much needs to be done to reach anywhere near the ideal, and will for ever need to be done, the way the sciences have progressed and the way some of them, once pursued independently of each other, have come together to form a new science (examples: microbiology, biochemistry and astrophysics), it is clear that science is not entirely the ramshackle structure that Kuhn believed it to be.

Quinton, agreeing with Stace, admits that unreasoned beliefs play a large part in our thinking, not only because we cannot hope to rationally justify every one of the beliefs we hold, but because many of them are held due to 'associative suggestion' which works along with scientific reasoning. The scientists have to be on their guard against mere association and unreasoned belief. One must also admit 'inarticulate diagnostic skill which is acquired from long-continued experience of a particular kind of subject-matter'. It has been admitted by surgeons that non-medical women workers can often diagnose breast cancer by palpating more accurately than surgeons can. But in most cases these hunches, until scientifically established by more sophisticated methods, are insecure and perilous.[29]

I have dealt with reasoning as traditional philosophy has seen it. Philosophy and science, particularly the physical sciences and especially physics, have been accepted as using reason at its best. I now turn to a kind of thinking – for thinking it is – that challenges these ideas. Rorty, the detractor-in-chief of traditional philosophy, 'believes that most of what passes for philosophy is either useless, clever puzzle-solving, with no relevance to the lives of real people, or potentially damaging, an attempt to ... put an end to inquiry.' This doughty champion of the new philosophy, however, does not believe in 'arguing for positions', but wants to 'simply try out'. What? Philosophical methods? No, he wants to try out 'the pragmatist's view of the nature and aims of inquiry' itself, 'and see what happens'. Is this trying out to be done by presenting views and arguments and testing them? It is to be done by a 'gradual inculcation of new ways of speaking, rather than of straightforward argument within old ways of speaking'.[30]

One of the standard ways in traditional philosophy, science and even common sense, to demolish an opposite view, is to expose some error or piece of nonsense in it. The assumption in such an enterprise is that you and your opponent accept the principles of reasoning and standard techniques of argument. Postmoderns, denying all this, are left without the right tools and weapons used by the traditionalists. But resourceful as they are, they have risen to the occasion. They deny the very possibility of error and nonsense. 'Continental philosophers,' writes Bouveresse, meaning, here, postmoderns, 'generally don't believe that such a thing as an error (or *a fortiori*, nonsense) can exist in philosophy,' or, indeed, anywhere. 'In order for there to be refutations,' says Bouveresse, 'there must be propositions,' but, for Rorty, interesting philosophy is a 'contest between an entrenched vocabulary which has become a nuisance and a half-formed new vocabulary'. Refuting is, for Rorty, a 'waste of time'. For Heidegger, 'refutation is nonsensical'.[31]

I turn to MacIntyre for some light on the subject of relativity.[32] MacIntyre's style of writing is such that he seems to be poised in unstable equilibrium: he sometimes unfolds a view at length as if he holds it and then you find that he doesn't. However, I am more concerned with the different views and not so much with which of them he holds. With this caveat, let us proceed.

MacIntyre rightly sees a connection between postmodern relativism and the views of some Nietzscheans and, further back, of the Sophists. The postmodern view is that all 'claims are made from some point of view, and any attempt to speak in a way that overcomes relativity and one-sidedness is foredoomed to failure.' The first part of this statement is innocuous; of course, every claim is made from some particular point of view and not in a vacuum. But once you adopt that point of view and possible ambiguities are straightened out, the truth-value of your statement is judged by objective standards, for, even from your point of view, you may see things right or otherwise. Hence, the second part of the statement quoted above neither follows from the first nor is it correct.

MacIntyre speaks of a way of regarding matters where 'a variety of theses have been advanced, defended ... and then refuted or abandoned, to be replaced by others; still no overall direction has emerged' and there is no 'progress'. What he seems to want to say is that no one thesis is any better or truer than another. This, of course, does happen sometimes in an inquiry; we still haven't got the true thesis or the truth about some matters. But it does not show that we never can or will find a thesis better and truer than any we have had so far. However, the words 'defended', 'refuted' and 'abandoned' clearly show that just because a thesis is 'advanced', it does not mean it must be accepted. So, where does relativism come in? The essence of relativism is that if I, from my point of view, advance a thesis, you, from your point of view, cannot refute it, because neither of us can overcome his own point of view. As Rorty would say, there is no error and no nonsense.

But MacIntyre says 'there might be progress pointing toward a goal', which is his way of saying that the successively advanced theses might be better and better, that is, truer and truer. *Such* theses would have certain necessary characteristics.

One of these is that a thesis advanced at a later stage of the inquiry would show why there was disagreement at an earlier stage. The 'later stages provide a theory of error ... to account for inadequacy at earlier stages' (he means a theory which explains that inadequacy).

An even more significant characteristic is that a 'gradually enriched conception of the goal' of the inquiry (the goal being, of course, the full truth), would show 'what it would be to have completed the inquiry' and so 'provide a single, unified explanation of the subject matter'. From this position it would be possible to 'deduce ... every relevant truth concerning the subject matter' and, most importantly, 'show that ... they [the truths] would not be other than they are'.

MacIntyre does not clearly say if he endorses this view of an inquiry. He does not say that it is wrong and that inquiries don't have such characteristics. In fact, he asks if adopting this view 'commits one to holding that one can finally exempt oneself from the one-sidedness of a point of view', that is, from relativism. He startles us with, 'Not at all.' He says this account, which is anti-relativist, 'is consistent *either* with' the conception of a 'single, unified explanation' which fully exempts one from one-sidedness (or, the same thing, relativism) '*or* with the rival and incompatible view'.

One would expect some clever move by which this anomaly could be smoothed out and some strong reasons for holding on to the one-sidedness view after the excellent analysis he has given of the other position. All one gets is the wishy-washy statement that 'although one can definitely progress toward the final completion of rational inquiry', that is, towards a finally true position regarding a subject matter, yet 'that completion lies at a point which cannot itself be attained.' This is an amazing point to make. No anti-relativist would think that he was bound to maintain that every inquiry must reach its goal. Many limited inquiries do reach their goal; crimes are often traced to their origins. Scientific investigation of nature is not expected to ever reach a final, all-encompassing truth. The point is that the admitted progress of an inquiry towards a goal shows that the elimination of 'one-sidedness and partiality' is conceivable and progressively attained, and this is enough to defeat relativism. MacIntyre springs another surprise on us: 'Hence we would be rescued by the progress of that inquiry from the one-sidedness of any particular point of view; we would still be guided by a conception of what it would be to understand things as they are absolutely and not just relating to some standpoint, even if such final understanding is not in fact to be attained.' Exactly what I just said in criticism of him! If the final and unattained understanding was, then, not crucial to the issue, why was print wasted on it? Just as the emperor complained that in Mozart's music there were too many notes, one can complain, with greater justification, that in MacIntyre's writing there are far too many words. The position that 'all claims are made from some point of view' is then quite compatible with the view that things can be understood 'as they are absolutely, and not just relating to some standpoint'. Can it be denied that MacIntyre stands on a 'fine equipoise' between conflicting positions?

I turn to an earlier discussion in MacIntyre's same book.[33] He refers to the 'concept of a kind of inquiry which is inseparable from the intellectual and social tradition in which it is embodied'. But why talk only of 'a kind of inquiry'? *All* inquiries, we have granted, are so embodied, because no inquiry 'floats on high' over particular contexts. The Enlightenment is very clear on this point, for, according to it, what contend 'are rival doctrines, doctrines which may as a matter of fact have been elaborated in particular times and places, but whose content and whose truth and falsity, whose possession or lack of rational justification, is quite independent of their historical origin.' The Enlightenment thinkers at least found no incompatibility here. That is found only by our postmoderns. About the kind of inquiry he has referred to, MacIntyre explains that theories have 'a structure in terms of which certain theses have the status of first principles; other claims within such a theory will be justified by derivation from these first principles.' (This formulation is inadequate because, in empirical science, everything is not, and cannot be, derived purely from the first principles; much comes from observation, but it has to be consistent with the first principles. However...) 'But what justifies the first principles themselves, or rather the whole structure of theory of which they are a part?' asks MacIntyre, and answers that it 'is the rational superiority of that particular structure to all previous attempts'. In case we pounce on him and say, 'But then, it is possible to assess the truth of a structure independently of its time and place of origin and by criteria that are part of, and within, the structure itself,' he is quick to add 'within that particular tradition'. So, that particular tradition supplies the criteria for assessing the merits of different structures within the tradition.

Are we not talking within the whole tradition of science, which tries to understand the world rationally? Seems not, for MacIntyre writes that: 'It is not a matter of those first principles being acceptable to all rational persons whatsoever.' So there are, on this view, different rational traditions to which persons with varying kinds of rationality owe allegiance and for whom totally different and perhaps opposed principles are acceptable, one in which '(p⊃q. p)⊃q' and another in which '(p⊃q.~p)⊃q'. There are, says MacIntyre, 'rationalities rather than rationality'. So, we wonder which rationality he is using in explaining and justifying all this. Of course the rationality of modern Western science, he would reply. But then, my dear Alasdair, if we are children of an ancient Indian tradition, would all that you are saying be Greek or double-Dutch to us? 'No,' MacIntyre would say, you people, due to years of British rule, have entered the modern Western scientific tradition. But, my sapient sir, if the traditions are different, how have we managed to perform this miracle?

'Doctrines, theses and arguments have all to be understood in terms of historical context.' We agree; understood, please note. Since every thesis has to be advanced by someone in some precise linguistic formulation of specific arguments and since linguistic idioms change over time and so does the manner of presenting them, if we want to understand the thought of earlier philosophers, we have to take account of the historical context. We must know, for example, that 'idea' for Locke meant sensation and its mental copy, whereas that is not what it means for us, and *dikaiosune*, usually translated as 'justice', meant, for Plato, not just justice (as we understand it), as one of the virtues but even the whole of morality. We need to know such things if we are to be fair to them in assessing the truth-claims of their doctrines. That does not mean that we, years or centuries later, cannot assess them, and assess them by using the very same principles of reasoning used by those philosophers in propounding their doctrines. Indeed, MacIntyre says precisely this when he follows up what he has just said with, 'Nor does it follow that claims to timeless truth are not being made.' But then, he proceeds to say something totally irrelevant: 'The concept of timelessness is itself a concept with a history!' Similarly, he says that 'rationality itself ... is a concept with a history'. So what? No one may have formulated the *concept* of rationality before Plato. But we are not discussing the concept of rationality; we are discussing rationality and, in doing so, we are using the concept of it, which concept was born perhaps some two and a half millennia ago. Rationality itself, on the other hand, presumably began with Adam, or at least Eve, if indeed they were our 'great grandparents' as Milton tells us they were, and the amazing thing is that it is still going strong and will, no doubt, continue to do so long after our 'fashionable nonsense' has vanished. Or has it already?

MacIntyre instances a number of controversial matters like abortion, human rights and justice.[34] Opinions with regard to such matters 'are strikingly at odds with one another', which shows that we are not educated into 'a coherent way of thinking' but into 'an amalgam of social and cultural fragments inherited ... from different traditions'. All very true and also trite. We would, in discussing such matters, want to apply 'standards of rationality'. But, alas! 'Disputes about the nature of rationality ... are apparently as manifold and intractable as disputes about justice', etc. Some say that rationality is to calculate costs and benefits before acting, others say it is to act for the greatest good of humanity, and so on. (These, of course, are not definitions of the nature of rationality at all, but different ways, so people think, of being rational; they are examples of what are thought to be rational actions.) What bothers MacIntyre is that we 'lack institutionalized forums within which these fundamental disagreements can be systematically explored and chartered' and then resolved. 'Private citizens are thus ... left to their own devices.' So, if there were such forums – a Royal Society for Discussing Concepts of Justice or an All India Congress for Deciding about Abortion – would resolutions passed by them be handed down to the citizens, which they would then simply apply to cases? Reminds me of a Mr. Blockhead (name slightly changed) who attended a meeting long ago of the Bombay Philosophical Society in Mumbai, wanting to know if God existed. 'I do not want to hear any arguments; just tell me, you philosophers, if God exists or not.' And if we had told him He doesn't, what would he have done?

Why does MacIntyre suppose that an institutionalized forum could do what individuals or informal groups could not do? Would the heavens somehow open out before an institutionalized forum? If he had attended a conference of the Indian Philosophical Congress or the Hegel Society in Oxford, his eyes would have opened; perhaps he has never attended any such forum. Citizens, due to the exigencies of practical life, have to accept and abide by the final pronouncements of a Supreme Court, but they may still not accept them as true. Judgements of the Supreme Court have been frequently criticized. Imagine a philosophical supreme forum proclaiming, 'From 1 April 2008, justice will mean so-and-so.' Or 'Abortion will be ethical', and 'No further appeal on these matters'. I suppose MacIntyre would be happy.

Even 'if Aristotle was successful, and I believe that he was,' writes MacIntyre, 'in showing that no one who understands the laws of logic can remain rational while rejecting them'. Yet the observance of these laws 'is only a necessary and not a sufficient condition for rationality... It is on what has to be added to observance of the laws of logic to justify ascriptions of rationality ... that disagreement arises concerning the fundamental nature of rationality and ... over how it is rationally appropriate to proceed in the face of these disagreements'.

First of all, it is heartening to hear that the laws of logic, such as Aristotle first formulated, are a necessary component of rationality and that there are not different laws for different rationalities. As for sufficiency, MacIntyre has misunderstood the nature of rationality and logic. Reason supplies the formal structure of argument. It cannot *supply* the material premises or vouch for their truth or reasonableness (reasonableness, as Toulmin has pointed out, being different from rationality). This depends on the available evidence, intelligence and knowledge of the thinker, or his gullibility, or serendipity, etc. Reason puts the material to the test, as shown by the Socratic method of 'cross-examination' which includes exposing contradictions, inadequacies (due to conceptions being too wide or too narrow), and other techniques.

The ultimate requirement is comprehensive consistency. MacIntyre puts the process quite inaccurately when he writes that something needs 'to be added to observance of' logical laws, as if adding tomato sauce to the spaghetti. The material is gathered according to appropriate methods of investigation, and all the while, as it is being gathered, it is sifted, arranged, and combined, and inferences are drawn, tested for their validity, and accepted or rejected. In this way a body of knowledge is built up. If an analogy is wanted, it is more like moulding the clay to form a piece of sculpture than cooking a meal by mixing ingredients. MacIntyre himself puts it well:

> The test for truth…is always to summon up as many questions and as many objections of the greatest strength possible; what can be justifiably claimed as true is what has sufficiently withstood such dialectical questioning and framing of objections.[35]

Sufficiency will consist, he continues, in competing answers being produced and 'the best answer to be proposed so far' being accepted. I have spent time on MacIntyre because he is an interesting specimen of postmodern wobbliness and verbosity.

Let us see if Charles Taylor is free from wobbling. Nothing shows, he writes, 'that the most worrying cases, those dividing people of very different cultures, can be arbitrated'. He is leaning, at least with regard to worrying cases, towards the old postmodern hobgoblin, incommensurability. 'Relativism still has something going for it, in the very diversity and mutual incomprehensibility of human moralities.' Why 'still'? Is relativism, then, more or less passé? And isn't speaking, at this stage, of the 'incomprehensibility of moralities' to commit a *petitio*? Postmoderns put disproportionate weight on the fact of diversity. Taylor doesn't want to 'give up on reason too early'; only in good time! He writes, 'We don't need to be so intimidated by distance and incomprehensibility that we take them as sufficient grounds to adopt relativism.' Not even incomprehensibility? 'There are resources in argument,' supposedly to counter relativism. But, 'at the same time, nothing assures us that relativism is false'. Like

Rorty, he says, 'We have to try and see.'[36] Try how and see what?

Taylor's general view seems to be that reason *can* arbitrate between cases. If this, in principle, is admitted to be possible, then, except for special reasons for showing that reason cannot, in special cases, arbitrate, I should think there is no reason to maintain that it cannot. I cannot see how such special reasons can be shown.

Let us dig into Taylor on this matter.[37] Practices of other cultures 'often make sense against the background of a certain cosmology, or of semi-articulate beliefs'. The important point is that Taylor holds that these 'can be successfully challenged and shown to be inadequate' and, presumably, also false.

Taylor instances human sacrifice (still practised in India occasionally) and subordinating women (still prevalent amongst us). The way to show that such practices are untenable is to show that they result from an error regarding the way things are, that human life has value, that humans – men, women and even children (for it is children that are generally sacrificed) – should be treated as ends. Those who differ from us here should be challenged to show facts and reasons for their position. What is there to show, for example, that women are, in such and such a way, different from men, and so they should be subordinated? What is there to show that a god likes children to be killed? Special pleadings which seek to support such evil practices can be 'found wanting, by rational argument'. Beliefs 'that seem utterly solid in one cultural setting just dissolve when one leaves this context.' Cross-cultural exposure, then, is the tool by which to exorcise false, stupid and wicked beliefs. This tool can be used only if cultures are commensurable.

If opponents of change (in the right direction) are confronted in this way, they are, says Taylor, 'thrown into a kind of strategic defensive' and find themselves in a position 'harder and harder to defend in reason'.

At this point someone is bound to pounce on my phrase 'in the right direction' and ask, defiantly: 'What makes you think that the change you want is in the right direction?' A common red herring. The present argument is not about which beliefs ought to be preserved and which discarded; it is about the question whether beliefs which we (for whatever reason) don't approve of, can or cannot be changed by rational argument. Taylor believes they can. For the purpose of the argument, it is postulated that we know what the right direction is. The point is that these questions can be argued out rationally and one need not give up the fight *ab initio*.

Seeing our society as one among many, says Taylor, is 'most difficult and painful', and 'may be virtually impossible', but what does this, he asks, 'say about the limitations of reason? Nothing, I would argue.' Even if there are some matters 'where reason cannot arbitrate', even then, says Taylor, it does not 'give us cause *a priori* to take refuge in agnostic relativism.'

Contrary to the idea of a neutral position that, according to postmoderns, would be required to pass judgement on different cultures, Taylor puts forward the notion of englobalizing.[38] 'When we struggle to get beyond our limited home understanding,' that is, understanding according to the principles and norms of our own culture, 'we struggle not toward a liberation from this understanding as such … but toward a wider understanding which can englobe the other undistortively.' The 'goal is to reach a common language, a common understanding, which would allow both us and them undistortively to be'. (We must always remember that 'language' in this context means a way of understanding, not 'language' in the ordinary sense.)

Taylor believes (as we have seen earlier) that, in the social sciences, a 'perspective free account', such as is possible in the natural sciences, cannot be given. Our understanding of the Romans 'could never be considered an objective reading' like the one we could have about subatomic particles. I have fully exposed Taylor's howler. Anyway, we are now happy to learn that we *can* 'get if successful ... an understanding that allows us not to distort the Romans'. (One would like to understand how this account about undistorted Romans differs from the objective readings about particles; but never mind.) So, even with only our own principles and norms, we can get some sort of correct account about the Romans, what they were really like, what were their desires and purposes, how they behaved. Taylor puzzles us by adding, 'some other culture' than ours 'would have to develop a rather different language and understanding to achieve their own account of the Romans'. Could we have two or more equally undistortive accounts of the same subject matter? Yes, if they were to be complementary. One account might tell us about the Roman war machine and the other about their legal system. But this is such an elementary logical point that surely this could not be what Taylor (and postmoderns) must mean. The only question that would be interesting (as Rorty would say) is whether two or more *conflicting* but equally undistortive accounts could be given. This is a question which postmoderns either cannot grasp or do not want to face. However, in spite of these different languages and understandings, Taylor says the 'aim is fusion of horizons, not escaping horizons'. We have at least got rid of the Archimedean point. 'The ultimate result is always tied to someone's point of view,' writes Taylor, rather unnecessarily. Naturally, if it is an understanding, it has to be at least one person's; it cannot hover like an unattached spirit. But that is not the point. The point is whether an account, say about the Romans, although and even necessarily tied to someone's point of view, can be objective *in the sense that, if true it is true for all who can understand it or if false is false for all who can understand it*. This, again, is a question that somehow eludes the postmodern mind.

Taylor instances Christian and Muslim groups who have 'elaborated a language in which their differences could be undistortively expressed, to the satisfaction of both sides.' (Again 'language' does not mean English or Arabic or Arabinglish; it means a *way* of understanding, which means that they have got rid of all those ticklish points which caused misunderstandings.) Let us suppose both groups agree that there is a personal God, that prophets could arise and bring messages from this God, and that Mohammed was a Prophet. Christians *believe* that Jesus was not a prophet but God's Son and Muslims *do not believe* this, but they *know* that Christians believe it and Christians *know* that Muslims do not believe it. I suggest that this is an accurate description of the Christian-Muslim religious belief scenario. 'This would still not be an objective, point-of-view-less language of religion,' says Taylor. What can he mean? It is true that it is not 'point-of-view-less', because it is a view, which the Christians and Muslims share, and, if *we* accept the description as a true undistorted picture of what Christians and Muslims believe, then it is true even from *our* point of view. But why is it not 'an objective' view? What more would have to be added to make it objective, or subtracted?

Perhaps what troubles and confuses Taylor is that the above account does not consider whether what Christians believe and Muslims don't believe is true or false, whether, that is, Jesus was or was not God's Son. But that question is irrelevant here, because the account which claims to be *objective* is about what Christians and Muslims believe, not about whether their beliefs are true or not. If *that* were the question, I doubt very much that they would have, jointly or separately, elaborated a 'language' satisfactory to both sides. However, Taylor manages to somehow clamber on to the truth (not about Jesus, but) about the nature of understanding, for he winds up the debate with: 'But all this doesn't mean there is no gain, no overcoming of ethno-centrism.'

Taylor explains how we overcome ethno-centrism. We 'find a way of placing the strange practice as corresponding to one (or some) of ours.' That is what the Spanish did when they 'explained' the ritual of the Aztecs by seeing that it was, like their own, a case of worship, but of the devil instead of their God. 'Understanding,' says Taylor here, 'is complete.' This is a very big step on Taylor's part, which many serious thinkers are unable to take – that one can understand, as the Spanish did, without accepting. All right; now what? Now we have to get at truth. To take Taylor's example, how do you show a man, who is waving his hands wildly to scare away flies, that he is mistaken because there are no flies about? The man has his own '(presumed) world' where there are flies bothering him. 'We understand the waving man against his world.' But 'we cannot but have our view about the contents' of his world, and 'we start to explain him in terms of illusion'. How do we manage this? Because the idea of illusion is common to both worlds and because there are not two worlds, his and ours, but only one world which he misconstrues as having flies that are bothering him right now. We would have to show him by tests, which he would understand and acknowledge as relevant, that there are no flies and that he is under an illusion. Taylor is actually saying this: 'Our account is shaped throughout by what we understand to be the reality of the case.' Here, 'we' includes him, and the reality of the case is the one reality or 'world' that we and he share. Taylor says, rightly, that 'our sense of reality is decisive for our understanding of these people', that is people like the man waving his hands wildly and the Aztecs. This man might be tempted to protest, 'This is *your* reality that there are no flies around; how can you say anything about *my* reality?' In the light of what Taylor has just said, such a question would be as nonsensical as MacIntyre's 'whose reason?' It is, again, disappointing to find that obscurantism still has a hold on Taylor. He begins to be shaky on his feet. Frazer, says Taylor, 'seemed to be saying that earlier people were simply mistaken about magic', that is, they mistakenly believed that certain acts produced certain results when, in fact, they didn't really do so at all. But when we 'begin to place magic differently', writes Taylor, 'we see it ... as an interpretation of the moral significance of things, and their relation to human purposes, we see it all in an altered light. These people no longer seem just wrong, inferior to us in knowledge.' They are not just wrong; they are wrong in a wise way, even superior to us in knowledge, but, of course, a different kind of knowledge from ours! There 'are things they know how to do'.

You see, you don't know how to perform voodoo rituals or do sorcery, do you? Perhaps they have 'come to terms with and treat the stresses of their lives'. The same can be said about sati and child sacrifice. How do you know these don't help people, even today among us, to treat the stresses of their lives – not of the widow or the child concerned of course? These are things 'we seem to have lost and could benefit by', sighs Taylor. But not to worry; we still have alternative medicine and reiki.

Suddenly, after this sympathetic, though foolish, approach to people with the other kind of knowledge, Taylor turns 180 degrees and says, 'It would be a mistake to think that this means we are no longer making judgments of truth;' we 'are still operating out of our conception of reality'. Whose? Ours or that of the early people? If ours, surely we must judge that they *were* simply wrong. And Taylor seems to agree, for, says he, 'We don't really think that dances have any effect whatever on rain.' Not even to relieve stress? Vaguely he says that 'we recognize other human purposes'. Other than what? Turns out they are not other purposes at all, but quite a common purpose – 'to make sense of their world', to 'find some meaning in the things they experience'. This is not denied; what is denied is that they *made* sense of their world; they only deluded themselves in thinking, like Taylor, that they did. They were, as Frazer rightly held, mistaken; but *they* may be excused. However, Taylor persists, 'Even disease can be more easily repelled … where the person can make sense of it all.' That it is, for example, sent by God for their lapses. Has Taylor never heard of psychosomatic diseases? False beliefs do not turn into true beliefs because sometimes they produce good results. This fact is very awkward for pragmatism.

Towards the end of the chapter entitled 'Comparison, History, Truth' Taylor comes round to think exactly as Frazer did. He says that 'making the other intelligible requires a language or mode of understanding which will allow both us and them to be undistortively described', but 'this has to be understood as compatible with our understanding them as, in important respects, wrong about their world'. So, please note carefully, they were wrong about their world – this *is* our understanding of them even when we have been quite fair to them and described them undistortively. But the paragraph ends with one more wobble: 'But this may have to be an account that also portrays them as being out of touch with important facets of reality.' Why 'also'? We have been saying all the time that they have been out of touch with reality. And why 'may have to be'? Isn't it the correct account?

Habermas, among the European thinkers, is one whom Aristotle would have described as a sane man, but he too occasionally babbles. He is 'critical of the Western metaphysical tradition and its exaggerated conception of reason'. We need not explore here what his conception of that concept is. Suffice it that he 'cautions against relinquishing that conception altogether'. He also 'argues that the wholesale rejection of the metaphysical tradition inevitably undercuts the possibility of rational critique itself', which implies that a rational critique is worth having. He holds that 'genuinely postmetaphysical thinking can remain critical only if it preserves the idea of reason derived from that tradition'.[39]

Two of the basic tenets of postmodernism are: when confronted with an opposite view, do not try to argue back but only 'converse'

(Rorty's prescription), or, if you do, foolishly, enter into an argument, see that you drag in everything that is logically extraneous to the issue. But Habermas says that 'in argument the "yes" and "no" positions … should be regulated by good reasons', and 'what may count as a "good reason" in any case has to be decided within argument itself', for there is 'no court of higher appeal than the agreement of others that is brought about within discourse and, in this respect, is rationally motivated.'[40]

In the above, 'brought about' is important. It means that the agreement which is the aim of the discussion is not simply a happening supplied by Providence, but is the result of the disputants' ability to marshal facts and arguments under the belief that arguments are not useless but do have the potential of reaching conclusions satisfactory to all parties. It is necessary that the parties should sincerely desire to reach a valid and true conclusion, and each party should not keep going at the other with: 'But who says so?' Or 'Whose reason?' Or the standard 'Why do you think you alone are right?' These ploys get us nowhere, for the other party can respond in exactly the same way.

Habermas further points out that 'the objectivity of experience cannot be made dependent on the agreement – no matter how rational – of a contingent number of participants'. When all participants agree on a particular conclusion, they have to accept that as the truth so far reached. This is the most reasonable stance to adopt; it would be highly unreasonable and strange to say that, in spite of all the arguments favourable to 'p' that we find cogent, and all the arguments against 'p' that we don't find convincing, we will not believe 'p' to be true and we think 'not-p' is probably true. This would mean to be unbiased with a vengeance. Of course, we must at the same time grant that better arguments 'might emerge ... on the basis of further experiences' and, we should also add, on seeing some logical flaw in the given arguments.

Says Habermas's translator, W. M. Hohengarten, that, according to Habermas, 'when speakers engage in argumentation, they must suppose that certain conditions hold that guarantee that the agreements they reach are based on reason alone', and these conditions are called 'the ideal speech situation'. For Habermas, 'ideal' means 'something that has a regulative function but is unattainable in actual fact'.[41] I do not think that we need to be so cynical and pessimistic about human ability. Humans are certainly fallible or likely to make mistakes, but it doesn't follow and it is not true that we are incapable of having good, sound irrefutable arguments and are making mistakes all the time. Science, too, accepts the view that a currently accepted theory may be false, but that is no reason to think that it is false.

Habermas speaks of three dimensions of validity, but it is only the truth-claim dimension that concerns us. A claim to validity must '*transcend* the particular context or the linguistic community in which the utterance is made'.[42] Of course this is so even if no utterance is made, for even when one thinks without uttering anything, a validity claim is made. This transcendence sets Habermas apart from postmoderns with whom, however, he seems to share some other ideas. 'The dimension in which self-distancing and self-critique are possible,' writes Habermas, 'is closed off as soon as that which is rationally valid collapses into that which is socially correct.' The phrase 'socially correct' means, I take it, according only to the norms of a community. Some cultures, Habermas states, 'have had more practice than others at distancing themselves from themselves', and all languages (literally, languages?) 'offer the possibility of distinguishing between what is true and what we hold to be true'.[43] However, we should add that we cannot know what is true except by holding or believing it to be true; there is no direct line to truth; you have to go through belief. Truth implies the 'supposition of a common objective world'. This supposition or, rather, incontestable postulate, makes possible a dialogue between different communities and cultures.

Referring to linguistic communities – our own and another, Habermas writes:

> The merging of interpretive horizons, which … is the goal of every process of reaching understanding, does not signify an assimilation to 'us'; rather, it must mean a convergence, steered through learning, of 'our' perspective *and* 'their' perspective – no matter whether 'they' or 'we' or both sides have to reformulate established practices of justification to a greater or lesser extent. For learning itself belongs neither to us nor to them; both sides are caught up in it in this same way… For, although they may be interpreted in various ways and applied according to different criteria, concepts like truth, rationality, or justification play the *same* grammatical role in *every* linguistic community.[44]

(Due to the unfortunate obsession with language, it becomes necessary to point out that 'linguistic community' means a community having an understanding that works through an appropriate linguistic form, and 'grammatical' here is roughly synonymous with 'logical'.)

What Habermas says in the above passage is worth pondering over. However, although it may be right, *in general*, to say that in a dispute both sides must be ready to give and take, and we should not want or expect the other party to get assimilated to *us*, there are cases where we do. In a dispute about land or about the relative merits, say, of Indian and Western philosophies, each party could very well learn from the other and reformulate or temper their respective stands to reach a common understanding, even if some minor matters stand out like sore thumbs. But with regard to, say, the dispute between proponents of the Ptolemaic and Copernican systems, or of modern science and the world view of the Aztecs, or between those who uphold honest citizenship and those who recommend shady practices – here, surely, there could be or should be no mutual 'assimilation', accommodation or compromise.

Habermas's entire trend is one with the view that the possibility of inter-subjective dialogue and assessment of the relative merits of different cultural positions does not need a neutral position. He writes, 'By no means do these universal pragmatic presuppositions of communicative action suggest', that 'we could take up the extramundane standpoint of a subject removed from the world'.[45] Nor need we. (I have a bone to pick with Habermas's use of 'pragmatic' and his apparent belief that the, on the whole, sensible views he has propounded are a species of the philosophical theory called 'pragmatism', at least of the sort spawned by William James and John Dewey. But let it pass.)

I conclude this chapter about reasoning with some general remarks.

Whenever the subject matter, particularly in the case of sociomoral problems, is very complex or 'thick', involving so many different viewpoints, we often just do not know how to proceed and we abandon the inquiry. We must, however, remember that this (maybe provisional) decision to call off the inquiry and entertain doubts about the competence of reason to make us see the way – this decision and these doubts are themselves the products of reasoning.

The resources at the command of human beings are limited. Time, energy required for sustained argumentation, and argumentative skill are all limited. Very often we are unable to collect enough evidence for a complete grasp of the issues with which we are struggling, and, as O'Grady points out, we 'cannot actually maximize coherence among beliefs' or even sort them out when they appear in a tangle. 'However,' O'Grady says, 'such cognitive limitations do not mean that one has to abandon,' in principle, the hope of ideal argument or satisfactory conclusion.[46] Calling off an argument with: 'Oh well, difference of opinion,' does not imply many rationalities or that there is no such thing as rationality.

References

1. Waugh, P., 1992, *Practising Postmodernism*, p. 71.
2. Ibid., p. 71.
3. Sokal, A. & J. Bricmont, 1998, pp. x, 4-5, 11, 14.
4. Toulmin, S., 2003, pp. 1-2.
5. Ibid., pp. 94-96.
6. McDowell, J., op. cit., p. 113.
7. Aristotle, *De Anima*, pp. 21-24, 33, 428a.

8. Pinkard, T., 'MacIntyre's Critique of Modernity' in Murphey, M.C. (Ed.), 2003, pp. 182-83.

9. Stebbing, L. S., 1950, pp. 6 ff.

10. Audi, R., 2001, p. 33.

11. O'Grady, 2002, pp. 138-39.

12. Ibid., pp. 140-42.

13. Cook Wilson, J., 1926, p. 35.

14. Joachim, H. H., 1948, pp. 99-100.

15. Stebbing, L.S., 1955, p. 14.

16. Ibid., p. 27.

17. For a fuller treatment of this see Ookerjee, S. K., 'Bosanquet on Bradley on Inference' in *Bradley Studies* (Oxford, Vol. 10, Nos. 1 and 2, Autumn 2004).

18. Bradley, F. H., 1928, p. 246.

19. Bosanquet, B., 1931, Vol. II, p. 8.

20. Wilson, J. Cook, 1926, p. 86.

21. Bosanquet, B., 1928, p. 138.

22. Sorabji, R., 1993, p. 68.

23. Joachim, H. H., 1948, p. 83.

24. Ibid., p. 85.

25. Ibid., p. 91.

26. Ibid., p. 96.

27. Blanshard, B., 1948, Vol. I, pp. 51-53.

28. Quinton, A., 1978, p. 109.

29. Ibid. p.124.

30. Guignon, C., & D.R. Hiley (Eds.), 2003, p. 31. R. Rorty's words quoted from his *Philosophy and Social Hope*, 1999, p. xix.

31. Bouveresse, J., op. cit., p. 143. Rorty's words quoted from his *Contingency, Irony and Solidarity*, p. 9.

32. MacIntyre, A., 1988, pp. 79-81.

33. Ibid., pp. 8-9.

34. Ibid., pp. 1-5.

35. Ibid., p. 358.

36. Taylor, C., 1997, p. 55.

37. Ibid., pp. 56-59.

38. Ibid., pp. 150-55.

39. Hohengarten, W. M., Translator's Introduction to Habermas, J., *Metaphysical Thinking*, 1995, rpt. 1998, p. vii.

40. Habermas, J., 1998, pp. 102-3.

41. Hohengarten, W. M., op. cit., p. xi.

42. Ibid., p. ix.

43. Habermas, J., 1998, p. 137.

44. Ibid., p. 138.

45. Ibid., p. 139.

46. O'Grady, P., 2002, pp. 144-45.

Chapter 8

The Golem

A Postmodern Portrait of Science

'Confounding, astounding,
Dizzying and deafening the ear with its sound.'

Robert Southey, *The Cataract at Lodore*

Science, according to post-modernism, is a golem. A golem, in Jewish mythology, is a man-made creature, not evil but daft and powerful, and who, if not controlled, would destroy its masters.

Writes Paul Feyerabend, a postmodern man of science, 'Western science has now infected the whole world like a contagious disease,' and non-scientific traditions have not survived the 'confrontation with science and rationalism'. The postmoderns' attitude to science is what is vulgarly called a love-hate one. Science is their foe, but they are fascinated by it, something like what happens to small animals when a cobra, erect with hood outspread, stares into their eyes. Feyerabend asks, rhetorically, if these non-scientific traditions were 'eliminated on rational grounds by letting them compete ... in an impartial and controlled way'; no, they were destroyed by 'military (political, economic, etc.) pressures'. A severe critic of science demanding that something should be allowed to compete on rational grounds, and that too in an impartial and scientifically controlled way! What next? The urge to legitimate their anti-scientific stance by scientific methods is painfully strong among postmoderns. They want to exploit the prestige of science to sell their own dubious wares. Science, according to Feyerabend, produced better weapons but destroyed spiritual values. It did not improve the lives of people. Not at all, ever? He, our science man, recommends the methods of primitive tribes for controlling plagues, floods and droughts. We in India better take a lesson from him; perhaps these methods could also help to *garibi hatao*. Feyerabend condemns not only the 'gangsters of colonialism' but also 'the humanitarians of developmental aid'. 'Back to the primitive' appears to be his call.[1]

Mary Midgley tells us that in the twentieth century, the term 'scientific' was an 'all-purpose justification for policies to which there were obvious moral objections'. 'Modern' was also such a word. Both terms are now 'discredited' but the 'reaction against them' has produced, says Midgley, 'the jumble of ideas now confusedly called "post-modern"'. Confusedly so called, and confused too.

Defenders of science claim that science is 'neutral, purely factual, a mere tool' or sometimes they heel over to the other side, holding that science can, and alone can, solve problems like those of hunger, sanitation, poverty and illiteracy, and can deal with 'superstitions and deadening custom and tradition'. These are Nehru's words and they express what he believed. This is called 'scientism'. Midgley rightly says that 'scientific values and ideals' must 'be placed in the context of other human ideals' and 'soberly assessed'.[2]

But postmoderns, by and large, think differently. Brian Appleyard is unsparing. Science is 'spiritually corrosive, burning away ancient authorities and traditions'; scientists 'take on the mantle of wizards, sorcerers and witch doctors'; experiments are rituals. Science's 'universally open-ended view' of the 'permanent possibility of change and progress' gives us a 'fluid, relative world'. This open-ended scientific view is, for Appleyard, a defect, because of which the scientist 'cannot argue absolutely' and there is 'only relative right and wrongness', and the scientist can offer 'not a fact but just another opinion'. Liberal man, claiming to be neutral, 'lapses into a form of spiritual fatigue' whose symptoms are 'pessimism, anguish, scepticism and despair'.[3]

If scientists are wizards, sorcerers and witch doctors, what are wizards, sorcerers and witch doctors? Have they become scientists? A kind of dialectical spiritualism.

In spite of their hostility to science, postmoderns can't shake off their craving for scientific acceptability. The 'comparative excellence of scientific and non-scientific procedures has never been examined in a truly scientific way', says Feyerabend.[4] Again, he says 'the choice of science over other forms of life is not a scientific choice.'[5] Naturally, though we can't guess what those other 'forms of life' might be over which science is chosen. Chosen for what? 'Strangely enough there are relativists who,' says Feyerabend, 'want to make general and – God help us! – objective statements about the nature of knowledge and truth.' It is not only strange, it is downright self-contradictory; the fact that a relativist has found it, at any rate, strange, is encouraging. 'The relativist who deserves his name,' Feyerabend goes on, 'may and often will generalize his findings but without assuming that he now has principles which by their nature are ... binding for all.'[6] Then in what sense are they general? Even if the relativist were to limit himself to describing his own private experience, it would still be binding for all; how can they dare to disagree, unless they doubt his honesty? Of course, to put the matter straight, if anyone were to generalize his findings, they are not 'binding' on anyone in the sense that they must be accepted as true; they *are* binding in the sense that they claim to be true for everyone.

Feyerabend continues: debating with objectivists, the relativist 'may of course use objectivist methods and assumptions, however his purpose will not be to establish universally acceptable truths ... but to embarrass the opponent – he is simply trying to defeat the objectivist with his own weapons. Relativist arguments are always *ad hominem.*'[7] An *ad hominem* argument is a well established mode of arguing: when someone makes a statement '*p*' and the other party can show, by drawing out implications, that if '*p*' were true, the consequences would be unpalatable to the person who propounded it. This is a weapon in Plato's armoury. Thrasymachus, in *Republic*, defines justice as the interest of the stronger party and Socrates argues that if we take that as true, it goes against Thrasymachus's own idea of a 'happy' life, the life of the tyrant. But (granting that Socrates's argument is flawless) this method works because both parties accept the universal truths or principles of reasoning. When these principles are the very issue in dispute, the relativist cannot take his stand on those very universal principles of reasoning (which the absolutist holds to) in order to deny them, for, in that case, he falls along with his denial of those principles.

Feyerabend makes a number of sensible and true statements about science, which, ironically, he thinks furnish a criticism of science. He writes:

> Many once utterly ridiculous views are now solid parts of our knowledge. Thus the idea that the earth moves was rejected in antiquity because it clashed with facts and the best theory of motion then available; a recheck … convinced scientists that it had been correct after all… The history of science is full of theories which were pronounced dead, then resurrected, then pronounced dead again only to celebrate another triumphant comeback. It makes sense to preserve faulty points of view for possible future use.[8]

Just as one should not throw away old furniture; it might fetch a good price in the antique market when fashions change.

What exactly is the moral Feyerabend wants to convey? I am sure he doesn't himself know. Instead of 'ridiculous views' he should have written '*ridiculed* views', for if they were really ridiculous, they could never become parts of knowledge at any time. Their resurrection shows that they were rejected due to a mistake, though often a pardonable one, on the part of the scientists of that time. They were acting according to their 'best theory'; what else could they have done? Should they have gone against the 'best theory then available'? That *would* have been *ridiculous*. Those so-believed best theories turned out (by the further and more exact use of the same scientific procedures as were used then) to be false. There is nothing to suggest they were ridiculous. The then rejected theories were, as Feyerabend says, 'pronounced dead', but they had not really died; they were zombies revived by a later treatment which showed that they had life.

This is how science works, but an important qualification is required. The resurrection also, surely, is accompanied by a modification in order to bring it in line with the knowledge that has gone ahead since the time when the so-called 'ridiculous' views were rejected. When, for example, the 'moving earth' view is revived many years later, the nature of that movement is much better understood and described than before. The old view is not simply attached like a cobbler's patch; it has to be assimilated into the current theory. The once-rejected view is not 'preserved' like a museum exhibit. Feyerabend has attempted to show science to be ridiculous by giving a more or less correct description of scientific procedure, which is the very strong point of science.

Let us hear Feyerabend on the Galileo-Bellarmino affair.[9] Bellarmino tells Galileo that his (Galileo's) hypothesis makes "excellent good sense" and explains the facts 'better than' does the theory using epicycles, but to accept it as a theory is to run a risk. What risk? Not the risk of finding it to be scientifically false or ridiculous, but the risk of injuring "our holy faith". (The words in double-quotes are Bellarmino's.) From Bellarmino's prudent advice to Galileo, Feyerabend jumps to saying that 'the fact that a model works does not by itself show that reality is structured like the model'. Why not? If the predictions made according to the model turn out to be true, if no better *scientific* model is suggested and if the opposite view (in this case, only the one given by the scriptures) has no observational or theoretical backing, why should the model not be accepted as a correct depiction of the structure of reality?

Feyerabend says that Schrodinger's mechanics were 'remarkably successful', but, 'by looking at a wider range of phenomena',

Bohr showed that Schrodinger's interpretation 'conflicted with important facts'. To show the agreement of a hypothesis with reality it is 'necessary to move to a wider domain', our author rightly says. Excellent, all this. But one must not forget that, when engaged in doing science, the wider range of phenomena and the wider domain are all within science and that, too, within that particular area of science in which the matter is being investigated. But the wider domain to which Bellarmino appeals is not science but theology, that too Christian theology of a certain brand, as interpreted by the Council of Trent, which 'forbids' any other interpretation. As for the 'wider range of phenomena', these were only the fantasies of 'the Scholastic philosophers'.

Feyerabend is unsurpassable. Theology, he says, 'was and still is a science, and a very rigorous science at that: textbooks in theology contain long methodological chapters, textbooks in physics do not'. Besides, 'scientific results, wrongly interpreted, may injure human beings'. 'Wrongly interpreted' here means "contrary to the common opinion of the Holy Fathers" (Bellarmino's words) and therefore, naturally, long methodological chapters are required to show how to discount recognized modes of interpretation and go behind science. If scientific results are wrongly interpreted, it can be shown where they have gone wrong and so can be corrected and set right, or, if they are beyond repair, they have to be discarded. Injury to human beings is not the test; if they are wrongly interpreted, they must be rejected *even if* they were beneficial to human beings.

Postmoderns are highly emotional people, and this often makes their qualities of heart play tricks with their qualities of head. So, quite irrelevantly, Feyerabend asks if a modern Galileo would have 'an easier life'. But who is talking of his life or even death? If a modern Galileo 'wants to teach evolution and Genesis on equal terms' (would he?), he would run foul of the concept of the separation of State and Church, or secularism – real or pseudo, in none of which does Feyerabend seem to have any faith. Galileo must thank his lucky stars (or planets) that in his times, scientists who challenged the 'rigorous science' of the Holy Fathers would not only be 'visited by the police' but ignited at the stake. So, Feyerabend seems to say we need not let our heart go 'out to poor Galileo'.

Feyerabend rounds off the discussion with: 'Church doctrine … is a boundary condition for the interpretation of scientific results. But it is not an absolute condition. Research can move it.'

So, science has the final word after all. Oh no! (Feyerabend would say), you are interpreting us quite wrongly. Scientific knowledge is 'connected with too narrow a vision of the world' and 'must be judged from a wider point of view', but not, this time, the view of the church, but one that 'includes human concerns and the values flowing therefrom'. The claims of scientific knowledge 'must be modified so that they agree with these values' – friendship, happiness, 'need for salvation'. Scientific claims about 'the ultimate constituents of everything have to be rejected and replaced by a more "instrumentalistic" position' which would 'temper the totalitarian and dehumanizing tendencies' of modern science and its notorious 'objectivism'.

Thomas Kuhn is the other authority on scientific matters and post-modernism's funny man. He too, poor soul, says all the right things about science, piously believing he is discrediting science.[10]

Old scientific views, he says, were 'neither less scientific nor more the product of human idiosyncrasy than those current today.' Correct, because they were the result of using scientific method as applied to facts then available. 'Out-of-date theories are not in principle unscientific because they have been discarded,' and if you call them myths, he says, then present scientific knowledge is also a myth. But we *don't* call them myths. A 'new theory … is seldom or never just an increment', and a new discovery, like oxygen, 'does not simply add one more item to the population of the scientist's world', because it has to be assimilated into it.

This, and much else that Kuhn writes, is a fairly accurate account of scientific activity. But in the wings another act is going on. All that has been so far described is called 'normal science', based on the scientific 'community's willingness to defend' the assumption that 'science knows what the world is like'. Why willingness? Is it a matter of choice?

Sometimes, normal science reveals an 'anomaly' and 'extraordinary investigations' lead to 'a new set of commitments'. These 'extraordinary episodes' are called 'revolutions'. The Copernican way of seeing the world is one such revolution. It is not really the investigation that is extraordinary. When a particular line of investigation reaches a particular stage, as a result of scientific imagination, a large conceptual change shows that problems which were defying solution can now be solved or that they can be tackled more easily, more quickly, more directly, more neatly (even more aesthetically) than before. All in all, Kuhn's account of scientific revolutions is unexceptionable.

Fiction now takes over. Normal science, says Kuhn, 'often suppresses fundamental novelties because they are necessarily subversive of its basic commitments'. (Postmoderns cannot get over their fixation on the language of politics and force.) Kuhn grants that the 'very nature of normal research ensures that novelty shall not be suppressed for very long'. This sees 'revolutions' quite wrongly because, as always with postmoderns, they long for novelty, but the merit of 'revolutions' in science is not their novelty but their truth; the novelty is incidental. The merit of, say, psychoanalysis lies not in the fact that it is something more novel than traditional psychology, but in the fact that it gives a more satisfactory explanation of pathological cases. However, this is not how Kuhn sees the matter. In 'these matters neither proof nor error is at issue', the 'transfer of allegiance' from an old theory to a new one 'is a conversion experience' like a religious awakening, and a new truth 'does not triumph by convincing its opponents and making them see the light, but rather because its opponents eventually die'.

After many pages of a clear and fairly correct account of scientific procedure, we enter the tunnel of postmodern prejudice. We may, says Kuhn, 'have to relinquish the notion ... that changes of paradigm carry scientists ... closer and closer to truth', and, although the process is one 'whose successive stages are characterized by an increasingly detailed and refined understanding of nature', yet 'nothing has been ... said [that] makes it a process of evolution *towards* anything'. The burden is surely on Kuhn to clarify how an understanding of nature fails to carry scientists closer to truth. What is Kuhn's concept of truth? We catch a glimpse when he says that 'we are deeply accustomed to seeing science as the one enterprise that draws constantly near to some goal set by nature in advance'. He thinks that science – at least normal science – is seeking something called Truth, which is some kind of entity out there, like a volcano or a galaxy, and, of course there is no such thing; there is only nature in which there are volcanoes and galaxies and many other things we don't know about yet. Nature sets no goal for the scientist; it is the scientists who set the goal of a better and truer understanding of nature, and to understand anything is to grasp the truth about it. Postmoderns don't believe in truth but they talk a lot about it, and have never squarely got down to clarify to themselves what it is they are talking about and dismissing.

Science, says Kuhn, is not a 'single monolithic and unified enterprise that must stand or fall with any one of its paradigms'. And asks, 'Does it help to imagine that there is some full, objective, true account of nature?' To the question and the earlier statement one can respond with: 'You are quite right; there is no full, true account of nature, and science is not a unified enterprise (like a military invasion or even a game of football). Not yet and will, it seems, never be. And that work is being done, up to a point, quite unconnectedly in diverse areas whose connections we are very far from grasping. Science is not a single enterprise in this sense, but it is a single enterprise in the sense that every scientist, however great or insignificant, is on the same task – understanding nature – and the contribution of each may be a world-shattering "revolution" or a very tiny gain, but both are part of the same enterprise.' So, it is not entirely the 'ramshackle structure' that Kuhn depicts. Its ideal is to find a place for all the different paradigms or conceptual frameworks in accordance with the principle of comprehensive coherence. Kuhn grants that a 'scientific theory is usually felt [felt!] to be better than its predecessors ... because it is somehow [somehow! just by chance?] a better presentation of what nature is really like'. However, he adds that there is no theory-independent way to reconstruct phrases like "really there"'.[11] This is, of course, the dread of the unwanted Archimedean point.

Evelyn Fox Keller, a reputed feminism mouthpiece, has plenty to say, like most feminists, on science, because, while they hate the male (remember science is male because reason is male), they want to make feminism an honest woman by marrying her to science, incompatibility of temperaments notwithstanding.

'Historians, philosophers and sociologists of science', she writes,[12] explore 'the influence of economic, political, and cultural factors' on 'scientific knowledge – on how questions are posed, how research programmes come to be legitimated, how theoretical disputes are resolved', and concludes that, therefore, the 'very distinction between internal ("scientific") and external ("extra scientific") dynamics have come to be thought of as an ideological fantasm'.

Every one of these questions is ambiguously posed. They can, for example, be taken up by sociology and answered like this: Questions are posed after considering the condition of the marginalized classes; research programmes are legitimated by, say, bribing the head of a department; and theoretical disputes are settled, not on merits, but by gagging one party. History can show you how these practices could have developed out of certain situations in the past. Fox Keller exposes her ignorance by lumping together sociology and history (which are fact-finding disciplines), on the one hand, and, on the other, philosophy (which is not). Of course, postmoderns, who are well versed in sociology, history and such subjects, are on very slippery ground when they talk, or talk about, philosophy.

The kind of answers that sociology and history would give to Fox Keller's questions would be 'external'; if they were to be answered philosophically or, more correctly, scientifically or, still more correctly, within science, they would be 'internal'. External answers to these questions could never show what she wants to show – that science, as such, is biased in favour of males, that it lacks objectivity and universality. If the questions were to be about questions being put in a scientifically significant manner or what scientific observations and reasoning was to be used to resolve scientific differences of opinion, they would fall in the internal domain.

Fox Keller herself occupies, she says, 'a "middle of the road" position'. Good Lord! Could it possibly be a neutral position? She leans 'more and more in the opposite direction' to the tendency towards the 'dissolution of all distinctive boundaries demarcating the sciences'. She feels the 'need for more attention to the logical and empirical constraints that make scientific claims so compelling to scientists'. Science, she admits, '"works" so extraordinarily well'![13] Let us not see too much in these statements. She only wants to see with greater attention what it is that makes scientific claims so compelling to scientists. It does not necessarily imply that she and her sort find them compelling. Her curiosity may not be philosophical at all and may be satisfied by a purely sociological or psychological explanation. Also, her recognition that science 'works' so well (how could she but recognize it?) does not mean that it does so because it is true or describes reality as it is; science's working so well might be, to her, something that just happens – a miracle.

Fox Keller soon leaves the middle of the road and veers to the culturalism side.[14] Nature, she says, is 'only accessible to us through representations', which are 'structured by language', which, in turn, is culture-dependent, and cultures are diverse. Therefore, no representation can ever '"correspond" to reality'. But Fox Keller is worried, for 'some representations are clearly better (more effective) than others'. The words 'more effective' make us wonder whether she means 'truer' or better in some pragmatic sense, but she does mean 'truer' because she says that recent philosophy of science is 'plagued' by this – how can representations be better or worse, she asks, 'in the absence of a copy theory of truth'? Her argument, at this point, seems to be: we can know only representations; in order to be true or truer they would have to correspond to reality; but the correspondence theory (according to postmodernism) is false; therefore representations don't correspond to reality; then how can they be true or truer (better)?

Recent philosophy may be plagued, but not she. In a flash of revelation the 'difficulty resolves' if we look at the practices which the representations 'facilitate'. So, our representations (whatever they are) make us succeed in this or that venture, and that success is our criterion of better or worse. Next step: scientific knowledge is, hence, 'value-laden', 'shaped by our choices'. What choices? What value? Not the only really relevant value – truth, which had seemed to plague recent scientific philosophy. But, first, the choice regarding 'what to seek representations *of* ' (that is, what are we going to investigate today, like asking which film shall we see this evening?) and, second, 'what to seek representations *for*' (that is, why do we want to do this particular research – to get a fellowship, to get a degree, just to pass the time...?) None of these are epistemic values or choices. Fox Keller, poor dear, cannot imagine why we should 'ever think of equating "good" science with the notion of "value-free"'; '*good science* is science that effectively facilitates the material realization of particular goods, that does in fact enable us to change the world in particular ways' (echoes of Marxism). That science should be 'value-free', in the sense that it should not be dictated to, in its search for truth, by any particular moralities that a community might favour – this Fox Keller cannot even think of. The 'true' has, as usual, dissolved into the 'good'; good science is not what brings our theories closer to nature, as we had so naively thought for so long, but it is what brings the 'material world in closer conformity with the ... expectations that a particular "we" bring with us as scientists embedded in particular cultural, economic, and political frames'. The mountain, after all, does come to Muhammad, and not only one mountain but many different mountains in many different cultures and frames. By this philosophy of science, since the Hopi believe that spirits live in trees, their scientists must prove that that is so, and since, in Indian culture, the male child is prized highly, our science must prove that, in fact, it is by nature superior and the female child, in consequence, should be....

Are there not scores of activities that facilitate the realization of particular goals, activities like growing food or building skyscrapers? What distinguishes science 'from other successful institutions and practices', says Fox Keller, 'is its disciplined interaction with the material constraints and opportunities supplied by "nature"' ('for lack of a better word'). What, incidentally, is this something for which a better word is missing? Anyway, 'scientific method' is just those 'assorted techniques … effective for assessing, subverting, or explaining those constraints'. Only assessing and explaining? Does 'assessing' them mean assessing their truth? And what is 'subverting' then? Explaining them away, if not found convenient for getting at our goals?

One is left in admiration to see how cunningly Fox Keller tries to find her way through a forest of confusions. One of the common confusions among postmoderns is that between philosophy and sociology. David Bloor and associates take umbrage at the fact that sociological explanations are often offered for errors in science but never for its truths.[15] When science is successful, its success is 'explicable in terms of its own internal, "rational" dynamic, so that a sociological explanation appealing to external influences is … unnecessary'. A truth or scientific success is reached when the scientist's mind has been working as a self-respecting human mind is supposed to work, according to logical principles. This is expected of it. When it falls short of expectation and so commits an error, there is a demand (particularly by some aggrieved party, if there is any) for explanation. If a person does the right thing, we don't ask for explanation; what can the explanation be except that it was the right thing to do? The explanation is available in terms of the '"rational" dynamic' of right actions. Explanations are needed when one runs off the straight and narrow path, be it of scientific truth or any other. The sociological explanation of a truth would be that it was obtained by a proper application of scientific method and that there were no deflecting circumstances like ignorance, bias or physical or other incapacities. 'Why did you get it right?' is a foolish question to ask; 'How did you go wrong?' is not.

Postmodern criticism of science takes two lines, and they are irreconcilable, for one says (a) truth is culture-relative and the other says (b) there is no truth.

1. I take position (b) first. It is voiced by Guy Claxton.[16] He says the sciences are just 'maps or collections of maps', and so the question of assessing or grading them against each other is meaningless. There is 'no "best" map of London', for there are different maps for different purposes – for locating museums or railway stations, for understanding the underground network, or whatever. So, 'scientific theories … are also, necessarily, multiple and complementary', and they are, like maps, 'judged by their utility, not their veracity'.

    As usual, a goulash of sense and nonsense, truth and half-truth. Maps of London museums are different from maps of the London underground. The two groups would, of course, be complementary, for one would consult the latter to get to a museum shown by the former. Though the two groups of maps are interrelated, they cannot, obviously, be inter-assessed. The same would apply to, say, physics and biology: a theory in biology may not clash with one in physics; a psychological theory may, in fact, support one in economics. But one can certainly compare two maps of London museums and throw one away as inaccurate or *false*. So, too, two theories within one science can be pitted against one another and one seen to be false. Once again let us remember Ptolemy and Copernicus. We have heard this story about maps and charts and signboards before. They can all be useful; they are useful when they give true information. The 'maps' of science, that is, theories, are, as Claxton so wisely informs us, 'good in so far as they enable us to predict, explain and control the behaviour of the natural world', but he seems unaware that they do this *because* of their truth. Sometimes, by chance, false theories may also help in predicting and controlling, which fact demonstrates the difference between truth and utility. His putting of 'explain' on par with 'predict' and 'control', exposes his naiveté regarding the nature of science.

Now Claxton gives a second criterion of good science. Theories are 'valuable if they allow us to talk interesting sense about interesting things, to have new thoughts about how things might be'. Let us not forget Rorty in this race for novelty. And even the new thoughts have to be, not of what is, but what might be, for we are like little children of bygone times (not of today) who want our fairy tales of beggars being kings and wishes being – scientific theories.

2. The most insidiously treacherous challenge to science (and to all knowledge) is the view that scientific truth (and all truth) is culture-relative, community-relative, contextual, historically determined, situated – different words for roughly the same idea. It is triumphantly announced that Wittgenstein, Quine, Rorty, Davidson, Derrida and Foucault have 'succeeded in demolishing that old "epistemological paradigm"' of absolute and universal

truth based on an 'independent ground or neutral observation language'.[17] The demolition squad includes MacIntyre.

From the notion of cultural relatedness postmodernism takes a dubious leap to the notion that science is biased and not objective, as it traditionally has claimed to be. It is dubious because firstly, *even* if a claim is assessed according to the values peculiar to a culture, it does not follow that, within that culture, bias and personal subjectivity cannot be avoided, and second, the very fact that you speak of bias in pejorative terms, means that you have a concept of unbiased objective scientific activity. If such a concept is not self-contradictory and makes sense, there is no reason (except a dogmatic and cynical fatalism) why you should not be able to achieve or, at least, approximate to it. If bias (whatever you mean by it) is, in the nature of the case unavoidable, you cannot complain about it. If a particular theory has not observed the requirements of scientific method, which aims, among other things, at impartiality, then that theory can be called biased; the whole of science or science as such cannot be described as biased.

Postmoderns have a propensity to believe that, every now and again, they make world-shattering discoveries, but, as Chalmers points out, 'The fact that perception has subjective and culturally relative elements has not escaped the notice of scientists.' Nor is it true that they have not devised methods and techniques for meeting this fact. This fact is a 'commonplace', says Chalmers, and therefore 'mere observation', like that of the layman, is replaced by observation under 'standardized circumstances following routinized procedures', by 'measurement and controlled experiment'.[18] That is how frauds are discovered. Bacon writes, 'I interpose everywhere admonitions and scruples and cautions, with a religious care to eject, repress, and as it were exorcise every kind of fantasm.'[19]

The relativist has an answer up his sleeve. He would say that these measures that science adopts are effective only within a particular culture, so we are back to relativism and bias. The answer to this argument is that if they work within one culture, at least there bias can be, if not entirely eliminated, at least controlled and reduced. So, in principle, we are not stuck with ineradicable bias. Other cultures, too, can devise their own methods of removing or controlling bias. And, again, in principle, and since the principles of reasoning are not different in different cultures, there is no reason to think that these methods are not, or cannot be, the same everywhere. If the relativist, belonging to a particular culture, still complains that, in spite of applying these methods within his culture, bias still exists, then that very complaint implies that he has transcended his own culture and is judging it by some criterion from outside. He is no longer a relativist.

I close this chapter with a delicious bonbon from the assorted confectionery of Luce Irigaray. 'Science always displays certain choices,' writes Irigaray 'and these are particularly determined by the sex of the scholars involved.'[20] Irigaray had earlier 'elaborated her critique of "masculine" physics', say the authors of *Fashionable Nonsense*, which claims that 'fluid mechanics is underdeveloped relative to solid mechanics because solidity is identified (according to her) with men and fluidity with women'. Irigaray's interpreter, N. Hayles, puts a gloss on her claim: 'Whereas men have sex organs that protrude and become rigid, women have openings that leak ... vaginal fluids.' This explains the rigidity of the male attitude to fluidity and the inability of science, which is so far male, to deal with it.[21] Hayles then describes a piece of her own writing:

> Whereas the flow of the argument has been female and feminist, the channel into which it has been directed is male and masculinist.
>
> (Hayles, 1992, p. 40)[22]

Sokal and Bricmont comment: 'Hayles thus appears to accept ... the identification of "rational discourse" with "male and masculinist".'[23]

References

1. Feyerabend, P., 1987, pp. 297-98, 303.
2. Midgley, M., 'Visions of Embattled Science' in Levinson, R. & J. Thomas, (Eds.), 1977, pp. 37-38.
3. Appleyard, B., 1993, pp. 9, 11-12.
4. Feyerabend, P., 1987, p. 31.
5. Ibid., p. 31.
6. Ibid., p. 78.
7. Ibid., p. 78.
8. Ibid., pp. 32-33.
9. Ibid., pp. 250-55, 259.
10. Kuhn, T., 1970, pp. 2-3, 5, 7, 8, 151, 170-71.
11. Ibid., p. 206.
12. Keller, E. F., 1992, pp. 2-3.
13. Ibid., p. 4.
14. Ibid., p. 5.

15. Chalmers, A., 1990, pp. 91-92.
16. Claxton, G., 'Science of the Times' in Levinson, R., & J. Thomas (Eds.), 1997, pp. 71-72.
17. Opinion of Stanley Fish cited by Norris, C., 1990, p. 6.
18. Chalmers, A., 1990, p. 46.
19. Bacon, F., quoted by Chalmers, A., 1990, p. 46.
20. Irigaray, L., 1993, p. 204 as quoted by Sokal, A. & J. Bricmont, 1998, p.106.
21. Sokal, A. & J. Bricmont, 1998, p. 110.
22. Ibid., p. 121, N. 148.
23. Ibid.

Chapter 9

Cultural Monadology

'...each in his narrow bed for ever laid'

Thomas Grey, *Elegy*

In 1996, a Parliamentary Commission was set up in Belgium to investigate inept police functioning.[1] In a television programme, a policeman named Lesage swore that he had sent a file to the judge and the judge, named Doutrewe, denied having received it. Professor Yves Winkin of the University of Liege, an 'anthropologist of communication', was interviewed by a Belgian newspaper (*Le Soir*, 20 December 1996). Referring to the conflicting statements made by Lesage and Doutrewe, Winkin was asked if truth existed and what to make of the two conflicting answers:

> I think all the work of the commission is based on a sort of presupposition that there exists, not *a* truth, but *the* truth – which, if one presses hard enough, will finally come out.
>
> However, anthropologically, there are only partial truths, shared by a larger or smaller number of people.... There is no transcendent truth. Therefore, I don't think

that Judge Doutrewe or Officer Lesage are hiding anything; both are telling their truth.

Truth is always linked to an organization, depending upon the elements that are perceived as important. It is not surprising that these two people, representing two very different universes, should each set forth a different truth.

Professor Yves Winkin's answer, comment Sokal and Bricmont, 'illustrates, in a striking way, the confusion into which some sectors of the social sciences have fallen through their use of a relativist vocabulary' and, I would add, through a cultivated habit of trying to hoodwink unsuspecting innocents.

Any ordinarily intelligent schoolgirl would have given the following answer to the Commission's question: Lesage could have truly said that he *had* sent the file, but due to some misunderstanding or other accident, it might have gone astray; therefore Doutrewe may also be telling the truth in saying he didn't receive it; hence, *prima facie*, neither may be a liar. The next thing for the Commission to have done was to investigate what happened to the file and where it had gone. That an anthropologist of communication had to be called upon to unravel such a simple matter shows the IQ of whosoever decided to seek his expert opinion.

After philosophizing and pronouncing *the* truth, as he saw it, about truth and partial truths, and after telling us about Lesage, Doutrewe and *their* truths, Winkin said, 'Having said that, I think that, in this context of public responsibility, the Commission can only proceed as it does.' That is, as it would have done had they not interviewed him. It reminds me of a world-famous guru, who, asked by a seriously handicapped person as to what he should do to be happy, (since the guru was holding forth on happiness) replied, 'Just go on doing, Sir, what you have been doing.'

Sokal and Bricmont are also right in saying that it makes no sense to say that 'both are telling *their* truth'. It is also pertinent to ask whether they could be telling *their* falsehood. To any non-relativist it is clear that both Lesage and Doutrewe could be telling the truth, or one of them could be telling a lie, and both these possibilities are logical possibilities without any need to refer to any organization or different professional universes.

There are two species of relativism: epistemological or epistemic, and ontological, the former being concerned with beliefs, theories, descriptions, reasonings; the latter about what exists. Epistemological (or discursive cultural) relativism holds that beliefs, etc. – if they are true or valid at all – are true or valid only according to the norms of a particular tradition, culture, context or community. Ontological relativism holds that there is no common objective world for all persons, no universal system of causation running through all phenomenal events, no social phenomena common for all people and no common, objectively recognized moral or social values. Such relativism shivers on the verge of nihilism and solipsism.[2]

I am not directly concerned in this essay with ontological relativism, though, of course, the truth of ontological relativism would strongly support epistemic relativism.

It is necessary to clarify that epistemic relativism is about beliefs, judgements, views and theories in their alethic aspect, that is, as claiming truth and not as psychological, social or historical facts. Of course, extreme relativism maintains that the alethic claim is bogus and that these things called beliefs, etc. have no aspect other than what psychology, sociology, history and similar disciplines can study.

Non-relativism (or absolutism) holds that, as regards truth-value, all humans belong to the one culture of rationality. In matters of taste or mere preference, we can comfortably belong to different cultures. A person may prefer to use the language of one culture, dress according to the codes of another, enjoy the arts of yet another and the culinary delights of a fourth. If a person maintains that one culture is superior, in any sense, to others, he makes an alethic claim, which he could be called upon to justify. Statements about taste and preference do not have to be justified as truths, though the honesty of the person reporting on her tastes or preferences may be doubted.

Moral preferences, however, function on a different plane. They claim to be, in some sense, correct; and actions are judged as better or worse. It may be a counsel of prudence not to judge others (at least, openly), but we always do judge others, and our judgements are either true or false, but it is often very difficult to decide which. It must be remembered that an action may be *explained* psychologically (he acted under stress or due to religious beliefs) and *judged* morally. The question about what part reason plays in the moral domain is, therefore, very relevant to relativism.

Epistemic cultural relativism does not, by and large, deny that there is something like a common objective world, the sense-experienced empirical world. The following is a fairly satisfactory account of cultural relativism:

> All arguments for relativism ... depend on the observation that there are, as a matter of fact, many languages, many

> theories for every phenomenon, many ... differing
> assessments of moral and aesthetic values. From ti.is
> observation it is concluded that phenomena are relative
> to which description is chosen, explanations are relative
> to which theory is favoured.... By a parallel line of
> argument it is supposed that moral and aesthetic
> assessments are relative to whatever criteria are current. [3]

Once again, 'languages' in this quotation means 'theories'. Ontological relativists might go to the extent of saying that phenomena are what they are according to the favoured theory, but epistemological relativists would be content to say that our understanding of the phenomena is related to the favoured theory.

The relativist claim splits into two irreconcilable claims: firstly, no beliefs, judgements, theories, etc. are true/privileged (malign relativism), and secondly, all beliefs, etc. are equally true/privileged (benign relativism).

'Relative truth is truth that is relative to some framework', 'historical, cultural, linguistic', and the 'core issue for alethic relativism is that something that is true in one framework may be false in another.' ('Framework', 'scheme', 'paradigm', 'view', 'culture' and 'tradition' are used, particularly in postmodern literature, more or less synonymously to mean a large theory or background of views, explicitly or hazily held by some group, regarding types of facts and ways of reasoning. The group usually referred to is called 'community'. We often come across, for instance, the 'scientific community'.)

This statement by O'Grady about relative truth is so imprecise that it could mean something that is true (and even trivial) or something that is false and dangerous. O'Grady tries to make it more precise by adding, 'The relativization of truth to framework avoids the kind of contradiction that occurs when the same thing is true and false in the same framework,'[5] but really makes it more confusing. Calling it 'strong relativism', he gives this as an example: The Hopi say 'spirits live in trees'. This is true in the Hopi framework but not 'when translated into normal English'. O'Grady seems hopelessly confused here due to the equivocation about 'language'. I suppose he means 'when it is said in the framework of modern Western thought'. If we amend his statement thus, we are still faced with vagueness. This could be just a statement of fact. The Hopi could simply be saying that 'we Hopis believe it is true that spirits live in trees, but you Westerners believe it is false', and *this* (statement of the Hopi) is, of course, true. The question is, whether 'spirits live in trees' is true? If relativism says it is true, as true as our belief that spirits don't live in trees or, for that matter, anywhere else, *because* the Hopi framework of beliefs is as true as that of modern Western thought, then *that* is relativism, and it is false.

Take 'A': 'Driving on the left side of the road is wrong.' In the framework of the USA traffic system, 'A' is true; in that of Britain and India, it is false. If this is strong relativism, it is perfectly innocent; it is true, and not worth making heavy weather of.

Consider 'B': 'Perseus slew the dragon to free a woman.' This statement is true in the framework of Greek mythology but false in the framework of everyday empirical reality, where 'C': 'Perseus did not slay the dragon and the woman is not free' is true. 'B' and 'C', if starkly juxtaposed, seem to be contradictories, but they are really not. They don't clash because they don't even make contact. We, who read Homer, do not believe the Homeric scenario to be real, myths to be true, and Perseus, the woman and dragons to have existed. But the Hopi framework and our framework clash, because we and the Hopi are talking about the *same* empirical world of trees and these trees do not house spirits. To suggest otherwise you would have to take recourse to a special kind of 'seeing' and a special kind of causation and, as we have fully considered when discussing Charles Taylor, make a virtue of ignorance to save a fiction.

The conclusion of the discussion so far is that the 'core issue of alethic relativism' that 'something that is true in one framework may be false in another', if properly understood and dealt with, does not jeopardize the law of non-contradiction, because, if the two frameworks are different, two apparently contradictory views are not really contradictory. It is when frameworks get mixed up so that a proposition has one leg in one framework and one leg in another, that we are in trouble.

So much for what O'Grady calls strong relativism. According to him, weak relativism holds that a statement may be 'true in one framework', but 'inexpressible in another'.[6] This, too, is an imprecise statement, and one is not clear whether it expresses the same idea which is called, by O'Grady, a 'very strong version' of relativism which holds 'that in different cultures and different historical epochs different standards of cognitive evaluation are used, leading to radically different sets of belief', so that 'cultures and epochs are closed off from each other' and thus raise 'the problem of incommensurability'. This is supposed to happen because there is 'no Archimedean position from which one can judge these different standards'.[7] I will discuss the Archimedean position later.

In the case of frameworks that are not so closed off but are, as they say, on speaking terms, something at least must be commonly held. There have to be, for example, gestures that naturally indicate what they are meant to convey and by means of which a parity of words in each language and then a parity of ideas, is reached. Probably onomatopoeic sounds also do the same job.

Since some rather elementary ideas seem to elude the postmodern mind, certain clarifications become necessary.

There can, obviously, be frameworks that are different from, but complementary to, each other. The same piece of land can be depicted in a geological map or a political one. A text can be studied linguistically (e.g. how many times does Dr. Radhakrishnan use a particular cliché in his writings?) or for its wisdom. In such cases there is no contradiction. If, however, one political map showed Kashmir in India and another showed it elsewhere, there would be a contradiction and would require something to be done about it.

MacIntyre writes:

> A tradition becomes mature just in so far as its adherents confront and find a rational way through and around those encounters with radically different and incompatible positions, which pose problems of incommensurability and untranslatability. An ability to recognize when one's conceptual resources are inadequate ... or when one is unable to frame satisfactorily what others have to say to one in criticism and rebuttal ... are all essential to the growth of a tradition whose conflicts are of any complexity or whose mutations involve transitions from one kind of social and cultural order to another...[8]

MacIntyre's writing is misleading. Are the radically incompatible positions within the tradition and between its adherents, or between the adherents, in the bulk, of one tradition and those of another? Similarly, does the inability to recognize one's conceptual resources as inadequate, and do the others who say something in criticism and rebuttal, refer to members within a tradition or to adherents of rival traditions? If the paragraph refers to encounters between adherents of the same tradition with its own concept of rationality, there should be no problems at all of commensurability and translation, for they would all subscribe to the same rational norms and the same language (meaning view or understanding). So, I expect he is talking of adherents, in the bulk, of rival traditions. It seems, therefore, that problems of incommensurability and untranslatability can and do arise between traditions and, even more importantly, a rational way can be found through and around the encounters between the traditions. MacIntyre, then, is not an extreme postmodern who holds that traditions, cultures or communities are completely 'windowless' and hermetically sealed. In fact, he admits 'transitions from one kind of social and cultural order to another'.

What he says soon after is perplexing: 'The standpoint of traditions is necessarily at odds with one of the central characteristics of cosmopolitan modernity', which is 'the confident belief that all cultural phenomena must be potentially translucent to understanding, that all texts must be capable of being translated into the language which the adherents of modernity speak to each other'[9]. (That is, of course the language or mode of understanding of modern science. Notice the equivocal use of 'language'!)

It is very difficult to decide on which side of the fence MacIntyre is standing. I doubt if he himself knows.

MacIntyre discusses frameworks.[10] Aristotle and Aquinas are taken to belong to the same tradition. So, one can ask, 'How far does the latter thinker solve ... the problems found insoluble by the earlier thinker?' or is 'able to resolve incoherences in the work of the earlier?' Presumably, these questions are meaningful and can, in principle, be answered. But in the case of Aristotle and Hume, 'accounts of practical reasoning and of justice ... are advanced within very different conceptual frameworks, which employ quite different modes of characterization and argument, and which yet are clearly incompatible'. It's not really that clear.

MacIntyre seems unaware that he is lumping together two different kinds of questions. One question is about substantive claims, where Aristotle holds that reason can educate the passions and that dessert has a place in the concept of justice, while Hume denies both these claims. The other question is about standards of rationality. Even if Aristotle and Hume differ profoundly about the substantive claims, they could not even see themselves as differing, nor could we (belonging to a still different framework) see them as differing unless their standards of rationality and ours were the same, and enough to show them both and us that their accounts about the substantive claims are incompatible.

And now MacIntyre asks, 'Is there some neutral tradition-independent standard of a rationally justifiable kind to which we may appeal?' Unless Aristotle, Aquinas, Hume and we share a common standard of rationality, how is it possible for any of us to judge whether the accounts are or are not compatible? MacIntyre has himself earlier shown (without, perhaps, realizing it) that a neutral tradition is not at all necessary and that two rival traditions can be reconciled by, and absorbed into, a third *tradition*, not a spot of nowhere-land. He tells us that Aristotle's understanding of the human agent was very different from that of Hebraic concepts, yet 'Aquinas's constructive discovery of a mode of understanding more comprehensive than either tradition had possessed' made it 'possible to integrate those two traditions.'[11]

MacIntyre raises another point.[12] To discover the nature of anything – say justice or reasoning – it is generally suggested that 'we ought not to begin from any theory' but 'from *the facts themselves*'; but this project also 'founders'. 'There are no pre-conceptual or even pre-theoretical data', and therefore no set of examples, 'no matter how comprehensive, can provide a neutral court of appeal for decision between rival theories'; 'How we describe any particular example will depend, therefore, upon which theory we have adopted.' MacIntyre is the victim here of the 'all-or-nothing' fallacy. Two theorists furnishing rival accounts about a certain phenomenon must at least be able to identify it, otherwise what are they theorizing and disputing about? Even a single theorist must distinguish what he is theorizing about *and* his theory about it. Otherwise he is like a person who says he is trying to find what he has lost, but doesn't know what it is he is searching for. If MacIntyre insists that you can start an investigation into a phenomenon only on the basis of a pre-theory, we can still point out that two theorists could identify their subject of investigation on the basis of a commonly held theory, and then give further accounts about it which differ from each other.

Aristotle and Hume could both agree on what reasoning is (enough to make a start at least), what passions are and the concept of slave and master; and Aristotle could conclude his inquiry with: 'Reason can direct or master the passions;' and Hume could conclude that Reason is their slave. They would start, I suggest, by picking on examples of voluntary action in the pursuit of satisfying the passions. Hume would not have much difficulty in showing Aristotle how humans with strong desires use rational means to satisfy them. Aristotle would have to show cases where persons having some very strong passions (say the desire to slap someone who has insulted them) nevertheless do not succumb to their passions because they know that such retaliation is not a reasonable or civilized way of behaving, etc. And, if courage is the phenomenon under investigation, different theorists would select cases of courage which no sensible person (including the theorists themselves) would seriously challenge.

I have been simply describing the Socratic procedure and there is no reason to doubt that it works. The aim is not to find examples that are neutral between two traditions or theories but those which both traditions or both theories admit are proper examples of the subject of study. They would have enough properties in common for identification as the wanted examples and yet would have other properties which would have to be discovered and may become matters of dispute between traditions and theories.

If, in a particular tradition, a certain act which is taken to be an example of a certain kind (say honesty), is, in another tradition, taken to be an example of exactly the opposite kind (dishonesty), then it would be almost impossible to establish any rational rapport between two such traditions. They would not be on speaking terms. This would be an ideal limit and such a case is highly unlikely to occur. Even the worst of criminals seek to justify their acts to those who find them unacceptable.

Two conclusions *do not* have to be drawn.

1. In order to morally assess a tradition, it is not necessary to find a 'tradition-independent moral standpoint' or features of 'human beings independently of and apart from those characteristics which belong to them as members of any particular social or cultural tradition'.[13] We do not need to quake before Archimedes' ghost.

2. The fact that, at times, with regard to social or moral issues we seem to confront almost insuperable difficulty, should not make us despair of reason's capacity. MacIntyre grants that 'very, very occasionally some particular thesis is conclusively refuted or at least rendered utterly implausible' and 'a good deal more often, the relationship of one argument to another or of one set of affirmations to another is clarified in respect of entailment ... or other logical and conceptual relations'. Only on 'major issues', he thinks, 'disagreement ... seems to be ineradicable,' and that too, 'seems to be'.[14]

What MacIntyre has to say about liberalism is very relevant and instructive.[15] Liberalism began as a project, writes MacIntyre, to found a social order in which 'individuals could emancipate themselves from the contingency and particularity of traditions by appealing to genuinely universal, tradition-independent norms'. But liberalism 'has itself been transformed into a tradition' and one 'whose continuities are partly defined by the interminability of the debate' over the 'alleged principles of shared rationality'.

This account brings out two points:

1. The activity of appraising the norms of a particular tradition by principles of shared rationality does not have to be performed from an uncommitted insubstantial platform, but is itself a tradition, which uses, like other traditions, its own norms and methods. MacIntyre himself says this. Liberalism is 'not at all ... an attempt to find a rationality independent of tradition'. MacIntyre, in writing this, thinks that it means that liberalism is not neutral and that its starting points are 'liberal starting points'. Yes, they are not neutral in the sense of being vacuous; they are the beliefs that there are principles of shared rationality, the principles by which all traditions, including itself, can be assessed. Liberalism is, he says, 'the articulation of an historically developed and developing set of social institutions.' The fact that liberalism has a history and continues to develop does not mean that it is so subjugated by its own history that it cannot rationally criticize its own principles. Self-criticism is the very essence of rationality, and it can be done *a*historically.[16]

2. Liberalism is indeed a tradition and a healthy one, but it is a tradition different from others (at least as these are thought of by postmodernism) in that it maintains that all traditions can be rationally compared, examined, critiqued, assessed and graded by standing back and reflecting on their ideas, norms and practices. It maintains also that this activity is performed by every tradition itself and is not performed by some external agency. The

> capacity of a tradition to critically examine itself and see its place among other traditions *is* the tradition called liberalism. Like hell or heaven, it is not a separate place; it is an attitude and a capacity.

MacIntyre proceeds: 'From the fact that liberalism does not provide a neutral tradition-independent ground from which a verdict may be passed upon the rival claims of conflicting traditions ... it does not follow that there is no such ground', and 'there can be no sound *a priori* argument to demonstrate' that such a ground is impossible.[17] (See how open and liberal MacIntyre can be!) But 'liberalism is by far the strongest claimant to provide such a ground which has so far appeared in human history....' One may ask what tradition-independent grounds MacIntyre has for this pontifical pronouncement. 'That liberalism fails in this respect, therefore, provides the strongest reason ... that there is no such neutral ground.' It also, however, shows that we can get along quite well without it. Nor does it follow, as MacIntyre thinks it does, that there is 'instead only the practical-rationality-of-this-or-that-tradition'.[18] We don't have to fall into Charybdis because there is no Scylla to fall into.

It 'may well appear to follow,' writes MacIntyre, 'that no tradition can claim rational superiority to any other. For each tradition has internal to itself its own view of what rational superiority consists in.' From this, he says, 'Two further conclusions may seem to follow:'[19]

1. At 'any fundamental level no rational debate between, rather than within, traditions can occur'. Within a tradition its adherents may share enough fundamental beliefs to conduct a debate, but 'the protagonists of rival

traditions will be precluded ... from justifying their views' to the outsiders or even learning anything from them. So, for example, the Hopi could debate among themselves whether the tree-dwelling spirits came down in the mornings or not, but *we* could neither take part in this debate nor point out that it's all a fairy tale. They, too, could not debate whether Ptolemy or Galileo was right. But debate within a tradition is allowed as possible. Surely, there would be groups (A and B) within a tradition, each having its own, often incompatible, ideas and norms (unless MacIntyre goes to the absurd extent of insisting that every tradition is or must be – on *a priori* grounds? – entirely homogeneous) and yet these groups can debate 'at any fundamental level'. So, in spite of their peculiar ideals and norms (which serve to make them different groups), they would have enough by way of rationality, to enter into debate to justify their several views and learn from each other. Then what prevents big rival groups from entering into a debate by using similar common principles of reasoning? Is it that between traditions there is some boundary or limit to rationally possible discussion – 'We'll discuss justice so far, but no further'? Is this limit fixed by each tradition according to *its* own norms or by an *a priori* principle or by a resolution? It is precisely the nature of reasoning that no external agency can impose a limit to it.

2. 'Given that each tradition will frame its own standpoint in terms of its own idiosyncratic concepts, and given that no fundamental correction of its conceptual scheme from

some external standpoint is possible, it may appear that each tradition must develop its own scheme in a way which is liable to preclude even translation from one tradition to another.'[20]

If we have to accept what is here said to be 'given', the conclusion drawn 'may appear' to follow, but there is nothing to compel us to accept it and every reason to reject it, because it is an arbitrary and gratuitous fiat. Further, MacIntyre writes that 'communication between traditions will at certain crucial points be too inadequate for each even to understand the other fully.'[21] This sentence clearly shows that, though he uses the word 'translation', he is not thinking in terms, literally, of language, as ordinarily understood, but of understanding. In the case of (for example) the understanding of the Hopi and modern Western science, the use of 'translation' is misleading, sophistical and mischievous. The understanding of the Hopi cannot, in any sense, be *translated* into that of modern science; it is simply rejected as incorrect and fanciful or *corrected* to such an extent that the original would be reduced to near invisibility. In the case of translation properly so-called, the translation and the text translated stand on the same level of acceptability.

MacIntyre ends Chapter XVII, which we have been concentrating on, with:

> A social universe composed exclusively of rival traditions, so it may seem, will be one in which there are a number of contending, incompatible, but only partially and inadequately communicating, overall views of the universe, each tradition ... unable to justify its claims over against those of its rivals...[22]

Where has 'only partially and inadequately communicating' dropped in from? We were made to think that there could be no communication at all. He now asks, 'Is this indeed what follows?' and says that to these problems 'we must now turn'.[23] He turns to them in the next chapter.

In emphatic terms MacIntyre tells us that 'the argument so far' has led to the conclusion that 'there is no other way to engage in the formulation, elaboration, rational justification, and criticism of accounts of practical rationality' or anything else 'except from within some one particular tradition' and that there is 'no standing ground' except that provided by a particular tradition. You can't put the cultural relativism case more strongly. But immediately following this, he writes, 'It does not follow that what *is* said from within one tradition cannot be heard or overheard by those in another.'[24] That *is* what we were made to think did follow from all that was said earlier. Is it suggested that there exists a *deus ex machina* who makes the outsiders hear or overhear what the insiders have been saying?

MacIntyre elaborates: [25]

> Traditions which differ in the most radical way over certain subject matters may in respect of others share beliefs, images and texts. Considerations urged from within one tradition may be ignored by ... another only at the cost, by their own standards, of excluding relevant good reasons for believing or disbelieving this or that.

If all this obtains, what is left of cultural relativism? Here also there is room for clarification. That traditions differ over certain subject matters and agree over others is irrelevant to the issue, which is whether they can agree and differ over the *same* subject matters, because each can engage, as we were told, in justification, etc. only from within and there *is* no common standing ground. It now seems that there *is* such a ground, a sort of marketplace where considerations can be brought for exchange by one tradition and accepted by another or ignored at its peril.

We are now informed that not only do different traditions share some common subject matters, they even 'share some standards'. Each is not condemned to stew in its own juice. 'All the traditions with which we have been concerned agree in according a certain authority to logic.' I have considered this point in Chapter 6. However, since 'that upon which they agree is insufficient to resolve those disagreements', says MacIntyre, it 'may therefore seem … that we are confronted with the rival and competing claims of a number of traditions', that 'no one tradition can deny legitimacy to its rivals', and every tradition 'has as much and as little claim to our allegiance as any other.' Unlike Orwell's animals, none here are more equal than others, even when they assert contrary 'truths'.[26]

But don't despair; there is a solution, and the solution, 'so the perspectivist argues, is to withdraw the ascription of truth and falsity'. The 'baby-bathwater' solution! 'Instead of interpreting rival traditions as mutually exclusive and incompatible ways of understanding one and the same world, one and the same subject matter, let us understand them instead as providing … complementary perspectives.'[27] We have here a very elementary logico-linguistic blunder. If the perspectives are rival and incompatible, they can't be complementary, and if they can be complementary, they are not rival and incompatible.

MacIntyre's writing resembles a river so clogged with flow-impeding matter and so often flowing away into streams and rivulets, that one is never quite sure which is the river and where it is heading. The suggestion about complementary perspectives seems to have been just dropped. From now on MacIntyre seems keen to meet the relativist and the perspectivist challenges which 'are often presented jointly as parts of a single argument', and, in so doing, he shows us a different (and complementary or incompatible?) face from the one we have so far seen.

The pendulum, never entirely steady, has altered its swing. MacIntyre now thinks that new situations reveal that beliefs within a tradition may be unable to deal with new questions. The tradition has then reached a crisis. 'The coming together of two previously separate communities, each with its own well-established institutions, practices, beliefs … may open up new alternative possibilities.' In place of the ideas on which postmodernism has so far and all along fed us about how traditions and communities can believe, and act on, only those norms which they happen to have and which cannot be questioned, we now have a plethora of changes that can occur. A 'stock of reasons and of questioning and reasoning abilities' will 'determine the possible range of outcomes in the rejection, emendation, and reformulation of beliefs, the revaluation of authorities, the reinterpretation of texts, the emergence of new forms of authority, and the production of new texts.'[28]

Elaborating the matter, MacIntyre continues, that a tradition 'will tend to recognize what it shares … with other traditions, and … common characteristic, if not universal patterns will appear'. (If 'common' is possible, why not 'universal'?) 'The identification of incoherence within established belief will always provide a reason for inquiring further' and the old belief will be rejected when 'something more adequate because less incoherent has been discovered'. This is a satisfactory description of what happens in scientific or any other systematic inquiry, but the important point is that something can come from another tradition and that traditions are no longer self-sufficient and isolated. New problems arise 'for the solution of which there seem to be insufficient or no resources within the established fabric of belief' and 'the invention or discovery of new concepts and ... a new type or types of theory' is required.[29]

It is clear from all this that the adherents of a tradition are not buried for life in their own tradition. G. Graham tells us that in 'Moral Relativism, Truth, and Justification' (1994), MacIntyre's 'basic thrust is that inter-traditional conflicts can in a sense be transcended' and that MacIntyre 'argues that all traditions of inquiry are committed to an assertion-transcendent concept of truth', so that the account which traditions give of morality (why only morality?) do not "suffer from the limitations, partialities and one-sidedness of a merely local point of view". Graham explains this position 'in terms of an underlying common nature that all human beings share in virtue of their evolved animality'; but MacIntyre does not seem to take this line.[30]

MacIntyre says that the adherents of a tradition often are 'compelled to recognize that within' another tradition it is possible to construct 'from concepts and theories peculiar to' that tradition 'what they were unable to provide from their own ... a cogent and illuminating explanation ... *by their own standards*' (italics mine).[31] Thus, for example, the Hopi could well be compelled, either by Western scientists or by their own gumption, to recognize the falsity of their own concepts, the correctness of those of Western science and how the latter is able to illuminatingly explain where they went wrong.

What I have italicized is very crucial. It means that all the silly talk about their standards and our standards should be given up. MacIntyre himself writes that if the relativist's thesis is that each tradition 'must always be vindicated in the light of' its own standards only, 'then on this at least the relativist is mistaken.' It is thus clear that the tradition that was in crisis must acknowledge that 'the alien tradition is superior in rationality and in respect of its claims to truth to their own'.[32] MacIntyre also admits that a tradition can 'defeat or be defeated by other traditions'.[33]

Jean Porter writes that 'on MacIntyre's view, the necessity for standing outside of any tradition whatsoever is obviated by the possibility of standing within two traditions at once in order to move between them in a comparative assessment of their claims'.[34] Physically this may be an impossible feat, but we know what Porter means.

MacIntyre quotes Donald Davidson, who goes the whole hog: 'A creature that cannot in principle be understood in terms of our own beliefs, values and modes of communication is not a creature that might have thoughts radically different from our own: it is a creature without what we mean by thoughts.'[35] MacIntyre gives a half-hearted support to this view of Davidson's.

MacIntyre has made, in Chapters VII and VIII of *Whose Justice?*, an extensive and unnecessarily involved tour from an apparently stoutly held relativist position to a near-complete surrender of it. He does not, perhaps, hold the former position at all and his stout defence of it was a technique of advocacy by stretching it to its utmost limit of plausibility. Anyway, he has presented it squarely before us and I have attempted to demolish it in my own way.

The view that the anomalies in a tradition can be resolved and absorbed by another, and that this is how knowledge grows, is, for Taylor, a case of 'supersession'. In every 'coping experience', that is, whenever we cope with a real situation that confronts us, even in our everyday life, 'we sense that we are in contact with a nature with a structure of its own that supports our coping', which means that 'it makes sense to think we can correctly describe that structure and that, indeed, there is evidence that our current science may well be progressively getting it right about (at least some aspects of) the universe.'[36]

I will expand this idea of supersession and then make some comments about the way Dreyfus looks at it.

When we enter a café that looks much larger than it seemed to be when we last entered it, we confront an anomaly, until we realize that the walls have been covered by full-sized mirrors. Now 'things snap into place'. In this way, we are always moving to a better grasp of the world around us; the criterion we are continuously using but, to a large extent, without being aware of it, is always comprehensive coherence. Understanding other cultures and frameworks that are foreign to the milieu in which we have been living and functioning, is far more difficult than dealing with the case about the mirrored café, but it is along the same lines. The difficulty is increasingly greater as we have to deal with cultures increasingly remote from ours. We have to see how the adherents of the foreign culture respond to our words, actions and the situation. When, for example, lovers of Western 'classical' music attend, for the first time, an Indian *jalsa*, they are shocked to find that the audience shouts its approval periodically while the artist is still performing, and appreciators of Indian music are equally surprised to find that Western audiences sit throughout a work for half an hour or more with serious faces and near-immobile bodies. Is a rapprochement possible? Of course it is; each party could be made to see what makes the other party behave as it does.

When we are up against a case of more extreme divergence, mutual understanding takes more out of each party. Dr. Niel Lamper, an American psychologist, told us that he could, without knowing their language, easily communicate with Koli fishermen – about catching fish. Doing it about psychology or atomic physics would not have been so easy, but, in principle, possible. Taylor's favourite example is that of the Aztecs eating the hearts of their sacrificial victims who even think they are honoured by this act. 'We can,' says Dreyfus, 'accept that there are radically different cultural understandings of being,' and 'yet,' he adds, 'rank their relation to reality'. Even the unbecoming practice of the Aztecs is, thus, not beyond our comprehension. And evaluation. It is because of our 'contact with a common world,' says Taylor, 'that we always have something to say to each other, something to point to in disputes about reality.' (Quoted by Dreyfus.) Our direct coping with the world 'gives us a sense of an independent nature that sets limits to what we can do unless we get in sync with it', and this is why and how our theories, we believe and have good reason to believe, 'correspond more and more adequately to the structure of the universe'. (This, mind, has nothing to do with the Correspondence Theory of Truth.)

I have quoted Dreyfus saying that according to Taylor, 'it makes sense to think we can correctly describe' the structure of the universe and that 'there is evidence that our current science may well be progressively right'. But he writes that Taylor 'does not have to hold that our current science is getting it right about the universe or that any science will ever get it right' or that 'current science is in fact on the right track'.[37]

What, here, is the concept of 'getting it right'? Science has, over centuries, developed criteria and methods in order to understand the universe, and, quite apart from its inherent rationally satisfactory nature, science's impressive practical achievements have shown that its criteria and methods have worked amazingly well, so that it satisfies the pragmatic test. In fact, the stance of postmodernism is nothing if not pragmatic. Do Dreyfus and Taylor (if accurately interpreted by Dreyfus) visualize some other kinds of criteria and methods which might make us feel more certain that we have got it right? In the total absence of any alternative criteria and methods, should we not accept the overall claims of current science? Dreyfus says that Taylor 'argues convincingly that, given our science's supersession claims, it makes sense to hold that our science is in fact zeroing in on (one aspect of) the physical universe as it is in itself'. Still it only 'makes sense' and nothing more.

Even in saying that current science's getting it right makes sense, Dreyfus writes, in parenthesis, 'at least some aspects of' and 'one aspect of'. In her introduction to *Charles Taylor*, editor Ruth Abbey writes, 'Dreyfus wrestles with the question of whether Taylor's arguments on this topic [coping with the world] can be squared with his cultural pluralism. Doesn't his belief, that science shows us the universe as it really is, 'necessarily consign other cultures' ways of looking at these same things to falsehoods?'[38]

This is where Dreyfus's parenthetical phrases come in handy. A distinction is made between essential and other properties. Abbey writes, 'In so far as other cultures do not claim to be describing the essential properties of things, their descriptions cannot be immediately weighed against those of modern science and found wanting.'[39] What on earth does this mean? When science says that gold has no magical or sacred properties and, as Dreyfus says, the Egyptians might have believed that 'gold's essential property might have been that it was sacred' (Dreyfus, p. 74), surely the Egyptians *would be* claiming to describe the same essential property that science describes as bogus.

The controversy is not about essential and inessential properties. Even if we say that the Egyptians were claiming that the sacredness of gold was an *in*essential property, science would still maintain that gold simply has no such property. Abbey's introduction of essential and other properties is one more instance of slipping a red herring into the argument. The controversy is really about scientifically claimed or established real properties (essential or otherwise) and fictitiously claimed properties, which no criteria or methods have established – established in any sense that 'makes sense'.

Abbey continues, 'In so far as there is no direct contradiction between the essential properties as revealed by science and those attributed by another culture to the same entity … both approaches can bring to light real aspects of that entity.'[40] I have shown that, in the case considered or any other similar case, there is certainly a direct contradiction. The hypothesized Egyptian account about gold does not bring anything to light except something concerning the Ancient Egyptian mind – that they, like many postmoderns, believed things for which they had no justifiable warrant. The Ancient Egyptians, however, can be excused.

'Taylor can accept,' Abbey writes, 'that there could be several true descriptions that correspond to various aspects of nature.'[41] Of course. Not could be, there are – the physical aspect, the environmental aspect, the aesthetic aspect; but not the mythical aspect, the mystical aspect and the fairy-tale aspect, because nature does not have such aspects. With that, let us say, *au revoir* to Taylor's robust realism.

Popular myths and superstitions die hard; they hold out, due to various reasons, for some time, but tend to disappear as the scientific view of the universe percolates down to the people. The scientific culture is slowly but steadily making inroads into the gradually shrinking territories of rival cultures and obscurantist ideas. O'Grady writes, 'Evans-Pritchard says of the Azande: "Most of their talk is common-sense talk, and their references to witchcraft, whilst frequent enough, bear no comparison in volume to their talk about other matters."… Furthermore, if cultures have their own standards of rationality, one would expect them to be immune to intellectual challenge from without. But in the history of traditional cultures, one can see a pattern of old beliefs dying out in the face of new systems (the prevalence of ghost stories in rural Ireland waned in the aftermath of rural electrification). This shouldn't happen if there are genuinely alternative rationalities.'[42]

All the claptrap about cultures unable to understand each other and their languages being untranslatable, is a concoction of the postmodern mind, such as it is. Instead of observation, it relies on its fertile imagination, for even a cursory look at the practice of anthropologists would tell them how wrong the postmodern take on the knowledge and understanding of traditional or primitive societies is. The anthropologist tries to 'translate their language into one familiar to the anthropologist'; he tries to 'ascertain the utterances that signify assent and dissent' and does it by projecting notions of contradiction, identity and inference' on to them. He also assumes, with good reason, that their perceptions are like his own and their utterances are similarly connected with their perceptions. O'Grady rightly says that 'they share a great deal of our way of thinking about the world' and this cuts against the claim about 'radically divergent rationalities'.[43]

To argue that the truth or even the meaning of a statement, *p*', is culture-dependent, it must, at least, be recognized as the same statement made in different cultures, and this recognition itself cannot be culture-dependent, for then it, in turn, will have to be recognized inter-culturally.

> 'I gave my BA exam last month,' says Mohun. 'That can't be,' says Tom,' 'because you are not even a graduate yourself!' 'Of course, I'm not; that's what I'm telling you; I gave my BA exam last month and I am waiting for the result.' 'I'm totally confused,' retorts Tom; 'how can you give an exam if you are still going to take it?' Pesy, who has been brought up in both the Indian and the British cultures (that being possible), clarifies the mystery. 'You see,' he explains, 'in our *desi* culture, "gave an exam" means "sat for an exam" because this is a direct translation of the vernacular, whereas in the British culture – they are so different from us – "give an exam" means "examine" – such an odd language, English!' 'Oh, now I understand,' says Tom, his eyes wide open. 'And, you see, what I told

you was true,' says Mohun, smiling. Pesy has done his good deed for the day.

And thus the meeting of the cultures. Mohun and Tom are concerned with the same '*p*' and, if Mohun is honest, '*p*' is true. If '*p*' is 'the same statement in each cultural/linguistic environment, then there is a universally intelligible statement … one absolute component in human thought'. This is '*the thesis of trans-cultural intelligibility*', which shows that either cultural relativism is false or, if '*p*' means different things in different cultures and can never mean the same thing, then, in the absence of God's eye (which *is* absent), it is impossible to know that different things in different cultures are different, and so relativism is unprovable.[44]

Quine expresses well the paradox of relativism: 'Truth, says the cultural relativist, is culture-bound. But if it were, then he, within his own culture, ought to see his own culture-bound truth as absolute. He cannot proclaim cultural relativism without rising above it, and he cannot rise above it without giving it up.'[45] If he means it to be true, not absolutely but only within his own culture, other cultures may well ignore it and go their own way. In asserting his identity the relativist has lost it, for he has entered the culture – and it *is* a culture – of the universality of reason.

References

1. Sokal, A. & J. Bricmont, 1997, pp. 99-101.
2. Harre, R. & M. Krausz, 1996, pp. 10-11.
3. Ibid., p. 7.
4. O'Grady, P., 2002, p. 35.
5. Ibid., p. 35.

6. Ibid., p. 36.
7. Ibid., p. 90.
8. MacIntyre, A., 1988, p. 327.
9. Ibid., p. 327.
10. Ibid., pp. 328-29.
11. Ibid., pp. 326-27.
12. Ibid., pp. 332-33.
13. Ibid., p. 334.
14. Ibid., pp. 334-35.
15. Ibid., p. 335.
16. Ibid., p. 345.
17. Ibid., p. 346.
18. Ibid., p. 346.
19. Ibid., p. 348.
20. Ibid., p. 348.
21. Ibid., p. 348.
22. Ibid., p. 348.
23. Ibid., p.348.
24. Ibid., p. 350.
25. Ibid., pp. 350-51.
26. Ibid., pp. 351-52.
27. Ibid., p. 352.
28. Ibid., pp. 355-57.
29. Ibid., pp. 359, 362.
30. Graham, G., 'MacIntyre on History and Philosophy' in Murphy, M. C. (Ed.), 2003, pp. 34-35. The words in double quotation marks are those of A. MacIntyre.
31. MacIntyre, A., 1988, p. 364.
32. Ibid., p. 364.
33. Ibid., p. 366.
34. Porter, J., 'Tradition in the Recent Work of Alasdair MacIntyre', in Murphy, M.C. (Ed.), 2003, p. 53.
35. MacIntyre, A., 1988, pp. 370-71. This quotation from Davidson is from *Expressing Evaluations*, 1984, p. 20.

36. Dreyfus, H. L., op. cit., pp. 68-69.
37. Ibid., pp. 69, 74-75.
38. Abbey, R. (Ed.), 2004, *Charles Taylor*, p. 8.
39. Ibid., p. 8.
40. Ibid., p. 8.
41. Ibid., p. 8.
42. O'Grady, P., 2002, p. 155.
43. Ibid., pp. 155-56.
44. Harre, R. & M. Krausz, 1996, pp. 26-27.
45. Quine quoted by Harre, R. & M. Krausz, 1996, p. 28.

Chapter 10

The Ghostly Point

The Archimedean Red Herring

T ruth and even meaning are culture-dependent; to relate, compare, contrast and in any way assess things which fall in different cultures, or different cultures themselves, would require a neutral position outside of the cultures, but there is or can be no such position, for everything falls within some culture or the other; therefore things that fall in different cultures or even different cultures themselves cannot be compared, contrasted or in any way assessed. This is the foundational argument for cultural relativism and relativists believe it to be a knock-down argument.

The supposed neutral position is nicknamed the Archimedean point. It is also called the God's-eye-view or view from nowhere.

Before going further we may remind ourselves of what Archimedes claimed. He claimed that, if he could occupy a particular spot in space and if he had a long enough pole and a fulcrum at the proper place, he could lift the earth, and the other planets too, with the strength of his arm. This is a straightforward deduction in mechanics. He didn't say he would have to be nowhere; he spoke of being somewhere in actual space, the same space in which the earth and other planets existed. So, the analogy about being nowhere and outside of all traditions breaks down.

Turning back to the argument for cultural relativism given above, it is a modus tollens '(p ⊃ q. ~ q)⊃~ p'. To which culture, one may ask, does this argument belong? And where has the implicatory premise, 'p ⊃ q', come from? It can't have come from experience. It is not an analytic truth either.

Stanley Fish, 'the latest in the line of debunking anti-philosophers', examined the idea that an individual can stand outside the prevailing norms 'constituted by historical and cultural forces to "see through" and thus stand to the side of his own convictions and beliefs'. He writes:

> But that is the one thing a historically conditioned consciousness cannot do – scrutinize its own beliefs, conduct a rational examination of its own convictions; for in order to begin such a scrutiny, it would first have to escape the grounds of its own possibility, and it could only do that if it were not historically conditioned.[1]

This is, of course, a *petitio*: a historically conditioned consciousness cannot stand to the side of his own beliefs and examine them rationally, because to do so, it would have to stand outside his own beliefs, but a historically conditioned consciousness cannot stand outside his own beliefs. However, this premise, which is also the conclusion, can be challenged for being gratuitously assumed. The anti-relativist claims that the human mind is not 'conditioned', like a knee-jerk or like Pavlov's dogs, and this is proved by the fact of this very controversy, which demonstrates that the anti-relativist has, in questioning the relativist's thesis, transcended the historical and cultural forces, and also demonstrates that the relativist, in trying to meet his adversary's contention by an argument, has also transcended those forces.

The controversy links up with the question of bias. Each person's understanding of any subject matter is from a particular perspective determined by the peculiar circumstances in which, due to historical and cultural causes, he finds himself. This, according to the relativist, makes each understanding 'biased', and not an understanding of the subject matter as it is in itself. All understandings and the truths they accept are, therefore, relative.

This view is well expressed by Tom Sorell,[2] who expounds the views of Bernard Williams:

> …someone's representation of the world from a certain perspective … is bound to contain things introduced by that perspective, things that are *not* 'there anyway'. From the standpoint of acquiring genuine knowledge, these subjective elements of one's perspective seem unwanted; yet, since it is always a person with a perspective who acquires knowledge, the elements seem ineradicable.

But, for Williams, 'the presence of subjective elements does not necessarily prevent a representation of the world from providing knowledge', for 'it may be possible to stand back from the differing representations and understand how a single independent world could have given rise to both' or all of them. This would be the 'inclusive conception', by which Williams presumably means that this conception would make it possible to spot, in the included

186 • Human Reason and Its Enemies

conceptions, those elements which are subjectively occasioned and those which are not, ignore the former and take the latter to be the correct representation of what is out there.

Increasing inclusive conceptions are possible and likely. If a conception 'faces no competition ... then this unrivalled conception will have the strongest claim to represent the world as it really is in itself'. Williams calls it 'the absolute conception'. Such a conception may, thinks Williams, create the illusion that it is independent of all representations or, in the relativist parlance, neutral. Sorell says Williams does not commit himself to the 'cogency' of the absolute conception, and 'it sometimes looks as if he thinks that there is no sense to be made of it'. Sorell, however, thinks we should be quite satisfied with the idea 'that the world as it is in itself is ... only the object of a representation that is ... unrivalled'.

The 'inside', 'outside' metaphor causes trouble and is mischievous. Thomas Nagel recommends, and rightly, that it should not be taken literally. While we cannot jump outside our individual point of view, we 'are to rely less and less on certain individual aspects of our point of view, and more and more on something else, less individual, which is also part of us', says Nagel. This 'something else', says Sorell, is the 'rational mind' and, we should note, is also part of us and not foreign to us. Indeed, it is the most distinctive part of us as humans. It 'cuts across the differences between individual human beings,' writes Sorell, and has the 'capacity, independent of experience, to generate hypotheses' about the world as it is. In other words, it is not 'conditioned' by Fish's historical and cultural forces. Sorell thinks this is clearly proved by our indisputable advances in knowledge.[3]

Let us turn once more to MacIntyre, the consummate trapeze artist who can swing from bar to bar with such ease.[4] He tells us that it would be wrong to suppose that Aristotle offered us an account of practical reasoning 'superior to those advanced from other rival, fundamentally different standpoints … by appeal to some neutral set of standards'; there is 'no neutral mode of stating the problems, let alone the solutions'.

'Progress in rationality,' he proceeds, meaning, presumably, rational progress, 'is achieved only from a point of view', that is, presumably, only within one tradition or framework and it is achieved where adherents of that viewpoint elaborate 'ever more comprehensive and adequate statements of their positions through the dialectical procedure of advancing objections which identify incoherences, omissions, explanatory failures, and other types of flaw and limitation, … of finding the strongest arguments available for supporting those objections, and then attempting to restate the position so that it is no longer vulnerable to those specific objections and arguments'. MacIntyre can write so well when he tries. An excellent summary of the Socratic method. This is how reason works, and it works within, and according to, a tradition (in this case, of the polis).

Is there anything to suggest that in other traditions reason can or does work in some other way? Instead of advancing objections, does it keep silent? Instead of identifying incoherences, omissions and other failures, does it ignore these failures? Instead of finding the strongest arguments for its position, does it seek and offer the weakest? What does MacIntyre suggest? Do the incoherences, failures, flaws and limitations, as they are understood in one tradition, become coherences, successes, merits and adequacies in another tradition? Do the very concepts of coherence, failure, success, omission, flaw and limitation differ from tradition to tradition? And if they *are* different, how would MacIntyre know this and tell us?

MacIntyre's next paragraph is bewildering:

> Any philosophical theory of any large degree of comprehensiveness has to include in what it explains the views of those intelligent, perceptive, and philosophically sophisticated persons who disagree with it... So Aristotle too...has a cogent and more comprehensive explanation for the varieties of error and disagreement. But it would be a mistake to suppose that it is the kind of explanation which could prove convincing to Aristotle's opponents and critics, ancient or modern.[5]

Aristotle could have said something like what Dr. Johnson said about argument and understanding. Whether the critics and opponents are convinced or not is a separate point, depending on the thickness of their heads. The point surely is whether Aristotle's explanation touched those varieties of error and disagreement, and whether his explanation was cogent and more comprehensive. *We* must judge this; what happened to Aristotle's opponents and critics is for historians to find out. If Aristotle's performance in this regard was satisfactory, and if his critics and opponents remained unconvinced, they must not have been intelligent, perceptive or philosophically sophisticated.

We jump some two dozen pages to observe Aquinas's miraculous feat.[6] In the thirteenth century, there were two 'apparently incompatible and conflicting demands of two distinct and rival traditions', the Aristotelian and the Augustinian. But if they were only apparently so (we may interrupt, excuse us), they obviously had something in common and were not bitter rivals; so where's the problem?

> When two rival large-scale intellectual traditions confront one another ... there is no neutral way of characterizing either the subject matter ... or the standards by which their claims are to be evaluated. Each standpoint has its own account of truth and knowledge, its own mode of characterizing the relevant subject matter. And the attempt to discover a neutral, independent set of standards or mode of characterizing data which is *both* such as must be acceptable to all rational persons *and* is sufficient to determine the truth ... has generally, and perhaps universally, proved to be a search for a chimera.[6]

Strong words! Bold too. But there are chinks in the armour. Firstly, 'generally' and 'perhaps' show that there is no impossibility *in principle* to find and use such neutral standards and modes of characterizing data. Secondly, 'there is no neutral way of characterizing ... the subject matter' contradicts the idea that there must be a 'relevant subject matter' which is commonly identified by the rival traditions about which each has its own account; otherwise, if the two traditions are talking about different matters, nothing is gained on behalf of relativism. If there is to be relevant subject matter, we may ask: Relevant to what? Obviously to the fact that both traditions are wrangling over a common topic. Surely, between theists and atheists, the common topic of dispute is God's existence, and to wrangle over it, they have to characterize God in a way which *both* parties agree to.

Before going further, I must point out here, as elsewhere in such discussions, there is confusion due to an ambiguity that runs right through. Is the controversy about substantive concepts like God, existence, etc. or about standards of truth and validity? If it is to be a 'genuine controversy', the standards must be the same for both parties, or they can't differ about the subject matter, which, also, has to be the same.

Let's see what MacIntyre has to say.[7]

> A genuine controversy proceeds 'in two stages'. Firstly, each party 'characterizes the contentions of its rivals in its own terms'. The qualification 'in its own terms' is vacuous because all it means is that the party makes 'explicit the grounds for rejecting what is incompatible with its own theses'. Surely they are also to be made explicit to the other party, otherwise, again, no genuine controversy. And surely, that is to be done in a manner, which is intelligible to the other party; that is, in the other party's terms also.

We are told that 'on marginal and subordinate questions', a tradition ('A') may allow that a rival tradition ('B') may teach it ('A') something on its own ('A's) 'standards of judgment' and from its ('A's) 'own point of view'. This would, no doubt, demand superhuman exertion on the part of 'B' to somehow leave behind its ('B's) own standards and viewpoint, slip out of its own skin, as it were, and enter the other party's ('A's). This confronts MacIntyre with four questions:

1. How *can* any tradition abandon, even temporarily, its own viewpoint and standards?

2. If it *can* do this trick, what happens to relativism?

3. If the trick can be performed regarding marginal and subordinate questions, what stops it from being performed regarding major and core questions?

4. By what criteria are the two sets of questions to be distinguished?

At the second stage (why is it a second stage?), the 'protagonists of each tradition' find it difficult to develop their respective enquiries 'beyond a certain point'. Then those of one tradition ('A') send an SOS to those of another ('B'), asking if they 'may not be able to provide resources to characterize and to explain the failings and defects of their own [that is, 'A's] tradition more adequately than they, using the resources of that tradition, have been able to do'. So, the flat-earth believers, who have come up against the fact that the earth's shadow on the moon during an eclipse is an arc, appeal to the spherical-earth believers if they could help; the latter would explain by saying the earth is spherical, which the former would either reject out of hand or accept, thus converting to the rival tradition. So, where does relativism fit in?

Once again, false analogy is a part cause of confusion. Standards and viewpoints are regarded as tools. Most physicians would bring their own sphygmomanometer when taking the patient's blood pressure, but some might use the patient's own. However, standards and viewpoints are not like sphygmomanometers and stethoscopes.

Let us recall that a tradition, in a genuine controversy, has rejected what is 'incompatible with its own central theses' in the theses of the rival tradition and also made explicit the grounds of rejection. So, how will the rescuing team come to the assistance of the tradition that has developed 'insoluble antinomies'?[7] What is the way out of this intellectual traffic snarl? We are told 'it requires a rare gift of empathy as well as of intellectual insight', such as, we are told, the Aristotelian and Augustinian traditions

192 • Human Reason and Its Enemies

lacked. If the protagonists of a tradition are fortunate enough to have this gift, they would 'be able to understand the theses, arguments, and concepts of their rival ... view themselves from such an alien standpoint and to characterize their own beliefs in an appropriate manner from the alien perspective'.

In carrying out this exchange, does a tradition have to surrender its own theses, arguments and concepts? Or do these exist side by side simultaneously with those of the rival tradition? Does each tradition doff its own intellectual garments and don its rival's? How, for example, would the Hopi (having this rare gift) 'characterize' their own belief about spirits in trees with the Western scientists' rejection of such beliefs, or vice versa? Would the Western scientists use the Hopi thesis, arguments and concepts to disprove their beliefs about spirits in trees? If so, success is ruled out *ab initio*; if they use their own, the Hopi would probably tell them to go to...

So, you see, nothing is explained by talking about the rare gift of empathy-cum-insight. If, by this gift, this mutual floor crossing is attained, does each tradition still maintain its earlier identity, its 'own account of truth and knowledge'? Will the flat-earth believers say to their rivals, 'Thanks very much for your help; we have now *understood* that the earth's shadow on the moon is an arc because, as you have explained to us, the earth is a sphere; but we still, of course, believe the earth is flat.' And what will their rivals say to the flat-earthwallas?

Aquinas enters the arena.[8] He was 'trained to understand' two 'distinct and in important ways incompatible philosophical traditions', and that, too, 'each from within'. Not only did he have one foot firmly set in each tradition, but he seems to have had a third foot, for his *Questiones Disputator* 'pointed towards a conception of truth, independent of either tradition'. He could juggle three balls.

Now, if Aquinas could understand and 'articulate' each of three traditions from *within*, why can't we? Because we are such tiny people? But that's not the point; the point is that it is humanly and logically feasible. If Aquinas could formulate his 'questions' so as to point to a conception of truth independent of any tradition, it seems, *prima facie*, that answers could also be furnished in a similar manner. Where did Aquinas's 'questions' exist? In a neutral place or in some tradition?

As was to be expected, 'some modern writers have rejected' Aquinas's conception of truth and his reasons for it. And what are *their* reasons for the rejection? Again, as was to be expected, 'an understanding of any reality, in relation to which truth and falsity … are judged, must be internal to our web of concepts and beliefs', which means that truth and falsity are not tradition-independent. Return to square one.

Which position does MacIntyre take? We will never know, because the acrobat swings away from the 'modern writers' and from Aquinas, to something else. Since there is, for the 'modern writers', nothing beyond their 'own web', 'they treat the concepts of truth as nothing more than an idealization of the concept of warranted assertibility'. This is a completely separate issue from what was discussed so far, and we are still left with the question as to how two rival traditions can understand each other, and how, if they can, they can still remain rivals. MacIntyre, too, gets back to the same question. He refers to the idea that there is 'only one overall community of inquiry', and asks, 'But what if there appears a second community whose tradition and procedures of inquiry are structured in terms of different, largely incompatible and largely incommensurable concepts and beliefs, defining warranted assertibility and truth in terms internal to its scheme of concepts and beliefs?'

This (perhaps intentionally) long sentence should not confuse us into thinking that we have got a new problem to face. We have gone through all this, with the only difference (which makes no difference) that now 'warranted assertibility' is added, while 'truth' is still retained, showing that pulling out this red herring was needless. Does MacIntyre, poor man, suffer from such a weak memory? He has lately, very lately, been spending pages over this very question and has told us – though not explained to us how – one such tradition, if gifted with empathy and insight, can rescue another in difficulty.

Now, instead of saying that even a rival community can understand and characterize the truth of what the other believes, he says that 'it can characterize the other as in error from its own point of view'.[9] Naturally, because truth and error are related; if it can characterize error, it can characterize truth too. 'But that after all is not the question,' he says, for both parties 'can agree' on that. But how can they agree? If their concepts of truth and/or warranted assertibility are defined 'in terms internal to' the scheme of concepts and beliefs of each, how can their concepts of error be the same? Does the concept of error somehow manage to get over the incompatibility and incommensurability barrier and get to the other community, while the concept of truth can't? Can error do what truth can't? Next question, please.

We move on.[10] MacIntyre writes:

> What the protagonists of each rival tradition must at
> this point do is choose between two alternatives, that of
> abandoning *any* claim that truth-value can be attached
> to the fundamental judgments underpinning their mode
> of enquiry *or* that of making a claim to truth of a kind
> which appeals beyond their own particular scheme of
> concepts and beliefs, to something external to that
> scheme.

We will not ask why, after it is admitted that traditions can come
to each other's rescue, they should still remain rivals. There are
more weighty questions to ask. Wrapped round and protected
by thick verbiage as the passage quoted above is, it may have
escaped the reader that MacIntyre has thrown in the sponge. Of
course he has not realized it himself.

The two alternatives he now puts before us are:

'A': Abandon the claim to any truth that is attached only to
   the concepts of your own tradition; or

'B': Make a claim to truth that goes beyond the concepts of
   your own tradition.

By a well-known law of logic (our logic, not Hopi logic or
any other), if you don't choose 'A', you must accept 'B'; if you
don't choose 'B', you must accept 'A'. If you *do not* make a claim
to truth that goes beyond the concepts of your own tradition
(this is the relativist's position), you must accept 'A' (that is,
abandon the claim to truth which is attached only to your own
tradition, which means you must give up relativism). If you do
not choose 'A' (that is, if you stick to your relativism), you must
accept that a claim to the truth goes beyond the concepts of your
own tradition (that is, you must accept non-relativism.). What

a mess MacIntyre is in! For, according to his disjunction, it comes to:

> If you are a relativist 'not-B', you cannot be a relativist 'not-A';
> If you are a relativist 'not-A', you must be a non-relativist (absolutist).

Perhaps, thanks to his imprecise language, we have misinterpreted MacIntyre, taking 'fundamental judgments underpinning their mode of enquiry' to mean 'truth attached only to the concepts of *your* tradition'. Let us be more charitable and take him to mean:

Either:

'A' – you abandon claim to any truth; or

'B' – you must accept truth to go beyond the concepts of your tradition.

Then: If I don't choose 'A', it means I claim some truth; then I must accept 'B' that truth goes beyond the concepts of any tradition.

And: If I don't choose 'B' (that is, if I do not accept that truth can go beyond any tradition); then I must accept 'A' and abandon claim to any truth.

In sum: If truth, then no relativism; and if relativism, then no truth. We have, on MacIntyre's own admission, really made progress.

Now which alternative will MacIntyre choose? He can't choose the first because that 'would have evacuated the concept of enquiry embodied in both the Aristotelian and the Augustinian traditions of its distinctive content,' that is, a claim to truth, 'the classical conception of truth'. Only that? Not the concept of enquiry altogether? But his relativist sympathies makes him want to cling to the first alternative – that is, he wants to abandon the classical conception of truth, and, luckily, he finds that this 'becomes possible' after the pragmatism of James and Dewey 'opened up new possibilities'.

Now that the first alternative can be embraced, there seems no need to worry about the second. It is allowed to RIP. But Aquinas is not buried yet.[11]

Aquinas makes certain distinctions (it doesn't matter which) 'whose justification lies in what they then enable him to achieve in reconstructing both Aristotelian and Augustinian positions within the framework of a unified metaphysical theology'. A man of rare gifts, Aquinas. Not only have two rival, incompatible and incommensurable traditions been unified, but it has been done by a third tradition, Thomism. We would have appreciated it if MacIntyre had told us how Aquinas managed this, but our author says, 'With the major part of that achievement I shall not be concerned here.' So, after this rigmarole, what have we got? As Akil Bilgrami might say, 'Bull– '.

The Archimedean point argument, which I have stated at the start of this chapter, is a bogeyman set up to frighten us and make us run into the arms of cultural relativism. The argument appears compelling because, once again, it conjures up a false analogy. In order to assess the relative merits of, say, two paintings, one has to take a position away from them and look at them. But when a person holding a theory claims that his theory is superior, in the matter of truth or validity, to another theory, he does not have to step outside his theory, give it up, and then compare it with the other, which he rejects. In fact, he rejects the other theory precisely because he holds his own theory, and holds it because he sees it to be true or truer than the other. It is by recognizing the merits of his own theory, Thomism, that Aquinas (so MacIntyre has assured us) was able to see what was true in Aristotelianism and Augustinianism and so to combine them with his own into a unified theory.

In the same way, Socrates can see that his desire, though subject to frustration, was more worth having than the desires of the pig. He did not have to forsake his desire, take up a neutral, desireless stance, and then compare his desire with that of the pig. It should be clear that the pig could not make any comparison, being totally unaware of Socrates's kind of desire. The modern Western scientist could, in principle, prove to the Aztecs (at least the ones with the required gift of empathy, etc.) that their 'science' was inadequate, while they, like the pig, could not return the compliment. A teacher, say, of mathematics can correct a student's error from his own grasp of mathematics; he does not shed his own mathematical knowledge in order to *compare* it with the student's by assuming a neutral position. Why, even in purely physical matters, one can stand on the terrace floor of the Mumbai Stock Exchange building and see that it is taller than Rajabai Tower; one does not have to hover in space away from both to see which is taller.

Another mischievous analogy is that of a judge and the disputants. To see the merits in a dispute, the disputants, unable to convince each other, may refer it to a third person whose judgement they trust. But this is not *logically* necessary, for they could see for themselves, rationally, which is the sounder position. All the disputes between humans are not taken to court or referred to a third person; rational people are able to settle their disputes through discussion. Logically, therefore, one *can* be judge in one's own case; in fact, one always is, whatever others might say.

If, therefore, we stare at the bogeyman, he will vamoose. Let us be vigilant and not allow him (or her) to bother us hereafter.

We may remember that we saw earlier how a particular framework (or tradition, as postmoderns are fond of saying) can be shown to be false or inadequate by another, rationally superior framework. The latter may itself be shown to be inadequate by, and absorbed within, a still more adequate and rationally superior framework. This has been the history of science.

This process of increasing inclusiveness may in most cases be endless. It would be so where the kind of knowledge sought depends on the discovery of new facts. But it need not be necessarily endless. The process may end with the satisfaction of all concerned parties. Aquinas, according to MacIntyre, did achieve a unified theory. Even if he did not – which is probably the general opinion – a unified theory is not theoretically meaningless or impossible. The goal of such a theory would be to give an account of 'that reality by reference to which the terminus of all intellectually adequate explanation and understanding ... has to be specified and in relation to which the ordering of all subordinate explanation and understanding has to be carried through.'[12] To this MacIntyre adds that such a reality and (we may say) framework 'cannot itself be explained ... by anything beyond itself'. Quite right. If it is what is claimed of it, it should require nothing outside itself to explain it. 'Substance,' says Spinoza, is 'that which is in itself and is conceived through itself'; the universe is, for him, the only substance. *If* a theory shows *no* contradictions, anomalies, antinomies, inadequacies or any other flaws, there should be no reason why it should not be unconditionally accepted as true. Its supremacy would be self-explaining and self-justifying. Such a consummation may never be achieved; it is not, therefore, to be despised, and the attempt to approximate it is not worthless. The guiding criterion throughout is, and only is, comprehensive coherence.

May Archimedes sleep in peace.

References

1. Quoted by Norris, C., 1990, p. 83.
2. Sorell, T., 'The World from its Own Point of View' in Malachowski, R. (Ed.), 1990, p. 13.
3. Ibid., p. 14. The words in double quotation marks are those of Nagel.
4. MacIntyre, A., 1988, p. 144.
5. Ibid., p. 145.
6. Ibid., p. 166.
7. Ibid., pp. 166-67.
8. Ibid., pp. 168-69.
9. Ibid., p. 170.
10. Ibid., pp. 170-71.
11. Ibid., p. 171.
12. Ibid., p. 171.

Chapter 11

Can Dinosaurs and Dragons Be Tamed?

Cultural Diversity and Moral Unity

I have so far argued that cultural relativism in respect of reasoning, truth, validity and knowledge, is a confused, fallacy-ridden, self-refuting position. To say that truth and rationality are culture-bound, in any unacceptable sense, is itself a universal claim, which transcends all cultures (except the culture of rationality). This argument of self-refutation has never been squarely met and can never be refuted.

If truth and rationality were culture-bound, a critical examination of any culture cannot be undertaken, but as a matter of fact, cultures, even the most hidebound and orthodox, have, at some time, examined themselves and changed to some extent in light of such self-examination. This is a theme which Plato could also have illustrated by his analogical story of the Cave.

When it comes, in a broad sense, to matters regarding values (values other than truth and other 'intellectual' values), particularly moral and social values, and questions about what *ought to be* done, a special treatment is needed. While thinking also involves an 'ought' – one ought to obey the laws of logic – it is not optional. If one violates the laws of logic one cannot think at all; nor does one choose or decide to obey those laws as one may decide to choose or decide to perform or not to perform a moral act. (This distinction between thinking and moral activity is made at a superficial level and may not stand deeper examination, but it should serve my purpose here.) Of course, in a sense even being moral is not optional. One cannot take a moral holiday, because even if, on a particular occasion one chooses to act immorally, one is still subject to moral judgement. On the other hand, aesthetic activity is entirely optional; one need not participate in it either as creator or appreciator.

While awake, one is continually making choices, many of which could hardly be described as moral, some could certainly be called so, and some, a much smaller number, would be very important and even crucial. Even a self-proclaimed moral sceptic and nihilist cannot escape putting to himself the question, 'What should I do?' Satan's 'Evil, be thou my good' is also a moral stand, moral in the sense that it falls within the moral domain. Thus, though one cannot jump out of the moral domain, one can, of course, variously decide to conform to or violate what are normally regarded as moral norms and obligations.

So much by way of introduction. Now, moral relativism: 'An adequate theory of rationality must do justice both to the variability that marks different ranges of experience and diverse cultural settings and to the constancies that, because of important elements in our humanity, can be expected as recurring elements.'[1] While – so I have argued – the principles of reasoning cannot differ from culture to culture, in the case of moral thinking, there are marked differences between cultures. Can such variety be squared with our view of a common rationality and a belief in common moral values?

When rival scientific traditions come into conflict, the dialogue 'is conducted in a context of observations about, and active engagement with, the natural world', writes J. Porter, and therefore, 'there must be some level, however rudimentary, at which shared description is possible' and which supplies the base for argument and agreement.[2] But moral claims seem to have no such 'objective' base to which disputants could point and agree on. As MacIntyre says, 'evaluative and normative concepts, maxims, arguments and judgments ... *are nowhere to be found except as embodied in the historical lives of particular social groups*'[3] (italics Porter's). 'Given this conception of morality,' writes Porter, 'it is not clear how rival claims of disparate moral traditions could be adjusted' and 'there could be sufficient genuine conflict between moral traditions'.[4] 'You, collectively, arrange your lives in one way,' so Porter spells out this idea, 'we arrange our lives in a different way. Is it clear that we even disagree? What is the shared subject matter of our disagreements?' It is admitted that, within a tradition, reasoning can be used to settle disputes.[5]

MacIntyre writes that even within a 'relatively coherent tradition ... there are just too many different and incompatible conceptions of virtue for there to be any real unity to the concept', and he cites Homer, Sophocles, Aristotle, the New Testament and medieval thinkers, all of whom 'differ from each other in too many ways'. (Surely it is an exaggeration to say this.)

If we add Japanese or American Indian cultures, the differences would increase. 'It would be all too easy to conclude,' he writes, that even within one tradition there is 'no single core conception' of virtue.[6] But does he so conclude? Four pages later he refers to what he has written as a '*prima facie* case for holding that ... there is no single, central, core conception of the virtues which might make a claim for universal allegiance', yet each tradition 'does embody such a claim'. He now says that he will 'argue that we can in fact discover such a core concept', at least in a tradition, and distinguish 'those beliefs about the virtues which genuinely belong to the tradition from those which do not'. (I said the earlier account was an exaggeration, and so it was.)

If it is possible to 'disentangle' such a core concept from rival claims within a tradition, there is no *prima facie* reason why it cannot be done between traditions. MacIntyre seems to have reached this idea, at least with regard to virtue if not the virtues. He formulates 'a first, even if partial and tentative definition', which implies that a fuller, more permanent definition is not impossible. '*A virtue is an acquired human quality the possession and exercise of which tends to enable us to achieve those goals which are internal to practices...*' (italics in the original).[8]

So, after ten pages of wordiness, MacIntyre cancels what he seemed to be putting forward so strongly earlier. We may not agree with his definition, but it is a big step to say that there can be a core concept in spite of differences. However, his definition gives us an inkling into some of his moral ideas.

MacIntyre's definition of virtue is utilitarian. A, B, C and D jointly pursue certain goods, 'share a practice'. A, knowing how D died, tells B the truth, but lies about it to C. C discovers the lie. According to MacIntyre, A has done wrong, not because lying is wrong, but by lying and C discovering it, 'some difference in the relationship now exists', with the result they may no longer be able to jointly pursue the goods they were pursuing. In short, there must be honour even among thieves, and honesty, courage and justice too (the virtues MacIntyre considers), otherwise it would create some differences in their relationship, resulting in inefficient thieving. These three, 'and perhaps some others' are 'genuine excellences', excellent tools, 'without which practices cannot be sustained', as long as they help us to achieve the 'goods' we have set our hearts on. This, irrespective of our 'private moral standpoint' and our society's moral code.[9] These are 'virtues' in the same way as it is the virtue of a knife to cut.

So, according to MacIntyre, whatever virtues make us succeed in a joint (why only joint?) venture are welcome. The virtue or morality of the venture itself – doing cancer research for the alleviation of human suffering or making bombs for killing humans – is evidently not to be considered.

These virtues can be defined. Courage, for example, is 'the capacity to risk harm or danger to oneself', but these definitions do not, naturally, indicate on which occasions we should display which virtue, what are the worthy ends for which the virtues should come into play. But these latter questions are the very ones that are important in discussing moral culturalism. However, before considering this, let us go back to the 'virtues' and consider a different question.

Could cultures differ on the very concepts of honesty, courage and other virtues usually spoken of? Extreme relativism would answer, 'Yes.' Is it possible that an act regarded in one culture as a

206 • Human Reason and Its Enemies

clear and undisputed act of courage or justice could be considered to be, in another, an act of cowardice or injustice, respectively? Some in the other culture might call our courageous act a case of foolhardiness. Suppose a woman rushed into heavy traffic to save a child from being run over or a man got out of a window of a fiftieth floor apartment to retrieve a pet dog. Could anybody in the world describe such acts as cowardly? Would even the Azandes or the Aztecs? This question assumes that they would agree at least to our 'thin' definition (given above, of courage). If they don't, then further talk with them would cease.

In the case of justice, a concept more complex than courage, the Marxists would definitely characterize the system of dispensing justice in a capitalist state as terribly unjust. If, however, they hope to convert (as they do) the capitalists to their own way of regarding justice, they would not succeed if they merely asserted what they believed justice to be. They would have to find some common ground and then show that their concept accords better with that than that of the capitalists.

Some philosophers hold that there could be a few moral concepts so peculiar to a certain society that they could not even be understood by outsiders. They would have to be called 'moral' only because the members of that society seem to approve or disapprove of them, and this can be seen from their behaviour. According to Hilary Putnam, 'chastity' as understood in the Medieval West is one such.

'Thick' moral concepts are distinguished from 'thin' ones.[10] 'Thick' concepts 'have a heavy descriptive content', a "halo of complementary significance that surrounds the primary, realistic signification" (O. Gusset's words). The primary significance or meaning of, say, 'generous' is 'free in giving' (*Concise Oxford Dictionary*, 1934), but it has a halo of different ideas connected with it according to different cultures. 'Elegance', 'courage', 'justice' are also halo-encircled. Examples of 'thin' concepts are: 'right', 'wrong', 'good', 'bad', 'duty', 'sin'. They are 'thin' because they run across all cultures, which appears to mean that all cultures would believe that some acts are good and others bad, some right and others wrong, that duties should be done and sins avoided. Knowing what 'duty' and 'wrong' mean, I cannot say what the Japanese consider to be their duty or the American Indians consider to be wrong. 'Thick' concepts differ from culture to culture; in addition to an evaluative content, they have a descriptive one, not the same in all cultures.

Bernard Williams, Putnam tells us, rejects that 'thick' ethical concepts can 'be explicitly factored' into a 'descriptive component' and an 'evaluative component', which means that for any 'thick' one you cannot get a value-free description. Some indication of approval (pro-attitude) or of disapproval (con-attitude) must enter the meaning of a 'thick' word. This seems to be the case with words like 'elegant', 'tasteful' and 'refined', but would it be so with all ethical words? What of 'generous', 'truthful' and 'outspoken'? We do approve of these, but they can be defined without reference to approval.

What Williams and McDowell seem to want to say is that you cannot have a concept like, say, courage, which is understood completely by different cultures, but towards which some have an approving attitude and some a disapproving attitude, as if these attitudes are simply added on to the concept. Which would mean that courage for those who approve of it is a *different* concept from those who don't. Therefore, it seems to follow for Williams that an act which *we* think *entails* that it is wrong, may not be so for another culture, it may not have the same ethical meaning at all. Expounding Williams' view, Putnam says, 'after all, "wrong" is *our* notion, and it is a kind of logical parochialism (Williams claims) to hold that valuations in all languages implicitly involve *our* thin ethical concepts.' The chosen example is 'sordid', which is a thick concept *for us*, but for, say, the Aztecs it may not be so. Among them, sordid acts may be as innocuous as having a walk or listening to music. Some do them on some occasions and some don't. The drift of this argument is clear: since 'sordid' for us means something quite different from what it means to the Aztecs, there is nothing here common between us and them; therefore we have no moral or logical right to criticize them. It comes to this: there are 'a number of local ethical outlooks, each of which can be regarded as "true" by its adherents, but whose truth does not have any universalistic implications whatsoever'.

Williams' view hinges on the notion that in each society the so-called moral concepts are all 'thick'. If so, we cannot meaningfully say even that the Aztecs perform sordid acts without the least moral discomfort. What would 'sordid' then mean? If they happen to perform acts which, when seen by us, we would call sordid, we would surely be entitled to judge them as wrong. We can deny the starting premises that all moral concepts are 'thick' in the sense that they have no core meaning which is common to all cultures. Take 'cruel' meaning causing suffering to others for no justifiable reason. Would Williams wish to say that if one of the Aztecs was torturing a child, we have no right to judge it as wrong and, if we could, to try and stop him?

Putnam takes 'chaste' as an example of a completely 'thick' concept. If it is a concept in a society that is so remote from us in time and space that we simply cannot imaginatively understand or adopt its way of life, then such a concept would be 'simply *irrelevant* to us'. What exactly is this supposed to prove? If all these conditions are met, we would just not know what to think about such a concept and not be able to approve of it or condemn it. Not understanding it, it would be silly to suggest that we have no right to pass moral judgement. Even if we did not fully understand the medieval concept of chastity, halo and all, if we could know which actions, in that society, were condemned as 'unchaste', we would be able to grasp a minimal part of the connotation of that word, and then we would not be debarred from passing moral judgement.

Let's forget 'chastity'; let's take jihad. Most of us may be quite unable to understand the idea and feelings produced by this 'word' when used by peoples who subscribe to the concept and are ready to act by it. But we can understand enough to know that it means an aggressive act in the name of religion. If this is denied, then we have nothing more to say. But if this much is granted, surely, whatever be the halo surrounding the concept for the believers, we are entitled to pass moral judgement that, no matter how deeply the religious feelings of a group may be hurt by those outside the group, to kill people on account of this, is not justified in any kind of society, religious or secular, primitive or civilized. This judgement can be debated, but the point is that a debate is possible, if not actually, at least in principle. Putnam is unequivocal on this point. Referring to a certain Greek word, he writes:

> ... any philosophical doctrine which requires for its
> defence the claim that this common Greek word is totally
> *uninterpretable* in English is as bankrupt as the bugaboo
> of total 'incommensurability' itself....[11]

He further adds, that 'every sane person does believe deep down
that there are universal human problems', which, I feel sure he
will agree, implies that these can, in principle, be rationally
considered and solved.

A brief look at Habermas on this topic will be worthwhile. In
what he calls 'communicative action' he says he hopes to achieve
a 'common understanding of the situation' by invoking 'a norm
that I implicitly take to be valid', and whose validity he claims to
be able to show if challenged.[12] This 'process of moral
argumentation' (as Habermas calls it) always implies a principle
of universalization, which is spelt out by J. D. Moon as follows:

> Whenever I invoke a norm... I implicitly recognize you
> as a partner in a dialogue in which that norm could be
> justified. We are able to coordinate our interactions
> consensually because we have or are able to achieve a
> common understanding of our situation. What is critical
> here is that 'a speaker can *rationally motivate* a hearer to
> accept his speech act offer because ... he can assume the
> *warranty* for providing, if necessary, convincing reasons
> that would stand up to a hearer's criticism of the validity
> claim'.... Thus communicative action can be said to
> 'presuppose those very relationships of reciprocity and
> mutual recognition around which *all* moral ideas revolve
> in everyday life.[13]

It is clear that Habermas allows reason considerable scope to work in moral life, but there is a limit. Habermas distinguishes *norms* which a person could be rationally motivated to adopt (e.g. to study regularly throughout the year to prepare for an examination) or give up (e.g. smoking) and *values* or ultimate ends which 'reflect views of what constitutes a good life and are based on our conception of ourselves and our basic identities', which are 'rooted in the culture in which we live and to which we are socialized'. To distance oneself from, and critically examine, "the forms of life in which his identity has been shaped", would be, in Habermas' words, to question "his very existence", which means that values cannot be questioned as norms evidently can.[14] Habermas, thus, seems not to be able to tear himself away from cultural relativism.

In spite of the fact that, as Moon says, there exists 'an irresolvable plurality of value configurations in modern, pluralist societies, and relations among different societies', Habermas holds that 'the "need-interpretations" that individuals bring to discourse can be challenged and may be revised in such a way as to discover common interests'. Individuals 'do not simply confront each other', for, in Habermas' words, "the principle of universalization requires each participant to project himself into the perspectives of all others".[15] We seem to be still confined to 'norms', which are revisable; but what about 'values'? Why can't the principle of universalization be applied to them also?

A breakthrough appears possible. Habermas' views are referred to as 'discourse ethics', which 'conceives of a universal "communication community that includes all subjects capable of speech and action"' (Habermas' words), of a 'solidarity', which in 'some form must extend to include all humans'. Then wouldn't this super-community – humanity, in short – have values which would override the lesser, more local values of different communities? Moon writes, 'To the extent that all humans are vulnerable in similar ways, it is plausible to suppose that there are "generalizable interests" that could provide the basis for norms that would command universal assent. Obvious examples include a right to life and bodily integrity.' If a basis for norms, why not for values? (For, after all, norms are distinguished from values only in that they are said to be revisable; they have no other distinguishing character.) Moon, however, still believes that 'deep conflicts' of a pluralist would not be overridden.[16]

One must grant, with Putnam, that there are 'alternative fulfilling conceptions of the good'. This is sometimes, wrongly, called cultural relativism, but, says Isaiah Berlin, it is not relativism because the "members of one culture can, by the force of imaginative insight, understand … the values, the ideals, the forms of life of another culture or society, even those remote in time or space." So much for understanding, but Berlin adds: "They may find those values unacceptable", but one may still be able to see them as "values, ends of life, by the realization of which men could be fulfilled".[17]

But this does not go far enough to get to relativism. The crucial question is not whether the members of a society can understand the values of another culture; understand them even as values through which members of the other culture could find self-fulfilment. The question is whether the members of a culture have any kind of right to fault the values of another culture or condemn the members of that culture for subscribing to values, which they themselves would think it wrong to subscribe to. The question is not whether Englishmen would understand but find unacceptable for themselves the practice of *sati*; it is whether they would have the right to condemn those who practise it, or to tell those who practise it that it is wrong, or the right to stop it if it was possible to do so. Berlin does not seem to grant that right. Putnam quotes him as saying:

> I conclude that the very notion of a final solution is not only impracticable but, if I am right, and some values cannot but clash, incoherent. The possibility of a final solution ... turns out to be an illusion, and a very dangerous one. For if one really believes that such a solution is possible, then surely no cost would be too high to obtain it... To make such an omelette, there is no limit to the number of eggs that should be broken – that was the faith of Lenin, of Trotsky, of Mao, of Pol Pot.[18]

Some would, perhaps, include Plato in this list. If you allow that it is quite all right to criticize a practice other than your own, then, in the name of making mankind happy forever, you would carry out the most horrendous acts to further your (real or imagined) objective.

It might be pointed out that the men mentioned above did not try to impose their will, by the most wicked methods, on the members of another culture, but on the members of their own society in the name of a culture which they claimed to be the true and real culture of their own society. This also shows that there can be and are conflicts of cultures within a society. This point will come up later.

Berlin's fear is very genuine. It is the same sort of fear that makes people reject the idea of euthanasia: unscrupulous and avaricious relatives and friends might polish off some poor soul in order to relieve her suffering and relieve her of her possessions. Remember the two sweet old ladies in *Arsenic and Old Lace*. But such possibilities cannot decide whether the idea of euthanasia is right or wrong; the doubt is regarding implementation. Nor can the actions of brutes like Pol Pot decide whether there is or is not a moral and logical right of one culture to morally criticize another. Is a society, in which injustice and cruelty to its own members flourish, right in saying to outsiders, 'Keep off, this is our business?' And would it be quite all right for the outsiders to turn their eyes away, shrug their shoulders and say, 'Well, their norms and values are different; how can we judge them by ours?' If the answer to this latter question is, 'No, we should not turn away our eyes and shrug off the matter,' then on what basis would we argue for our stand? Ultimately we would have to take our stand on the concept of humanity and human nature.

Putnam asks if Berlin is 'not just saying that there are a number of optimal moral … philosophies around, and that one must just make one's own subjective choice from among the optional ones?'[19] Or, maybe invent one for oneself? Putnam writes:

> Every way of life, every system of values … that humans have so far invented has defects as well as virtues. Not only are there imperfections that can be exposed from within the way of life … but there are defects that we come to see from the outside, as a result of increased knowledge and/or a wide sense of justice…[20]

I suppose 'increased knowledge' indicates knowledge derived from contact with cultures other than one's own, now made so much easier to obtain due to information technology.

Moral scepticism, says Taylor, is widely evident today, and 'the seriousness with which a thinker like Nietzsche is regarded shows that this is no marginal position'. It has two aspects: first, a disbelief in morality altogether, with morality's claims globally challenged, and second, the suggestion that we must 'plump' for what we feel most suitable. Unfortunately, young students take this to be 'the intellectually respectable' position.[21]

Not only in different cultures, but even within the same culture, people have different and conflicting values and moral intuitions. Can we rest here? Taylor asks, and just accept that some people do not 'share our most basic and crucial moral intuitions', such as, for example, that innocent human beings should not be killed under the belief that it would achieve a particular end? 'Is there no way to show them wrong?' he asks; is 'reason powerless before such people?'[22]

This opens up a large inquiry into the nature of moral life and of the concept of agency. I turn to Terry Pinkard's 'Taylor, "History", and the History of Philosophy',[23] which considers Taylor's views on agency.

Humans, unlike other animals, are 'self-interpreting animals' who continuously keep asking themselves what it means to be a human being. 'Our nature is to be never simply what it is but consists in part in how we take it to be, how we conceive of ourselves, how we interpret our complex embodied social existence.' We are always agents who assume a 'stance toward ourselves, a kind of self-conscious distance from ourselves', and our 'grasp of anything in our encounters with the world is always mediated in terms of what we "take" that experience to mean'. These are ways of saying that we do not, as animals presumably do, have an experience, encounter things and just react in certain ways; we try to understand the experience or the situation and *our part in it*. This at once brings in the function of reason, because reason is our only tool for understanding. (I do not dispute insights, intuitions and such like which make it possible for us to understand, and particularly understand people and their ways; but, unless that 'understanding' can be translated or formulated in reason's terms, as judgements to be accepted or rejected, one has not understood in the sense here being considered.)

Being self-interpreting animals does not mean that we consciously and explicitly keep thinking all the time of the full meaning of what we are, what we are doing and how we are playing our part, but it means that we are ready, if challenged, to 'respond with an articulation of what it is that we took ourselves to be doing, and, in more complex cases, with some kind of account that would (attempt to) justify it'.[24] Why only in the more complex cases? Surely, always. In being an agent, which every one of us always is, one is 'oriented to a basic good or set of goods'. This is what each of us takes – however vaguely, hazily, inadequately, even subconsciously – to be 'what ultimately matters to oneself', an 'end worthy for its own sake' and which makes an agent (in Taylor's terms) a 'strong evaluator'.[25] Taylor calls such an ultimate good a 'hypergood', which is 'determinative of all lesser goods'; they take their character from it.[26] All the various ends, in varying degrees of generality and specificity, that one pursues, are meant – even if they do not always do so – to contribute to this hypergood; contribute as constitutive elements of it. It has been called a *summum bonum*. It constantly calls upon us to evaluate and re-evaluate our purposes and actions. In order to incorporate the lesser goods into our lives so that we get progressively, though often blunderingly and not always consistently, closer to the *summum bonum*, 'we must reason about them', says Pinkard.

It is a commonplace to say that none of us starts out on life with a *tabula rasa*, untouched by the ideas and norms of the society and culture in which we are born and have grown up. Our moral ideas are shaped and develop in ways of which we are not explicitly conscious. We believe that our parents and elders follow worthy norms and their actions are good and right (even when, in fact, they are not). We are (to use a common postmodern word) situated creatures.

All this has to be granted. So a problem arises. I state it in Pinkard's words; referring to our talk about the goods we seek to obtain. He writes:

As the product of cultures and languages, these articulations are contingent expressions; as normative, they also call out for, if not demand, justification… [This] places a particular type of strain on our conceptions of agency and the good. Justification, if it is to hold, has to be in terms of reasons that are acceptable to others; but the contingency of our norms suggests that what counts as a reason is itself only contingent, that its acceptability is as much a matter of circumstance as it is of its inherent rationality or universalizability. The demand for justification pushes us in the direction of non-contingent rationality. The recognition of the contingency of norms pushes us in the direction of scepticism about whether any such justifications are even possible.[27]

'The response to this dilemma has typically been to look for some kind of viewpoint that is external to the norms in question,' writes Pinkard, 'some set of criteria that all sides must accept.' But these are not available to Taylor, who does not accept the possibility of 'standing outside of all human practices and viewing them from no point of view'.[28] Archimedes has popped up again.

'Yet there is such a thing as moral objectivity, Taylor insists.' So Fergus Kerr assures us. Although, as we have seen, we begin our lives and grow up within a particular culture, yet, according to Taylor (so says Kerr), 'we should treat our deepest moral instincts ... as our modes of access to the world in which ontological claims are discernible and can be rationally argued about and sifted'.[29]

These deepest moral instincts provide us a passage from our narrow parochial cultural world to – not an Archimedean point but – the common world of morality that humans must, whether they like it or not, share. Kerr, expanding Taylor's view, writes that there is a 'range of discriminations of right and wrong, better and worse', which 'stand independent of' our desires and choices, and 'offer standards by which these discriminations are ... judged.'[30]

Taylor believes that humans have 'certain moral intuitions, rooted in our animal nature, as one is inclined to say,' and which 'cut across all cultural differences' of environment and upbringing. And what intuitions are these? They are, for example, a 'reluctance to inflict death or injury on our own kind, and the inclination to come to the help of the injured'. Didn't we always know that animals were morally more advanced than us? Such reactions are 'natural' in the sense that we expect to find them in 'any culture, ancient or modern, religious or secular'.

Taylor even compares these deep moral reactions, rather absurdly, to 'vomiting with disgust' or 'fainting with fear'. The important point is that they, the moral reactions, can be 'trained, redirected and refined' in forms 'specific to a certain local culture'.[31] Does this mean that the less local ones cannot be? Even the 'greatest violators' of human rights, Taylor thinks, have deep moral instincts, and it is because of this fact, when they perpetrate heinous crimes, they still 'hide behind a smoke-screen of lies and special pleading'.[32]

It may stretch credibility too far to suppose that Genghis Khan or Hitler or Stalin could have any moral instincts, deep or shallow; but no matter. If such instincts do exist among ordinary people who constitute the majority of a nation, it means that a common morality obtains and that such human monsters are an aberration.

In an almost Socratic vein, Taylor, says Melissa Orlie, 'characterizes our stance toward the good as part of the "transcendental conditions of human agency"'; without making evaluations 'we simply cannot make sense of our lives'; we cannot help but make 'qualitative discriminations' of right and wrong, good and bad, better and worse, and higher and lower.[33] Everyone acts, or is inclined to act, according to one's concept, such as it is, of the good, the hypergood. This is the Socratic theory usually referred to as 'virtue is knowledge'.

On the basis of this moral psychology, we can hope to resolve the dilemma posed by Pinkard: moral ideas arise and develop in a particular culture but the demand for justification pushes us towards non-contingent rationality. If the members of another community do not share our basic moral intuitions, Taylor has asked, 'is there no way to show them wrong?' (One must understand that to ask, 'why do we assume that our intuitions are right?' is to activate a red herring, because deciding what the right intuitions are is not the issue; the issue is whether moral conversion – irrespective of who is right or wrong – is rationally possible. So let's shoo away the herring.)

To start with, we must agree with O'Grady that the 'mere presence of widespread disagreement between cultures … doesn't preclude the possibility of that disagreement being rational and amenable to argumentation'.[34]

Taylor considers how one can argue about morals with a person who proclaims a position that is grossly opposed to what we most cherish.[35] To confront such a person head-on with propositions and principles which he flatly and doggedly rejects, is not going to help. We would have to argue 'from the ground up', after digging down to the point from which our disagreement begins and hitting upon some common ground. (Let us note, once again, that we are not hankering after an Archimedean point that is nowhere.) Taylor thinks that even the worst offenders would not 'lucidly reject' a principle like the 'inviolability of human life'. Perhaps Taylor is too sanguine here, but some such strategy is our only hope of making our opponent start examining his own beliefs. Also, convincing or converting an opponent and producing cogent reasons and arguments against his position are two different undertakings, and failure in the former does not, *ipso facto*, disqualify the latter. Reason is ineffective, says Taylor, with those who have a maniacal urge to cause harm to others, but 'this is not to say that reason is powerless to show them wrong' – that is, of course, to those who are not such maniacs. There is a school of postmodernism that identifies reason with power.

Taylor is sure that the special pleading by wrongdoers is a symptom of inner acknowledgement of guilt and an implicit awareness, however dim, of moral intuitions. The Nazis gave 'reasons' for eliminating the Jews; they even produced 'scientific' evidence to show that the Jews were polluting the purity of the human race. Often noble considerations are produced for the most 'mad and irrational' acts. Thus, rather than succumbing to the usual argument that reason cannot prove or establish moral ideas, Taylor, on the contrary, holds that immoral positions cannot be rationally defended, that 'there are limits beyond which *rational* challenges to morality have great trouble in going'. The best way to deal with an immoral claim is not to try to justify a moral one but to throw the burden of establishing the immoral one on its proposer. He will 'barely stand up to the cold light of untroubled thought'. R.M. Hare argues that if it is incontestably proved to a Nazi that he himself was a Jew, he would either have to abandon the principle that Jews ought to be exterminated or commit suicide with his family. Hare thinks it less likely that he will hold on to the principle.[36] He would have to choose between the two actions, because *reason* shows he can't hold on to both. A moral principle is open to rational refutation.

To get back to Taylor; we have to show the wrongdoer, or one who pleads on his behalf, that the special pleadings are hollow, that, for example, the 'evidence' is either non-existent or cooked. Then (if he still wishes to carry on the discussion) we have to find some moral idea or principle that we share with him and show him that the immoral act which he defends clashes with that idea or principle, and that he does not realize this because of some confusion in his mind or his unwillingness to face the implications of his admissions. 'Changing someone's moral view by reasoning is always at the same time increasing his self-clarity and self-understanding'; in fact, it is the effect of clarifying his mind. The method of arguing is Socratic – your views do not follow from, or are exactly opposed to, your deepest convictions, convictions that both you and we share.

If an individual can be made to see, or is able, by self-reflection, to see for himself, the moral confusion of his earlier position, then a group of individuals holding a moral position can also come to see how its purposes and acts actually conflict with its cherished ideals. For example, a union that sincerely has the objective of benefiting its community may come to realize that, by its aggressive acts, it is actually harming its cause, and may, therefore, desist from them. There is no *a priori* reason why a similar change of heart cannot occur in a whole culture or a nation, brought about, among other causes, by intercultural or international dialogue. A particular culture may well act as a Socrates to deconfuse another culture and so cure it of its inhuman and therefore immoral practices. Apart from the question about whether a culture could perform, not by force of arms but by reasonable argument, such a messianic role vis-à-vis another culture or not, would it not have a moral right to try?

It is obvious that Taylor takes his stand ultimately on a conception of human nature. The deep moral intuitions that he pins his faith on as a base from which to argue with the wrongdoer are those that are expected to belong to all humans, except, perhaps, the Jurassic monsters among them. Even these, Taylor believes, must have a spark in them. These intuitions surely constitute a crucial part of the essence of human nature as distinct from our animal nature. They serve as the foundation of morality. Taylor, Pinkard tells us,[37] is opposed to any 'foundational' approach, but his position regarding deep intuitions is foundational, though not viciously so. Not viciously so because there is no bar to revising our concepts of human nature or deep intuitions in light of more knowledge.

Towards the end of the Introduction to *Alasdair MacIntyre* (2003), M.C. Murphy writes, 'The path out of the moral wilderness is the formulation of an ethics of human nature – where human nature is not merely a biological nature but also an historical and social nature – and the formulation of an historical, but not relativistic, account of rationality in inquiry.'[38] There's the rub – three rubs, in fact. Why should an account of rationality be historical? What sort of historical account would it be? Just a catalogue of different views about rationality down the ages? And most interestingly, how could it be historical and yet not relativistic? Anyway, MacIntyre, writing in 1959, says that a "concept of human nature … has to be the centre of any discussion of moral theory".[39]

On reading David Solomon,[40] one gets the impression that MacIntyre has abandoned relativism: 'MacIntyre is clear that there need be no conflict between regarding moral norms as ultimately rooted in the particularity of community life and … as aspiring to universality and genuine truth.' In fact, communities themselves 'see no inconsistency' in this, since they 'typically – and perhaps necessarily – seek to combat the opposing ethical claims of distant communities'. So, the ghostly point has completely vanished. MacIntyre further insists that in settling intercultural disputes 'we must strive to avoid the use of power' and use 'rational inquiry alone'. Indeed, power cannot settle the matter at all. The postmodern coupling of reasoning with power is not only wrong but also absurd. MacIntyre wants us to 'make our arguments more persuasive to our interlocutors'.

Feyerabend, our man of science, cites an example to illustrate how *his* philosophy, relativism, 'undermines the very basis of Reason'.[41] 'My aim,' he says, without blushing, 'is to show that relativism is reasonable.' It is to be 'expected that actions that seem perfectly normal in one culture are rejected and condemned in another. To take an example (an actual case I heard from…)':

> A physician suggests X-rays to pinpoint the illness of the member of a Central African tribe. His patient wants him to use other methods: 'What is going on in my inside is nobody's business.' Here the desire to know and, on the basis of knowledge, to cure in the most effective way possible clashes with the wish to maintain privacy and integrity of the body.

Gandhiji's refusal to allow his ailing wife to have beef tea advised by the physician is an example of the same sort, and so is the refusal of Christian scientists either to receive or even donate blood.

Our science-man's example is meant, by him, to show that cultures and their different values are incommensurable. Ironically, it shows how a rationally superior culture, in being more liberal and respectful of human rights, is able to deal with another, which does not have such ideas. The tribal culture, instanced by Feyerabend, is not able to deal with a civilized culture in the same way. Feyerabend himself (unwittingly) explains how this is. The African's refusal to have an X-ray of his body taken is seen as 'unreasonable for a community where efficiency and the pursuit of knowledge overrule everything', but though seen as unreasonable, it is 'tolerated in a society' that 'makes room for personal idiosyncrasies' and, he should have added, the right to stick to them. (This itself shows, incidentally, that in civilized society, efficiency and the pursuit of knowledge *do not* overrule everything; human rights are respected.) The tribal society, on the other hand, would be very unlikely to tolerate a member who wanted his X-ray to be taken (if that was unacceptable in that culture) and to make it possible for him to have it taken. In the Central African or any similar tribal society there would probably be no space for arguing about and examining its values.

Feyerabend's African does not only devalue efficiency and the pursuit of knowledge, but also devalues logic, because by what logic does he refuse to have an X-ray taken on the ground that he doesn't want the physician (or anyone else) to know what is going on inside his body and yet want the physician to use other methods to find out the same thing – what is happening inside his (the patient's, that is) body, without knowing which, the physician could not suggest a cure? This, of course, is where the witch doctor is superior, for he doesn't even *want* to know what is going on inside the patient's body!

A few words on Rorty's inimitable style of dealing with our problem.[42]

All 'vocabularies' are 'human creations', therefore 'this would mean giving up the idea that liberalism could be justified, and Nazi or Marxist enemies of liberalism refuted, by driving the latter up against an argumentative wall – forcing them to admit that liberal freedom has a "moral privilege" which their own values

lacked'. Such an attempt fails when the 'wall' 'comes to be seen
as one more vocabulary', just 'one more way of describing things'
no better or worse than other ways (that is, other than
argumentation), just 'a painted backdrop ... one more bit of
cultural stage-setting'.

Rorty has the gift of the gab, but, in plain English vocabulary,
it means that reasoning, giving reasons, justifying, is only one
way of, only one *reason* for, preferring, say, liberalism to fascism,
and so may not, on a particular occasion be used if we prefer not
to use it. After all, it's just a tool; its use is optional. But when it
is used, is it any superior to other tools? Is its result more binding?
However, Rorty himself clearly recommends 'a poeticized culture',
and goes on to give *reasons* for it.

'To sum up', he writes, 'the moral I want to draw' regarding a
charge of relativism is that such a charge 'should not be answered,
but rather evaded'. As he explains two pages earlier, 'there is no
one way to break standoffs'; there are a 'vast number of ways
of ... trying to outflank one's opponent'; in fact 'there never
are ... any standoffs'. And no opponents either.

Putnam rejects the view, 'accepted by many people as if it
were common sense', that 'value judgements are subjective',
'incapable of objective truth and objective warrant', while
statements of fact alone are capable of being objectively true and
objectively warranted. Putnam calls this the '"fact/value"
dichotomy', according to which value judgements 'are completely
outside the sphere of reason'. These views, for Putnam, rest on
'untenable arguments and on over-inflated dichotomies'.

Putnam believes, and I think rightly, that value judgements
can be objective (just as factual judgements can also be subjective)

and have truth-value; can be correct or incorrect. People think otherwise because they equate objectivity with description. Putnam is also right in holding that though our value judgements 'are shaped by a particular culture and by a particular problematic situation' (this, latter, may not always be the case), this is not incompatible with holding that they 'claim objective validity'. In *this*, value judgements are like scientific truths or descriptive judgements. Neither of these two types of judgement requires us, Putnam adds, 'to seek an Archimedean point ... outside of all contexts and problematic situations', nor to 'give up on the very possibility of rational discussion'.[44] Putnam further suggests that to deal with value judgements to determine their truth or validity, we must employ the procedure which he attributes to Socrates – 'to examine who we are and what our deepest convictions are'.[45]

However, I must point out that, in order to establish the objectivity of value judgements and their claim to objective truth and warrantability, Putnam provides an utterly confused and unconvincing argument against the '"fact/value" dichotomy' and speaks, rather smugly, of 'the collapse of the fact/value dichotomy.'[46] I am not going to delve into this because admitting the '"fact/value" dichotomy' does not compel one to surrender the objectivity of value judgements and because Putnam seems to have chosen an inappropriate way to establish it. Strangely, in the very book entitled *The Collapse of the Fact/Value Dichotomy*, after claiming to have engineered this collapse, Putnam writes, 'Any inquiry has both "factual" presuppositions ... and "value" presuppositions', which means that the said dichotomy is still kicking and has not kicked the bucket.

Putnam uses an argument to combat cultural relativism which is worth looking into briefly.[47] He says that 'judgments of coherence, simplicity and so on are presupposed by physical science', yet these concepts are values; if the 'familiar arguments for relativism with respect to values' were correct, they would 'apply to our epistemic values as well' (that is, to our values of coherence, simplicity and so on); but this would make science (which presupposes such values) and all knowledge relative; however, this is 'self-refuting', for it would apply to relativism as well. Thus Putnam dismisses the 'fashionable, but wholly untenable, pictures of different cultures as "incommensurable"'.

With his final verdict, I agree, but the foregoing argument is a bad one. Coherence, simplicity and other epistemic requirements, and truth itself, are values. Without accepting these, inquiry, truth and knowledge would be impossible. When *cultural* relativists, however, talk about values as relative and thus making cultures incommensurable, the values generally meant are not the epistemic values but the moral values, which they claim are peculiar to each culture. Cultural relativists could maintain the relativity and incommensurability of *these* values without upholding the relativity of epistemic values. Of course, Putnam's argument as against epistemic relativism is quite valid and it has never been, and cannot be, refuted.

A complete and definitive refutation of cultural relativism would have to be an extensive undertaking. I am confident it could be done, but I cannot do it here even if I were competent to do so. I can only outline two main arguments against it.

Firstly, cultural relativism takes its stand on a disbelief in human reason. The culture of anti-reason is a fraud that does not hoodwink anyone except those who claim to belong to that culture. The very notion of their claim involves them, as has often been shown, in self-refutation. As long as they keep on, pugnaciously and tendentiously, retorting, 'Whose reason?' to every attempt to reason with them, there is, of course, no hope of convincing them regarding the rational impossibility of their venture. But, equally, they cannot hope to convince those who are outside the circle of their thesis without having to give it up.

Secondly, we can speak of psychological relativism or normative relativism. The former would mean that we simply cannot help thinking and acting according to the norms prevalent in our culture or community. This is a positive claim and falls in the domain of psychology. The cultural relativism we have been concerned with is normative. It holds that we should think and act according to the norms of the culture or community to which we belong. We should do so, not because we are psychologically incapacitated to do otherwise and follow some other norms, but because there *are* no norms other than those of our culture and community. To follow these is the right and proper thing to do. In other words, morality is internal to a particular culture or community. Which community? There are so many different ones, smaller and larger, to which each individual simultaneously belongs.

Relativists sometimes think in terms of the family or sometimes of the nation. But in between the two, there are dozens of others. One is, let us say, a citizen of India; but he is also a citizen of a state within India, say Maharashtra; and is also a resident in a neighbourhood, a member of a housing colony, of a particular building which has its own unwritten norms, and, of course, of a family. He also belongs to an ethnic group, a clan or a caste.

One may be a member of a college, a club, a library, a hospital, a local council, or of world bodies like Rotary, WHO, the Catholic Church; or be a freemason or a Lion. The list can be as long as Don Juan's range of amours.

If all these 'communities' or associations or groups could neatly fit into each other, each having norms which do not clash with the norms of any other, things would be hunky-dory. But this is absurdly far from being the case. So, at times of conflict, which community would have a stronger claim on one? If the accepted and expected practices of a social group to which one belongs were to be completely opposed to norms prescribed by one's religion or those which are accepted in my neighbourhood, which do I consider more morally binding? Does one consider oneself to be an Indian first, or a Maharashtrian or a Mumbaikar? How far down, or up, does one go to determine one's proper 'community'?

Take an actual, rather gruesome case. A Parsi Zoroastrian died in Mumbai and his body was put in the *dokhma* (tower of silence). A murder was suspected and it was necessary to bring the body out for a postmortem examination. The trustees in charge of the *dokhmas* faced a terrible dilemma. According to the religious norms of the community, a body once placed in the *dokhma* cannot be taken out; the norms of the larger civic community demand that the criminal investigation must not be hampered. What were the trustees to do? They would have had to decide according to their moral sense and moral principles, which transcend the norms of the two communities concerned. In this case, of course, they had to allow the body to be brought out, because they could not obstruct criminal investigation.

A conflict of obligations due to different allegiances is not a new invention; cultural relativists seem not to have heard of it. It may be granted that the culture of any whole to which one belongs has some influence on one's beliefs and actions. Non-relativists, however, maintain that human reason, which is referred to as 'natural reason', is such that one can, by using it, reflect upon these beliefs and accept or reject these beliefs on merits. On this basic conviction, education is distinguished from indoctrination, critical assessment from mere acceptance, reasoning from brainwashing. According to cultural relativism, all of us are brainwashed by our culture, including themselves. They are not curious to know, and are not able to explain, how a person brought up in a devout religious family could turn atheist or how a Gorbachev could arise out of Soviet Russia.

References

1. Audi, R., 2001, p. 9.
2. Porter, J., op. cit., p. 53.
3. Quoted by Porter, op. cit., p. 54, from *After Virtue*, pp. 255-56.
4. Porter, J, op. cit., p. 54.
5. Ibid., p. 54.
6. MacIntyre, A., 1985, p. 181.
7. Ibid., p. 186.
8. Ibid., p. 191.
9. Ibid., p. 192.
10. Putnam, H., 1995, pp. 189-90.
11. Ibid., p. 191.
12. Quoted by J. D. Moon, 'Practical Discourse and Communicative Ethics' in White, S. K. (Ed.), 1995, p. 146.

13. Moon, J. D., op. cit., p. 150.
14. Ibid., pp. 150-51.
15. Ibid., p. 151.
16. Ibid., p. 152.
17. Putnam H., 1995, p. 192. The words in double quotation marks are those of Berlin.
18. Berlin quoted by Putnam, 1995, p. 193.
19. Putnam, J., 1995, p. 193.
20. Ibid., p. 194.
21. Taylor, C., 1997, p. 34.
22. Ibid., p. 35.
23. Pinkard, T., 'Taylor, "History", and the History of Philosophy' in Abbey, R. (Ed.), 2004, pp. 191-92.
24. Ibid., p. 194.
25. Ibid., p. 195.
26. Ibid., p. 210, N. 14.
27. Ibid., p. 196.
28. Ibid., p. 196.
29. Kerr, F., 'The Self and the Good: Taylor's Moral Ontology' in Abbey, R. (Ed.), 2004, p. 96.
30. Ibid., p. 92.
31. Ibid., p. 93.
32. Quoted by Kerr, op.cit., p. 93, from Taylor's *Sources of the Self,* 1989, p. 9.
33. Ortie, M. A., 'Taylor and Feminism', in Abbey, R. (Ed.), 2004, pp. 146-47.
34. O'Grady, P., 2002, p. 170.
35. Taylor, C., 1997, pp. 35-37.
36. Baldwin, T., 2001, p. 230.
37. Pinkard, T., op. cit., p. 196.
38. Murphy, M. C., 2003, p. 7.
39. Quoted by Murphy, (Ed.), 2003, p. 6 from MacIntyre's 'Notes from the Moral Wilderness II' in *New Reason 8,* p. 45.
40. Solomon, D., 'MacIntyre and Contemporary Moral Philosophy' in Murphy (Ed.), 2003 pp. 147-48.

41. Feyerabend, P., 1987, pp. 13, 24-25.
42. Rorty, R., 1989, pp. 53-55.
43. Putnam, H., 2003, p. 1.
44. Ibid., p. 45.
45. Ibid., p. 44.
46. Ibid., Ch. 2 and Putnam, H., 1995, pp. 205-6.
47. Putnam, H., 2003, pp. 142-43.

Chapter 12

The Roar of the Paper Tiger

'Smooth and Slippery'
Advertisement for Amul Butter

I n the kingdom of Post-modernism, who is king (or queen) is a matter of doubt. There are many claimants. There are many princes and princesses ready to wear the crown. There are clowns too. But there is one court jester, and his name is Richard Rorty. Many of his views he shares with the postmoderns; others are peculiar to him. They are also 'peculiar' in the colloquial sense. He deserves a chapter to himself.

The Game Called Philosophy

'Traditional philosophy', as it has recently been called, has always, along with the natural sciences, been a rational activity par excellence. Rorty, looking upon himself as some kind of philosopher, therefore gives us a series of pictures of philosophy and science. Of a portrait done of him by Graham Sutherland, Churchill said, 'It is a remarkable example of modern art!' Of Rorty's pictorial series it can be said, 'It is a remarkable example of postmodern art.' Because of his hit-and-run style of writing, it is impossible to give a systematically developed account of what Rorty believes, if indeed he believes in anything. One can dip into the fishpond and pick up some strange specimens. Brandom tells us that Rorty has been pictured as 'an analytic philosopher unfortunately seduced by the fashionable but unsound ideas of postmodern literary theorists', but adds that this is 'quite wrongheaded'. Rorty is also 'sometimes taken to demean science by his denial that scientific uses of language hook up with reality in a way that is privileged as more *ontologically revealing*' than other uses.[1] But listen to Rorty himself (as quoted by Brandom):

> Fifteen years ago, when I found that almost the only other American academics who are reading the Hegel-Nietzsche-Heidegger-Derrida sequence were people who taught literature rather than philosophy, I optimistically assumed that this European cultural tradition would now, at last, be represented in American universities, to everyone's benefit... That was one of the reasons I switched jobs, moving from the Princeton philosophy department to ... the University of Virginia (a university that has distinguished departments of literature...).

Rorty's preference for non-analytic philosophy cannot be doubted.

Rorty writes that 'our purposes' (whatever they are) 'would be served best by ceasing to see the truth as a deep matter, as a topic of philosophical interest, or "true" as a term which repays "analysis"'; again, the '"nature of truth" is an unprofitable topic', and so also is 'the nature of man' and of God. The *nature* of anything is anathema to Rorty. What he always wants is something to dispel his boredom. 'Interesting philosophy is rarely an examination of the pros and cons of a thesis', and, true to this thesis, he commends the attitude of Wittgenstein, Heidegger and Dewey in setting aside epistemology and metaphysics as possible disciplines; 'I say "set aside" rather than "argue against"' because 'they do not devote themselves to discovering false propositions or bad arguments in the works of their predecessors', but see 'the vocabulary of philosophical reflection' as 'pointless'.[2]

Rorty certainly sees himself as a messiah, the prophet of a new philosophy,[3] edifying philosophy whose method is 'to re-describe lots and lots of things in new ways', a philosophy that 'does not work piece by piece, analyzing concept after concept, or testing thesis after thesis', not at all in the manner of a scientist, patiently, ploddingly and systematically exploring his subject. No, Rorty will have none of that. For him, philosophy does everything at one go, 'holistically'; and, of course, 'pragmatically'. It tries to 'ignore the apparently futile traditional questions by substituting ... new and possibly interesting questions', to 'want to stop doing those things' we were doing 'and do something else'. But don't imagine that this new thing that we are to do is done by using the old common criteria, for 'just in so far as the new language really is new, there will be no such criteria'. In fact, since we are now dealing only with a new language with new rules, there is no place for criteria at all. We have often heard that language is just a tool, and so is thinking. When you want to do some thinking, edifying philosophy 'says things like "try to think of it this way"', as a carpenter might show you how to use a hammer: 'Hold it this way, not that way.' To Rorty anything old is an abomination, but all this codswallop about games and tools is itself rather old and faded now.

Jane Heal, in defending Rorty, exhibits, unintentionally, his eel-like qualities:[4]

> There is a difficulty right at the start in being sure that we have done justice to Rorty in attributing to him certain 'claims' for which he 'offers arguments'. He would see himself as doing (at least in part) what he calls 'edifying' rather than 'systematic' philosophy – that is, as offering remarks which encourage us 'to break the crust of convention' ... to conceive ourselves free to invent and move on to new and exciting forms of discourse. There are, according to him, no (agreed) forms of argument by which one can persuade people to think of themselves one way rather than another; the activities by which these changes ... are accomplished (activities which Rorty calls 'conversation') are more like poetry and literature than like mathematics and science....

What is expounded here is an oft-tried sleight of hand practised by all intellectual conjurors. It works out as saying, 'I will argue for my position, but when you counter my arguments, I will remind you that I was not arguing, that I don't believe in argument, that I'm only offering remarks, maintaining an attitude, creating poetry.' Heads I win, tails you lose.

According to Rorty, mathematics and science 'do sometimes proceed by agreed rules of argument' and this he calls 'inquiry'. So, there are such things as rules of argument and so there is no reason why Rorty should not be obliged to defend his position by using them instead of hiding behind 'conversation'. What is it but a species of cowardice?

But Rorty is not the only eel; his defender is also one. How else can she defend one? After protecting Rorty against the charge of being inconsistent by telling us that he is not doing 'systematic' philosophy (that is, philosophy by argument), Heal now withdraws that defence and says that Rorty is, in fact all for argument and was only indulging in a little playful exaggeration:[5]

> But since it is an implication of my claims that these contrasts are exaggerated by Rorty ... I shall not scruple to represent him as proceeding in the customary fashion by offering claims and defending them with argument.

So, with those new and exciting forms of discourse we only went on a picnic and are now back at good old philosophical argumentation. But please don't run away with the idea that we are back at traditional philosophy which tries to understand the nature of the universe, man's place in it, or anything of that sort. For Rorty, it is a 'contemporary language game' among other games we play. It is 'an exercise in imagination'; traditional philosophers 'have their eye on eternity', but the gamester philosophers 'have their eye on the current preoccupations of the age', and this is called, by Rorty, 'edification'. The 'search for objective knowledge is replaced by ... novel descriptions and vocabularies'.[6] Are we going on another picnic?

It has been pointed out that Rorty himself propounds a number of substantive philosophical theses. James Conant culls eight of them, which I mention briefly:[7]

1. 'Solidarity ... should replace objectivity';
2. 'Truth cannot exist independently of the human activity of employing language';
3. Vocabularies are not mirrors of nature, but tools which should be evaluated according to 'how well they help us *cope*';

4. Moral beliefs are those which 'my community's current practices … will let me get away with';

5. Historical processes are 'fundamentally *contingent*' and 'understanding is always *situated*';

6. 'Public and private goods are incommensurable';

7. Liberalism is 'nothing more than a function of … commitment to [one's] community';

8. Ironism believes that 'anything can be made to look good or bad by being re-described in an alternative vocabulary'.

There are surely many more such theses, one major one being that philosophy itself is a game.

These philosophical theses are either argued for or not argued for. If argued for, Rorty stands self-refuted; if not argued for, they are only emotional outbursts and non-Rortyian philosophers may ignore them and get on with their work.

Intellectual Darwinism and the Extinction of Truth

Rorty declares he doesn't want to give up on reason but wants only to 'reinterpret' it 'naturalistically' in a way compatible with 'Nietzsche's Darwinian claim that we are just "clever animals"'. This implies 'giving up the notion of scientific truth as accurate representation' of what there is. The Darwinian claim also gives up the claim that mind, matter and self have an intrinsic nature owing nothing to our cognitive activities.[8]

Rorty always wants to give up something or hold on to something, assert something or deny something, but he never wants to tell us exactly why he wants to do this, or how it can be done.

Rorty's pronouncements on truth and understanding are sprayed all over his writings like bullets from a terrorist's gun. Of course, for him, truth and understanding don't exist. Since there is next to no systematic development in his writing, it is extremely difficult to deal with it. In keeping with his own views of reason and rational argument, what he says cannot seriously be taken to be the conclusions or findings of a rational inquiry. They are more like eruptions of deep-rooted phobias or manias. The phobias are against truth, argument and such things; his manias are for originality, 'revolutions', excitement and something called 'conversation'. Towards warrants and justification his attitude is one of uncertainty.

Let us start with truth. One of Rorty's techniques for dealing with any subject is to recommend something else as being in some way better to do. It reminds me of the time when I went to buy a pair of black shorts. The shopkeeper hunted for them, didn't have them, and said, 'Buy blue; black tears easily.'

Where ordinary thinkers speak of an argument being valid or invalid, or more cogent than another, Rorty speaks of a 'discursive strategy', and allows that one strategy can 'transcend' another, which means – not that it solves a problem more correctly than the other, but – that it aims at some 'other, better goals', such as 'greater honesty, greater clarity, greater patience'. He doesn't see how he could aim at truth. Thus, he shuffles off the question of truth by embracing morality.[9]

Postmoderns, as we know, have power on their minds. 'I think Nietzsche and Foucault were right in saying that truth is always an effect of power, and that it is a waste of time to try to replace power with truth.' (As it, no doubt, would be to try to replace a cause with its effect.) Might, we have heard, is right, but now might is also truth. So, what do we good people do? Rorty says, 'we should try to keep power ... in the hands of us good guys', forget truth, and 'just aim at ... a better (fairer, more just, more open) society'.[10] But isn't better, fairer and more just also the result of power, or do they have some existence and meaning not derived from power? Otherwise, better, fairer, etc. are what people in power think or say they are; so if we good guys are at present not in power, we can have no idea what better, fairer, etc. really mean; and if we do not know what they mean, how can we aim at them?

'Truth cannot be out there,' writes Rorty, because 'sentences cannot so exist, or be out there'; 'sentences are elements of human languages' and 'human languages are human creations'.[11]

Rorty is a purveyor of half-truths dressed up as truths. First: sentences. Sentences, as physical entities (sounds and marks) are human creations but have no truth-value. It is what they signify or symbolize, their content or meaning (often referred to as 'proposition') that can have meaning and, therefore, can be true or false. This is first-year philosophy. It is true that neither sentences nor propositions could exist unless some human being believed propositions and expressed them in sentences. To believe something, a psychological activity (the *believing*) has to occur. But a belief or a proposition is not a thing, like a table, and is not made or created. It is also true that you may choose to think or not to think of a certain subject matter, but once you take the plunge, think of something and tell us what you are thinking and so believe to be true, you are making a claim which has slipped out of your control. The claim is made good or is justified by factors not made by you – that is, in the very act of making that claim. This point needs to be clarified: I may say, 'That building is unsafe,' and I might have built that building; but, once built, it is a thing, whether built by me or someone else, which will have to be examined to decide whether my proposition is true or false. None of all this requires, as Rorty thinks it does, 'sentence-shaped chunks called "facts"' or making 'truth' identical with God (as Rorty thinks).

If there is one philosophical theory which postmoderns are right in opposing, it is the 'correspondence theory of truth'. 'Correspondence', as Bradley has pointed out, is a very general word and idea, for there are many kinds of correspondence. A portrait corresponds to its original in so far as it resembles it, and ordinary maps resemble, to a certain extent, the aerial view of the areas they are maps of, and so correspond to them. But a relief map corresponds to the elevation of a mountain, musical notation corresponds to musical sounds, and the Morse code corresponds to the English alphabet, without there being any resemblance between what is said to correspond and that to which it claims to correspond to.

The 'correspondence theory of truth', from Locke to later empiricists, uses correspondence in the sense of copying and thinks of truth as some kind of duplication of the reality, so that we are supposed to be able to confront, at one and the same time, two entities, the reality (whatever it is) and its copy, compare the two and pronounce judgement on the exactness of the copy. The obvious question this raises is, if we can confront the reality directly in order to compare the copy with it, why do we need the copy, and, if the copy is thus redundant, what happens to the 'correspondence theory'? And if we cannot confront the reality and can only have the copy, we cannot carry out the test of comparing copy with reality, and so never know if we have got truth or not.

There is another altogether different view of truth that maintains that, though truth does indeed 'correspond' to reality in that it *is* reality as understood by the human mind, it is not a separate entity or a duplicate of reality. The human mind confronts what it takes to be real, what it constantly has to take into account, and what it tries progressively to understand better and better. This theory of truth and knowledge has been propounded by the Absolutists, in particular, Bradley and Bosanquet. They make an important distinction, on the one hand, between the nature and definition of truth, and, on the other, the criterion of truth. The latter is not, as it is for the 'correspondence theory', a comparison between copy and original, but comprehensive coherence. Donald Davidson seems to corroborate this view when he writes: 'Truth as correspondence with reality may be an idea we are better off without': 'the formulation is not so much wrong as empty, but it does have the merit of suggesting that something is not true simply because it is believed', and it 'does capture the thought that truth depends on how the world is'.[12]

It is not possible or necessary for me to defend the Absolutist theory of truth here. Rorty is on the right lines in rejecting the view that thinking *mirrors* reality. He, however, uses the word 'epistemology' in a sense peculiar, I believe, to postmodernism, as a theory for which thinking mirrors nature. For him, hermeneutics takes the place of epistemology, 'once the mirroring notion has lost its grip' (which, I hope, has happened or is happening). At present I am not concerned with Rorty's other point that hermeneutics studies 'various different ways of looking at … the world'. I have no quarrel, either, with Rorty maintaining that there are 'different kinds of discourse (scientific, literary, moral)', which the hermeneutic philosopher sees and which are different ways of coping with the world. But he proceeds to describe them as 'kinds of linguistic strategy', which means that these 'discourses' are not taken as accounts or arguments which seek to reach valid and true conclusions. It is, therefore, not clear as to how they are supposed to cope with the world.

Surely, in scientific and, arguably, in moral discourses the concepts of truth and validity are involved. Since we are not told what is meant by 'literary' discourse, I cannot say whether truth and validity are supposed to be involved in it. Instead of enlightening us about how these discourses cope with the world and, also, with 'living our lives', Rorty shuffles away into declaring how philosophers (except those of his breed) are 'absurdly frightened of disagreement, inconclusiveness or mutual misunderstanding'. He believes that 'clashes between world-views … involve incommensurable concepts', and yet he hopes that the proponents of these 'will enter into some sort of dialogue'. How can they? What sort of dialogue can it be?

The account in the paragraph above is taken from Jane Heal and the quoted words are hers, not Rorty's.[13] She is sympathetic to Rorty and says that, 'it seems central to the pragmatist stance' which Rorty takes, that 'acquiring beliefs, theories or views can be regarded as a matter of *choice*'. When the mind 'takes large views' (she quotes Rorty) 'its activity is more like deciding what to *do* than deciding that a representation is accurate'. 'But are our beliefs' – large or small – 'things that we can in any sense choose?' asks Heal, and answers, 'I shall suggest that they cannot.'[14] Nevertheless, she cannot bring herself to declare that Rorty is talking through his hat. In a sense, of course, we do choose our beliefs. We do choose, again, up to a point, the subject-matter about which we want to know something and are therefore prepared to believe what we will find to be true. But we do not choose that truth; we accept it.

In contrast to Rorty's position on truth, Davidson writes:

> Sentences are understood on condition that one has the concept of objective truth. This goes also for the various propositional attitudes sentences are used to express. It is possible to have a belief only if one knows that beliefs may be true or false. I can believe it is now raining … because I know that whether or not it is raining does not depend on whether I believe it, or everyone believes it, or it is useful to believe it; it is up to nature, not to me or my society or the entire history of the human race… Truth enters into the other attitudes in other ways. We desire that a certain state of affairs be true, we fear, hope or doubt that things are one way or another. We intend by our actions to make it true that we have a good sleep… Since all these, and many more attitudes have a propositional content – the sort of content that can be expressed by a sentence – to have any of these attitudes is necessarily to know what it would be for the corresponding sentence to be true. Without a grasp of the concept of truth, not only language, but thought itself, is impossible … without the idea of truth we would not be thinking creatures, nor would we understand what it is for someone else to be a thinking creature.[15]

Davidson has also highlighted the fact that it is not sentences themselves but what they are used to express that has truth-value. It is the propositional content of beliefs, the proposition, that claims truth; but belief, being a mental state, also has a psychological component. People like Rorty need to straighten out all this for themselves, because they are obsessed with language and sentences instead of being concerned with thinking and propositions. This is, of course, partly the pernicious influence of Wittgenstein's talk of language games.

Although postmodernism rejects the 'correspondence theory of truth', it is not at all certain whether Rorty and the rest of them are quite clear about what they are rejecting and what they believe. Rorty is quite right in asking, rhetorically, if true beliefs or sentences can be 'treated on the model of realistic portraiture', but he goes on to say, 'Obviously some sentences can', such as '"the cat is on the mat"'. A correctly understood rejection of the 'correspondence theory' would not concede even this. Obviously, the sentence 'the cat is on the mat' does not look like the cat sitting on the mat. The idea of correspondence, as understood in the theory, is a totally incorrect idea of truth, any kind of truth, and truth's criterion. Even to find out if the belief that the cat is on the mat is true, a comparison is not made between the actual situation and the belief. How could it be done? To be fair to Rorty, however, I must mention that after 'obviously some sentences can', he adds 'at least *prima facie*'; so, perhaps, he has correctly grasped the matter.[16]

Conversation

> 'Words, words, words ...' 'But what is the matter?'
>
> Shakespeare, *Hamlet*

Justification and truth (even truth!) are topics from traditional philosophy which Rorty, strangely, doesn't find boring, as he does some others. What he says about them is not boring either, but quite entertaining.

As a true, blue-blooded postmodern, he never tires of telling us that there is no such thing as truth. But humans do make claims to knowledge and truth, and they even try to justify them. Such justifying, says Rorty, 'is not a matter of special relation between ideas (words) and objects, but of conversation, social practice'.[17] Guignon and Hiley explain this by saying, 'Forming beliefs, determining what we know, defending our claims – these are all matters of interacting with others in a linguistic community where the members exchange justifications of assertions with one another,' in the way in which, one supposes, the English at one time used to say, 'How do you do?' on meeting each other, without meaning anything and without expecting a relevant reply. At no point is there any suggestion of any member of the community making contact in any way with the facts, making observations, gathering and sifting evidence, claiming truth. 'There is no basis for deciding what counts as knowledge and truth other than what one's peers will let one get away with,' write Guignon and Hiley, and, then, 'justification reaches bedrock when it has reached the actual practices of a particular community.'[18] It all comes to playing a linguistic game, with each community having different rules of play.

'Conversation' simply means intellectual slavery to one's community's norms of truth and inquiry. There is no escape into the wide world of facts and arguments transcending the narrow bounds of one's community. Even so, it still does not mean that one leaves the concept of truth; it only means that different communities may have different concepts of truth. 'Sellarsian anti-foundationalism tells us,' say Guignon and Hiley, that 'there is no exit from the beliefs and reasons we currently accept as a community',[19] but is this not a kind of foundationalism where one is shackled to the unalterable, unchallenged bedrock of one's community's intellectual beliefs?

For Rorty, 'nothing counts as justification unless by reference to what we already accept'. He is right, for premises have to be accepted if the conclusion is to be accepted. He further says, 'there is no easy way to get outside of our beliefs … so as to find some test other than coherence'.[20] Right again. But it does not follow and it is not true that the beliefs we accept on a particular occasion (and from which we draw a particular conclusion) cannot themselves be questioned and questioned to the extent that we are driven outside the beliefs and norms of our community. And we are so driven precisely because we want to find that coherence which, Rorty rightly holds, will settle the truth of our beliefs. 'A foolish consistency is the hobgoblin of little minds,' said Emerson, 'adored by little … philosophers.' To be bound irrevocably to one's community norms is that foolish consistency; one has to, and can, break out of it to reach that more comprehensive coherence demanded by common human reason in its search for truth. To say that one has to remain enclosed within the circle of one's community's ideas is a caricature of the Coherence Theory, a caricature that supplies a basis for the usual and misconceived criticism of the theory. A proper understanding of it makes one realize that, when one feels uneasy (to use Rortyian language) with a set of irreconcilable ideas, one has to push farther out to regain consistency.

So far there is nothing really new in the notion of 'conversation'; it is just cultural relativism coupled with incommensurability. But Rorty's notions about it go further than this. Conversation 'presupposes no disciplinary matrix which unites the speakers', not even warranted justifiability, leave alone truth. The speakers do not 'hope for the discovery of antecedently existing common ground', that is, each one just starts from anywhere. Tom says, 'It's a fine day,' (even though it is raining heavily). Dick replies, 'Yes, London is very far away,' and Harry (who's Harry?) says, 'No, philosophy is rubbish.' This may very well put a stop to the conversation, but it could go on. The speakers could live, like all good men, in hope; for, says Rorty, 'the hope of agreement is never lost so long as conversation lasts', and, if not agreement, of 'at least, exciting and fruitful disagreement'.[21] Neither agreement nor disagreement are to be aimed at; one of them might just happen if they converse long enough, just as all the works of Shakespeare might be produced if a team of persevering monkeys typed away long enough. So, keep up the pressure, Tom, Dick and Harry; keep the conversation going. This vision of human discourse is vouchsafed to a science called hermeneutics.

We are eager to know something more about this disagreement that could be useful, but we are not taken into confidence. Exciting? Conversation is always exciting, because we are not trying to get anywhere; 'we play back and forth between guesses … until gradually we feel at ease with what was hitherto strange.'[22] But then, oh horror! The excitement will cease and how will we survive? We will have to feel uneasy again.

There are more illuminating accounts of 'conversation'. 'Free and open conversations take unpredictable directions, swerve in unforeseeable ways for unforeseeable reasons.' This trite statement is true of all discussions, for, obviously, before the discussion, nobody could say how it would go; if one *could* say it, there would be no point in embarking on it. But this does not mean what Rorty intends to convey, that a discussion proceeds, *essentially*, randomly and haphazardly, without purpose, aim or principle. We can normally review a discussion or a complex argument to gauge how it has gone, to see whether it is relevant to the issue, valid, cogent and convincing. But not so for a Rortyian 'conversation': 'There is no way to rise above the conversational moment in which one finds oneself, survey the conversation as a whole, and make principled recommendations. The most one can do is say something like: "This segment of the conversation … is getting a bit boring"'[23] and so turn to something else. It's very stuffy in this room with these old fogies; let's go to the next room where there is some dancing. Also very like some gurus who, not appreciating your questionings, turn away to another questioner.

Smashing the Mirror

Knowledge is something postmoderns talk a lot about; it is also something they don't like and, in fact, don't believe in. Alternatively, they have their own ideas of what it is.

The declared aim of Rorty's *Philosophy and the Mirror of Nature* is 'to undermine the reader's confidence in … "knowledge" about which there ought to be a "theory" and has "foundations"'. Theories too, generally, are to be shot down. Sensible people like Wittgenstein, Heidegger and Dewey, says Rorty, do not have '*alternative* "theories of knowledge"'; they simply 'set aside epistemology and metaphysics as possible disciplines'.[24] That they should be set aside – is that not their *theory*? Of course not; they have nought to do with should and should not; they simply set them aside and get on with their work.

But, though knowledge is nothing, it is such a bewitching nothing that Rorty simply cannot put it aside. Since he doesn't believe in truth, he cannot believe in knowledge, because knowledge, whatever else it might be, is made up of truths; truths systematically connected. Isolated truths, flying about like birds in an aviary (recall Plato), do not amount to knowledge. But connecting is the work of reason and argument, of formulating and solving problems, and we know Rorty's opinion on reason and argument.

Traditionally, knowledge has been taken to be our (true) understanding of the universe or whatever we consider to be real. Our basic contact with the real world is through sense-experience. As soon as we are aware of what comes to us in this way, we characterize it as such-and-such. We make judgements (of various degrees of explicitness) the moment we rise above the stage of brute sensation (if there is ever such a stage). One job of traditional philosophy has been to try to figure out the relation between what is given in immediate sensory experience and making judgements about it, and, further, how, by getting back to experience, we can assess the truth-value of these judgements. 'The dominant outlook in Anglo-American philosophy assumes that the world consists of natural kinds of items and that our task is to achieve a correct mapping of these types,' write Guignon and Hiley, but 'Rorty thinks this entire conception of our epistemic situation is shot through with conceptual logjams and insoluble puzzles', the 'prime offender' being our 'uncritical assumption that representation gives us the right picture'.[25] Rorty wants to replace this with a 'pragmatic conception of knowledge which eliminates' the contrast 'between representing the world and coping with it'.[26] He sees knowledge 'as based on social practices', whatever that means, an approach which he calls 'behaviourism'. This 'behaviourism' is said to be supported by the famous three – Wittgenstein, Dewey and Heidegger – and argued for by Quine and Sellars.[27]

Admittedly, the dominant philosophical outlook is shot through with logjams and puzzles, perhaps even insoluble ones. If it were not, philosophy would not be worth doing. But, instead of offering solutions (or showing philosophically that, in particular cases, solutions are, in principle, not possible) and instead of trying to find a way out of the jams, the easy way is, of course, to pass the buck to social practices. Which practices? If we were to be told what these are, and in what way precisely knowledge is based on them, we would be able to try and assess the situation and find a way out of the logjams. But Rorty and his peers do not care to reveal their secrets.

Wilfrid Sellars questions 'the traditional assumption that our ... knowledge of the world must be grounded in immediate sensory experience'. He holds 'that "all awareness is a linguistic affair"', and though he does not deny that we are affected by stimuli in the environment, these 'have no role to play in grounding knowledge'. Knowledge, for Sellars, is 'justified true belief' and always has 'a propositional structure', but sensory experience has nothing to do with it. But, then, what are these beliefs and propositions about? What is their content? What do they get at? How are they to be justified? Answer: 'The only way a proposition can be justified is by means of inferences from other propositions.' In Rorty's words, 'there is no such thing as justification which is not a relation between propositions.' 'Sellars, like Wittgenstein before him, argues that one must already possess a fairly wide range of concepts before one can have sensory experience in the epistemically relevant sense.'[28] Let us accept this as true, though it requires further analysis. It still does not prove that sensory experience plays no part in the acquisition and structure of knowledge.

The Sellars-Rorty view may be likened to a case of roads leading to or issuing from other roads, but never reaching or coming from any particular destination or source. Imagine a map that shows only roads. It is a strange meeting of extremes that the philosophers who reject the 'correspondence theory of truth' and those who embrace it are equally unable to see an obvious philosophical truth – that we are directly, through sense experience, in touch with the real, sensible world and that this awareness is always in the form of propositions and beliefs. The holders of the 'correspondence theory' think that those who reject it are floundering inside a ring of mere propositions and the world is left outside; our present rejectors of the theory think that knowledge is concerned exclusively with propositions that have nothing to do with the world. But we know the world directly only by means of the mechanism of beliefs and propositions.

Holding on to the idea that knowledge is exclusively concerned with propositions (nay, not even propositions, but sentences), our philosophers quickly mount their favourite hobby-horse – that one is bound by the norms of 'the linguistic community in which justifying claims is carried out'.

Vocabularies

Rorty is always telling us that a language or (what he calls) vocabulary is a tool, having nothing to do with 'truth' or 'reference'.[29] Wittgenstein and Davidson (and Rorty himself) 'treat alternative vocabularies', says Rorty, as 'alternative tools'. While ordinary folk sometimes ask if one sentence or judgement contradicts another, the Rortyian philosopher asks, 'Does our use of these words get in the way of our use of those other words?' and this amounts to the same as asking, in a particular case, 'whether our use of tools is efficient, not a question about whether our beliefs are contradictory'. Vocabularies are often found 'interfering with each other'. Normally, in such a case, we try to reconcile them in some way by reinterpreting their meaning or by discovering which of them gives a true account of their subject matter. According to Rorty, 'we invent a new vocabulary to replace both', just like throwing away your old car on the junk heap and buying a new one. Even on its own terms, this account is untrue. When the Ptolemaic and Copernican theories clashed, a third theory was not formulated.

'Inventing' is the key word here. Galileo, Hegel and Yeats (what a strange get-together) are credited with having, by 'gradual trial-

and-error', invented new vocabularies and discarded the old. Rorty says that 'we must resist the temptation to think the re-descriptions of reality offered by contemporary physical or biological science are somehow closer to "the things themselves"' than earlier descriptions.[30] They are just different. But why was the new description invented and the old discarded? Because the former was more suitable, more efficient. If we probe further and ask, 'In what way more suitable, more efficient?' we are clearly shown that we are making a nuisance of ourselves and do not deserve an answer. Next question, please.

Rorty performs the unique feat of riding a see-saw all by himself. He is at one end of the plank when he says that 'it may be as difficult to know which scientists are actually offering reasonable explanations as it is to know which painters are destined for immortality'. Difficult but presumably not impossible. At least it seems to Rorty to make sense to want the explanations to be reasonable. Almost at the same time, he clambers on to the other end of the plank and holds that there are no '"objective" and "rational" standards' to distinguish science from other things, and that Galileo, too, was performing a unique feat – lifting himself, as it were, off the ground by his bootstraps, for, in claiming to be objective and reasonable, he was actually 'creating the notion of "scientific values" as he went along', which implies that all notions of objectivity and reasonableness are what a scientist creates as he goes along, and therefore subjective. And 'the question of whether he was "rational" in doing so is out of place'.[31] So also, 'notions of criteria', says Rorty, 'are no longer in point when it comes to changes from one language game to another'. This means that within a particular language game, say

Western science or Aztec mythology, there are rules and criteria to be followed and used, but there are no over-arching ones that apply to several games.

Rorty goes even further to say that the shift from playing one language game to another is not a result of choice or decision, depending on some reason for the change; so even some kind of pragmatism doesn't come into play. And, quite obviously, arguments do not remotely enter the scene. Change just happens.[32] 'Europe gradually lost the habit of using certain words and gradually acquired the habit of using others.' Just as, in the forties, old ladies played mahjong, but now they play housie, or just as teenagers then said, 'Rubbish,' but now say, 'Bullshit'. Since habits change and fashions sometimes return, we may expect that we may go back one day to accepting Egyptian cosmology or even prehistoric animism. In fact, many have rejected evolution for spontaneous creation and many have adopted barbaric practices 'made more sinister by the lights of perverted science'. These things should not trouble Rorty or his friends at all, for on what grounds and by what criteria can you condemn or correct any of it?

In speaking of vocabularies, the analogy of tools, admits Rorty, 'has one obvious drawback'.[33] A craftsman knows what he is trying to make and then chooses the appropriate tool, but a Galileo or Hegel 'is typically unable to make clear exactly what it is that he wants to do before developing the language in which he succeeds in doing it.' His new vocabulary formulates, 'for the first time', 'its own purpose'. The science of hermeneutics would give several interpretations of such cryptic utterances of Rorty's, but on the face of it this particular utterance implies that a Galileo or a Hegel always succeeds, because, since he had no prior ideas as to what he wanted or where he was heading, whatever his new vocabulary takes him to, is success. Or failure, since there are no criteria of assessment. Such are the advantages of aimless bumming. For all his cynicism and nihilism, Rorty is a dreamer for whom the function and purpose of a language are 'to make something that never had been dreamed of before.'[34]

The Magic 'Jharoo'

'Representation' is a bad word in postmodern Rortyian language, but, like 'correspondence', it is quite innocuous, for everything depends on what concept of representation you have. Rorty seems to be on the right lines when he denies that knowledge, and particularly, philosophy, 'mirror' reality, for a mirror image or a picture is not the only kind of representation possible.

Rorty is naturally worried about this reality that is not mirrored by knowledge. Whether it is mind-dependent or not is a 'vexed and confusing' question. The trouble with Rorty is that, instead of arguing out the matter and considering different answers and reaching the least implausible one, he slips into talking of language, and the matter is left hanging. He writes:

> Searle sometimes writes as if philosophers who, like myself, do not believe in 'mind-independent reality' must deny that there were mountains before people had the idea of 'mountain' in their minds or the word 'mountain' in their language. But nobody denies that. Nobody thinks that there is a chain of causes that makes mountains an effect of thoughts or words.[35]

We would very much have liked to know what, then, Rorty does believe about mountains before people thought of them, and, if nobody denies that mountains existed before people, what meaning would he give to his insistence that there is no mind-independent reality. That would have been an extremely worthwhile contribution to ontology and epistemology. He robs us of that favour. What he does tell us is that 'people like Kuhn, Derrida and I, believe that it is pointless to ask whether there really are mountains or whether it is merely convenient for us to talk about mountains'. After which, he again confidently asserts that 'one of the obvious truths about mountains is that they were here before we talked about them'. (Surely, even before we saw them.) Seeing our astonishment, he turns on us with: 'If you do not believe that, you probably do not know how to play the language games that employ the word "mountain".' But we do believe that and we believe we do know how to play the relevant language game. Our astonishment is about how, like some of our senior politicians, you have the temerity to say, one moment, that talking about the existence of mountains is pointless and, at the next, assert categorically that they do exist and did exist before we talked about them. We are also grateful to Rorty for reminding us that 'we can get along quite nicely without the notion of "Reality as It Is in Itself"'.[36] But can we engage in philosophy without it? The magic 'jharoo' will undoubtedly sweep this question under the carpet (and carpets certainly did not exist before mankind thought of them and spoke of them).

'Although Richard Rorty is famous for denying that there is any correspondence between our words and elements of reality,' writes H. Putnam, 'virtually all Rorty's writings contain passages intended to reassure us that he is not denying that there is a world, or even denying that we are in unmediated touch with the world… In "Pragmatism, Davidson and Truth" the tone of reassurance is strident: "Using those vocables [the words and sentences of 'our language'] is *as direct as contact with reality can get* (as direct as kicking rocks, for instance)…."' Yet to Putnam these 'reassurances seem … utterly inadequate'.[37]

They are inadequate because, having asserted something of importance, Rorty is disinclined or unable to pursue the matter, to elucidate or explain his position. For example, regarding the distinction between what exists in itself and what exists in relation to human minds, he writes, 'This project, like the project of underwriting the sanctity of the Eucharist, once looked interesting, promising, and potentially useful… It has turned out to be a dead end.'[38] A question about a religious dogma (the Eucharist and its sanctity or its very possibility) is simply put on par with a basic philosophical problem that has plagued, on Rorty's own showing, philosophers from Aristotle, through Locke and Kant, to Searle. Maybe it is a pseudo-problem, but surely that has to be shown to be so. Rorty just orders the magic 'jharoo' to do its work – indiscriminately.

The notion of objectivity is anathema to Rorty and the postmoderns. As one would expect, these concepts are not considered worth serious discussion, only a serious application of the all-purpose 'jharoo'.

Rorty backs a culture which is 'more sensitive to the marvellous diversity of human languages, and of the social practices associated with those languages' than one which keeps asking whether our language '"corresponds to" some nonhuman, eternal entity', such as (he means) a universal or some sort of Platonic 'idea'. (Remember, 'language' does not mean, literally, language, but view, account, theory, etc.) Instead of asking about 'the intrinsic nature of reality', 'we should ask whether each of the various descriptions of reality employed in our various cultural activities is the best we can imagine – the best means to the ends served by those activities'.[39]

We need not dwell on the intrinsic vagueness of these sentences: Which cultural activities of ours? Which ends? What is meant by 'best'? Best in what respect? Could it, by any chance, mean 'truest'? Why should we not ask about the intrinsic nature of reality, if we are doing philosophy? The 'marvellous diversity of human languages' – what else can it mean except views about reality in different cultures, the liberal Western culture, that of the Aztecs, the Hottentots, the Dark Ages, the Freemasons and of those who perform human sacrifices? All are to be treated as equal. We should ask what is the best way to save fuel consumption or to preserve peace or to placate the spirits that live in the trees, or to perform human sacrifices or to roast and eat your fellowmen.

Rorty, like a cleric issuing a *fatwa*, tells us what we should and should not ask. We should not ask, for instance, 'idle questions like: "Are there objective facts about right and wrong in the same sense that there are objective facts about electrons and protons?"' For 'there is nothing to the notion of objectivity save that of inter-subjective agreement'. And 'agreement is to be reached by free and open discussion of all available hypotheses and policies.'[40] We would have gratefully appreciated Rorty telling us how such a discussion is to be carried on while keeping truth out of it. What, in the absence of wanting to find out whether the hypotheses are true or not, are we to do with them? But, perhaps, when Rorty talks of discussion here, he means 'conversation', which, of course, is said to be possible without worrying about truth or falsehood.

Agreeing with Nelson Goodman, Rorty writes that 'all the logician can do is tell you what deductive arguments people usually accept as valid; she cannot correct their notions of deductive validity.'[41] If, perchance, most people, in course of time, drop, when arguing, the rules of *modus ponens* and embrace the opposite rules, she, our logician, would henceforth maintain that asserting the consequent asserts the antecedent. How very convenient for all who argue. When, by using the *usual* logical principles, I cannot win my point, I turn maverick and begin using other principles, which would favour my case. All that the other party could do would be to protest, 'Hey! You are not using the usual rules of logic.' To which I would blandly reply, 'So what? I'm different.' The other party would then, following my example, select or invent new logical rules which would help him (or her) to win his (or her) case. I would then respond with ... This is the chameleon mode of arguing which is of a piece with the other well-known postmodern techniques of changing colour when the situation becomes hot and also similar to getting out of an intellectual logjam by declaring it to be 'pointless' to continue the discussion. Logic would, accordingly, become a branch of the sociology of human cunning.

Again Rorty writes, 'Similarly, all we philosophers can do when asked for standards or methods of disinterested and objective inquiry is to describe how the people we most admire conduct their inquiries.' We do not, of course, admire them because they use the correct standards and methods, but because, maybe, they are so handsome, or wealthy or well mannered. The people *we* admire most are film stars, *crorepatis*, builders and 'dons', and we long to be able to follow their standards and methods of 'getting on'. 'We have no independent information about how objective truth is to be obtained.' For Rorty, the only alternatives which are open are accepting what is done by the people we most admire or getting some 'information' from somewhere. Since there is no such source of information, we are left with the first alternative. It doesn't strike Rorty that we can do a third thing – study the conduct of the most admired people and try to understand why they used the standards and the methods they used and what makes them worth using or discarding. In keeping with his philosophy, Rorty would answer that they just used them, they had no reason why they used these particular standards and methods, and they could very well have chosen to use any others. No, not even chosen. 'The wind bloweth where it listeth' and they were simply blown in one direction rather than another.

Once again we get an assurance: 'nobody ever said there was no such thing as objective truth and validity.' Nobody? Not even Rorty? No, but they are rather different from what we had so far believed them to be. 'All there is to talk about are the procedures we use for bringing about agreement among inquirers.' This may be achieved by careful and systematic observation of what is real and by rational argument, or it may be achieved by alternative procedures like threats, torture, trial by fire and water, brainwashing. Agreement is all.[42]

If you actually look beneath all this democratic and cosmopolitan talk about the marvellous diversity and equality of languages, you find a covert conviction that there is only one language which is superior to all others. Taking up Putnam's view that truth is 'idealized rational acceptability', Rorty interprets it as equivalent to truth being 'rational acceptability to an ideal community', and this he seems to agree with. So there are not different truths acceptable to different communities; it makes sense (so it now seems) to speak of an ideal community and truth being what is acceptable to that community. Now, is this ideal community an idle dream, a community which has, *per impossibile*, a God's-eye view of things? Can you believe our good fortune? There really *is* such a community. 'Nor can I see how, given that no such community is going to have a God's-eye view, this ideal community can be anything more than *us*,' says Rorty; not us as we are, but 'as we should like to be'. So we can conceive of an ideal community and of truth as what is acceptable to that community. And can we fill out this idea of an ideal community with some more detail? Yes, we can. 'Nor can I see,' says Rorty, 'what "us" can mean here except us educated, sophisticated, tolerant, wet liberals, the people who are always willing to hear the other side, to think out all the implications, and so on – the sort of people, in short, whom both Putnam and I hope, at our best, to be.'

So, now it is clear that beliefs held by uneducated, un-sophisticated people who, for instance, believe that spirits live in trees, are not true. Truth is no longer what is acceptable to a particular community, different for different communities. But Rorty is quick to warn us against thinking that 'rational acceptability' means acceptable to 'human beings *qua* human'; there is no such in-built 'guidance system' for all humans, Aztecs and witch-doctors included. While terms like 'rational', he says, 'will always invite the question "to whom?"' it 'will always lead us back ... to the answer "*us*, at our best"'[43]. And all this time we didn't know it!

Jack in the Box

Rorty and the postmoderns have a horror of universals. It is linked to their fear of objectivity. 'The desire for objectivity', says Rorty, is the 'motivated attempt to provide a firm basis for community by grounding social practices in something that is not itself a social practice – namely, truth, rationality, or some other ultimate ground'. Common human nature is also a candidate. We know Rorty's opinion (albeit confused) of truth and rationality, and he also holds that 'there is no "common human nature" that necessarily binds us to our fellows, grounding our community values'.[44] With lofty contempt, he writes, 'We will not get anywhere by asking our philosophy professors to make sure that there really are such things as human rights.'[45]

Though our desire for objectivity is a desire for a fiction and can be explained away, we also have, according to Rorty, a desire for solidarity, which is quite respectable and seeks an 'ethical basis for cooperative inquiry and human community'.[46]

Much as postmoderns disbelieve in the existence of these ghostly presences called universals and essences, they are haunted by them. Solidarity is as much a universal as truth, objectivity, or human nature. It is not relevant here to raise the big and complex problem of the ontological and epistemological status of universals. From the time of Locke, if not much earlier, philosophers have found universals or 'general ideas' an embarrassment. Various means (for example, substituting resemblance) have been tried to exorcise them, but with little success. They keep popping up when least wanted in the writings of philosophers who, however different in their persuasions, dislike them. They refuse to be ostracized even from Rortyian conversations.

Habermas and Apel, says Rorty, speak of 'something called "rationality" which all human beings share', but, retorts Rorty, 'suppose we say that all that rationality amounts to – all that marks human beings off from other species of animals – is the ability to use language and thus to have beliefs and desires'.[47] However, whether we speak of this ability or of rationality, we are speaking equally of a feature shared by all humans, a feature that marks them apart from non-humans, and is, as such, a universal. Again, in place of 'desire for truth', which Apel and Habermas invoke as a universal, Rorty suggests *curiosity* – 'the urge to expand one's horizon of inquiry', and he also suggests that the desire for truth or curiosity or whatever exists only within a community and not necessarily in all mankind.[48] But whether a particular quality exists in a limited group of individuals or among all humans, even if it exists between two individuals, it is still a universal. A universal is that which is other than a particular or individual, to be a universal it does not have to belong to *all* the members of a class. The thesis of 'family resemblance' (made famous by Wittgenstein) does not manage to get rid of the notion of universal, for even though all the members of a family, say the Cursetjees, are not deaf, in so far as some are, deafness is a universal.

Some metaphysical and theological theories want us to acknowledge a common human nature and even sceptics like Nietzsche, who will have none of metaphysics and theology, bemoans Rorty, 'have their own theories of human nature' – 'there is something common to all human beings – for example, the will to power.' Dear, dear! Not only something common to all humans, but they even have theories, and what are theories if not universals claiming truth? How different a Rortyian 'conversation'!

However, 'historicist thinkers', like Rorty himself, have gone beyond even Old Major. 'They have denied that there is such a thing as "human nature";' They insist there is only 'socialization' and that 'the question, "What is it to be a human being?" should be replaced by questions like "What is it to inhabit a rich twentieth-century democratic society?"'[49] Whatever it is, it is sure to be a universal popping up again and grinning at Rorty.

In place of 'essence' and objectivity, Rorty backs something he calls 'solidarity', which 'seeks only an ethical basis for cooperative inquiry and human community'. Whatever that ethical basis is (isn't it human nature, after all?), it would have to be universal and objective if it is to be at all effective. Rorty seems to think that solidarity and objectivity are mutually exclusive, but there is no reason to think that one of them comes in the way of the other. In a new version of the myth of the Cave, Rorty, like the Platonic Socrates, wants to come to the succour of 'human beings clinging together against the dark', but unlike Socrates, without any 'hope of getting things right'.[51]

Scientific Conversations

'....the fairy tales of science'

Alfred Lord Tennyson, *Locksley Hall*

Let's talk about Rorty's talks on science. You can't call them views or theories; they echo the familiar noises made by postmoderns about the subject.

Rorty's main thrust is that science does not reveal nature to us (and, of course, that philosophy does not reveal something even bigger, called reality.)[52] He sees science 'as one more human activity' rather than 'as the place at which human beings encounter a "hard", non-human reality'. But, then, what kind of activity is it? Great scientists 'invent descriptions of the world which are useful for purposes of predicting and controlling what happens, just as poets and political thinkers invent other descriptions of it for other purposes', and 'there is no sense in which *any* of these descriptions is an accurate representation of the way the world is in itself'. We may ask why we should accept the assertion that scientific claims are 'inventions' like those of the poets and also whether it is, in principle, impossible for any descriptions to be reasonably accurate representations of anything. To the former question no answer is ever preferred; to the second the answer is, yes. 'These philosophers', of whom Rorty is proud to be one, 'regard the very idea of such a representation as pointless'. 'Pointless', mind you; he doesn't categorically say, 'impossible'.

As usual, there is, here, an invocation of the uncanny. For scientific descriptions (which do not describe) are able, presumably, to, on the whole, effectively and successfully predict and control what happens, but this is miraculously so, since it has nothing to do with the nature of scientific reality. We have no idea, so it seems, why scientific predictions are so often successful and why events can be scientifically controlled. Just as the witch doctor or his patients have no idea why the slitting of a cock's neck drives the spirit out of their souls.

I suppose it would be admitted by 'these philosophers' that there are limits to scientific predictions and control. This means that we know that there *are* happenings which we know, or come in due course to know, to be such and such, which it is not yet possible to predict or control. Here we have representative description without prediction or control.

Predicting and controlling are not the only or even primary functions of science. To suggest that they are, is a gratuitous and groundless denial of an obvious fact that prediction and control are possible because of, and to the extent that, the descriptions are accurate and true. The cart doesn't draw the horse. However, 'philosophers of science' such as Kuhn and Hesse 'explain why there is no way to explain the fact that a Galilean vocabulary enables us to make better predictions than an Aristotelian vocabulary'.[53]

Rorty himself has a number of inventions to his credit. One of them is the notion that when non-Rortyians think of nature or the real world as not made by humans, they visualize some reality over and above what is presented to us in sense perception. Some metaphysicians may think of it that way, but what is ordinarily meant is that the world has a nature that goes beyond our present perception and knowledge of it, that its existence and nature are not determined by our wishes and that it reveals itself to scientific inquiry as well as to ordinary non-scientific human experience. Rorty thinks that when one speaks of the 'intrinsic nature of the world', one 'takes for granted an outmoded conception of the world as God's artefact', which 'commits us to believing in a person who made the world, or to thinking of the world itself as a person', itself having 'a point of view and preferences about how it is described'. This is pure poetic imagination, and so is the idea that those who think thus of science, 'see the scientist (or the philosopher, or the poet, or *somebody*) as having a priestly function, as putting us in touch with a realm which transcends the human'.[54] Tom Sorell rightly considers all this to be a caricature of science, for which Rorty 'gives us no very compelling reason'. We should remember that it is a Rortyian philosophy that reduces the scientist to the status of a shaman or witch doctor.

The concepts of 'language' and 'tool' are used to present this caricature. Galileo 'hit upon a tool which happened to work better for certain purposes than any previous tool'. The 'tool' here is Galileo's theory. What could those mysterious purposes be? Maybe, they have something to do with reaching a correct representation of the world. And 'better' might, perhaps, have some connection with 'truer'? 'Once we found out what could be done with a Galilean vocabulary, nobody was much interested in doing things which used to be done with an Aristotelian theory.'[55] Just as when people found what computers could do, they were not interested in typewriters any more. We have here, once again, the working of mysterious forces. Once you substitute 'tool' (and 'language') by 'theory', you see how Rorty's sophistry fails. An old theory is not dropped because it has become uninteresting but because it fails to explain or explain as well as the new one. For Rorty, science is a hit-and-miss affair, playing blind-man's-buff, a game not of skill or expertise, but of luck. Often (intentional?) vagueness is a component of that game. The difficulty in trying to engage his arguments is that 'they are cast at such a level of generality and diffuseness that it is hard to know what one is endorsing ... or what it might mean to oppose what is being said', and Rorty seems always to be shouting at us as he skips from one track to another, 'Watch me whiz by, catch me if you can.'[56]

It is not only that 'the language of science' (that is, scientific theories) does not describe or gives no truth about the world. It is, for Rorty, not even a literal language.[57] Science and the actual language (I mean, language) that it uses to give expression to its theories (for example, that the earth's gravity attracts at the rate of 32 feet per second) speak in metaphors (a word often on postmodern lips). A metaphor is a 'figure of speech in which a term is transferred from the object it ordinarily designates to an object it may designate only by implicit comparison or analogy' (*Webster's II New Riverside University Dictionary, 1994*), as when, for example, God is called 'a mighty fortress'. So, the metaphor is actually used to refer to the former object by means of the latter. In Rorty's concept of science, the metaphors which science uses in its talk and the metaphor that science itself is, never let us know what they are to be transferred to, what they are actually supposed to refer to, metaphorically. They remain, as it were, suspended in mid air. Rorty allows science (and us) a free choice between 'alternative metaphors', because since science completely ignores the world, the world retaliates by not providing us 'with any criterion of choice' between metaphors, particularly as the world (and we) do not know what the metaphors are meant to refer to. All we can do is to 'compare ... metaphors with each other, not with something beyond ... called "fact"'. And after comparing, what? Nothing, of course; after all it is only a language game. (It may be noticed, in passing, how the idea of 'comparing' is again at the bottom of the mischief.)

'The only way to argue for this claim is to ... exhibit the sterility of attempts to give a sense to phrases like "the way the world is",' says Rorty. We should be happy to be assured that, at least, there *is* a world, though it does nothing for us; also to hear that Rorty is trying to 'argue' for a 'claim', and not merely indulging in a 'conversation' *sans* arguments and claims. Is it, by any chance, a claim to a truth, which he wants us to accept, or just a claim, take it or leave it?

Galileo vs Bellarmine

Rorty cannot bring himself to admit outright that Bellarmine was wrong and Galileo right.[58] 'If one endorses the values,' he writes, 'common to Galileo and Kant', the values of truth and rational argument of course, 'then indeed Bellarmime was being "unscientific"'. In other words, if you are thinking of science as ordinarily understood, then Bellarmine was trying to make falsity look like truth. But if you take science in some other sense (where, say, truth is what suits you or what you want to be accepted), then Bellarmine was 'scientific'. And he has a right, of course, to cherish his own values, particularly when they happen to be backed by a powerful Church. Truth is power, remember! And convenience. Rorty writes:

> But, of course, almost all of us (including Kuhn, though
> perhaps not including Feyerabend) are happy to endorse
> them [Galileo's values]. We are the heirs of three hundred
> years of rhetoric about the importance of distinguishing
> sharply between science and religion....

Our happiness is simply the result of efficient and persistent
advertising and conspiracy by a group who called themselves
'scientists' and who decided to keep poor Bellarmine out of the
club. In spite of his clout at the time, he lost out in the long run
and 'Galileo won the argument' because of this and his followers'
superior rhetoric and sophistry. However, thanks to a new group
of conspiring rhetoricians, the tide is turning or has already turned
and we are back to the Middle Ages in Europe. Britain and the
US are fast catching up. But who knows! Tides have a habit of
turning and we may once again have an Enlightenment.

Were the values Bellarmine invoked – loyalty to the Scriptures
and the Church – 'properly scientific', involving 'rationality' and
'disinterestedness'? Rorty answers, 'At this point, it seems to me,
we would do well to...' Have a guess; no marks for the correct
answer, which is 'to abandon the notion of certain values
("rationality, disinterestedness")', and then we are told that Galileo
was '*creating* the notion of "scientific values" as he went along',
those very values which we have just been advised to abandon.
What the misguided Galileo created we must now destroy. Why
should we? No reason; just like that; it's time to change, otherwise
it becomes boring.

If we say, as we do, that for Bellarmine truth was a matter of
convenience, Rorty would spring to his defence and assert that

convenience is indeed the basis of making a statement. Rorty quotes 'an anti-Rorty argument attributed to Putnam by Bernard Williams': [59]

> If, as Rorty is fond of putting it, the correct description of the world (for us) is a matter of what we find it convenient to say, and if, as Rorty admits, we find it convenient to say that science discovers a world that is already there, there is simply no perspective from which Rorty can say, as he does, that science does not really discover a world that is already there, but (more or less) invents it.

In other words, writes Williams, Rorty's views 'simply tear themselves apart'. The point of this argument is this: *if* it is only convenient (for whatever purpose) to say that 'science discovers a world that is already there', and if convenience is our only criterion and basis for making what is called a 'correct description of the world', *then*, in saying also that 'science does not *really* discover a world that is already there' (italics mine), Rorty is assuming a God's-eye view and telling us that the latter statement is, not convenient, but true, whereas the former is only convenient. So, on his own theory, Rorty has no right to make the latter statement.

Rorty could have replied that each of the two statements is convenient in its own way, that there are different types of conveniences, and which you choose is decided by a kind of super-convenience. Rorty responds that convenience is a matter of degree. It is, therefore, convenient to say 'science discovers a world that is already there', but if this puts you in an awkward situation, it is more convenient to say the opposite. 'The convenience of the idea that there is a 'Way the World Is' would … be superseded by the still greater convenience of the idea that there is not.'

The old nagging questions arise: Why does ' $\sim p$ ' have 'still greater convenience' than 'p'? Is it true that '$\sim p$' is more convenient than 'p', or is it only more convenient to think so? What is your criterion for deciding that one convenience has been 'superseded' by another? Is it only convenient to say so, or has it really been superseded? The magician has another trick in waiting: '"Convenience" in this context means' – not convenience at all, but it 'means something like: ability to avoid fruitless disagreements on dead-end issues.' To say that some of these issues are quite fruitful, alive and likely to go on being discussed, would be rather inconvenient for Rorty.

Truth Wears a 'Burka'

When Rorty talks about truth in connection with justifiability or warranted assertibility, he forgets all his gobbledygook about convenience and plays a language game more comprehensible to old-fashioned philosophers.

It is unclear whether he believes that, since there is no such thing as truth, we can't, obviously, get at it, or, since we can never get at it, there is no such thing. Is there a face behind the burka? Rorty sometimes seems to think there is, and sometimes that there is not. Not only is there no truth, there is not even a concept of truth, or, at least, that we do not need such a concept. His mode of writing makes it very difficult to decide what his views of the matter are, and this may, in fact, be due to the fact that he himself doesn't know or hasn't decided. For example, he writes that 'the universal desire for truth is better described as the universal desire for justification'. Is this so because he believes that there is no such thing as truth? Even if there is, we cannot know it or pursue it, because we are unable to recognize it even if we have got it. 'We can never know for sure whether a given belief is true'; all that we can know is that nobody so far has been able to 'summon up any residual objections to it' and 'everybody agrees that it ought to be held'. Normally we would say that if this is so and we have sound reasons in support of our belief, then we take it to be true, but Rorty holds back. 'True', for Rorty, only means 'so far not unjustified', and since (we have earlier noted) justification can only be for an audience, it means only that we 'are concerned about the danger that some day an audience will come into being before which' our 'presently justified beliefs cannot be justified'.[61]

If, however, that dreaded audience does emerge, would we not admit that our previously held and now unjustifiedly held belief was and is false? And what concept of 'false' can we have without having its correlative concept of 'true'? Truth is reached progressively. That position which has withstood all so-far-proffered objections is taken as true, with the proviso that one day it might be seen to be false; but there is no reason to think that, until then, it is not true. Truth also has degrees. The Copernican theory is truer than the Ptolemaic, but that doesn't mean that the latter has no truth, for it is certainly truer than earlier accounts.

The nature of the warrant for taking a belief to be true determines the degree of conviction with which we take it to be true; the strength of our right to take it to be true. The belief that yetis do not exist has a much stronger warrant, and so we have a greater right to believe it to be true, than the belief, at one time, that all swans are white. The latter was based on an insufficient and limited observation, whereas the former is based on a far more thorough and sophisticated search for the creature.

At times Rorty talks like any of us. Listen to this:[62]

> There is, to be sure, something unconditional about truth. This unconditionality is expressed by the fact that once true, always true: we regard people who use the word in such expressions as "once true, but not now" as using it incorrectly.

He adds that '"once justified, always justified" is obviously false', and that to 'say that truth is eternal and unchangeable is just a picturesque way of *restating* this fact about our linguistic practices'. These practices are, of course, based on our concepts of truth and justification.

Rorty is here quite right and sensible. He is, as it were, warning us against the tendency people sometimes have of saying something like this: 'The Ptolemaic theory was once true, but is not so now.' Or: 'It was once true that to go from Bombay to London took about two weeks, but it is not true now.' Rorty's point is: if 'X' was true at any time, it is true for all time; if it is false now, it was false then too. The Ptolemaic theory was not true even when Ptolemy held it (though it was truer than earlier theories), and, if the Bombay-London statement was true then, it is still true, for it appears not to be so only because it is not fully stated, its full statement being: 'When people travelled by ship, to go from Bombay to London took about two weeks'. This statement will remain true even if ships now go much faster.

But even though the Ptolemaic theory was not true when Ptolemy propounded it, he was, we might suppose, warranted and justified in believing it, given the state of scientific knowledge in his day.

We have heard Rorty say that 'justification is relative to an audience'; 'we can never exclude the possibility that some better audience might exist, or come to exist, to whom a belief that is justifiable to us would not be justifiable.' 'But,' he adds, 'there can be no such thing as an "ideal audience" before which justification would be sufficient to ensure truth.'[63] Actually there may be no such thing, now or in the future, but, unless such a thing is conceivable (and even, in general terms, be definable), Rorty cannot make even this statement. But we won't haggle over this. There is much in what Rorty says here that is quite acceptable. Truth can be got at only by way of what, at a particular time, is assessed to be warranted by the facts known and on the basis of the argumentation that is furnished. And truth can only exist in the form of judgements. Every judgement's truth is conditional, depending on innumerable factors. No person making a judgement can guarantee that he has considered all of them or even be sure that he has (explicitly) thought of all of them. One audience may be 'better-informed' than another but may still be ill-informed; not sufficiently informed. Rorty may be surprised to learn that this view (if indeed this formulation by me is his view) is fairly close to that of the British Absolute Idealists. But at this point he parts company from them. For them, each better-informed audience has got nearer the truth, and they believe that, because you cannot ever get at the whole truth (as they also believe), it does not follow that you have got no truth or that it is pointless to forge further in search of it. Rorty holds that you can never get at the truth, big or small. Indeed, on *his* premises, 'better-informed' makes no sense, for information, being about facts or the world, plays no part in knowledge. Galileo was no better informed than Ptolemy, a doctor of medicine than a shaman, or we than the Aztecs.

More recently, Rorty seems to see sense in the idea of an ideal to be aimed at in discourse. In 'conversation' we just had to talk without aiming at anything. 'I think the *only* ideal presupposed by discourse is that of being able to justify your beliefs to a *competent* audience.' He adds, 'But everything depends upon what constitutes a competent audience.'[63] At least and at last we have been extricated out of the notion that one audience is as good as another. And we are also able to answer Rorty's earlier challenging question as to whom we are to address our arguments to – children aged four or convinced Nazis. Answer: Not to children aged four unless they are very precocious. To Nazis? It depends on the subject matter and provided that they are open enough to want a rational discussion. If the discussion is about quantum mechanics, then the answer, in most cases would be a 'No'. If it is about human rights, why not? You may not convince them of your point of view even after months of discussion, but convincing an opponent is different from providing cogent arguments.

But 'competent audience' only takes us half the way. Once again the question pops up: Who is to decide which audience is competent? In this maze we will flounder forever. In matters of argument, there can be no court of final appeal that will give a verdict from outside the argument. The required competence must come out of the arguments and counter-arguments themselves. If a propounder of a new theory believes that nobody with whom he has engaged in discussion is able to refute or even, perhaps, understand his theory, all he can do is hope for a competent audience. Rorty's summing up of the discussion is typical:

> We philosophers who are concerned with democratic politics should leave truth alone, as a sublimely undiscussable topic, and instead turn to the question of how to persuade people to broaden the size of the audience they take to be competent, to increase the size of the relevant community of justification.[65]

This only means that, being democratic (but why should we be?), we should try, through proper education, to make more and more people competent to assess the assertibility of any subject matter. With truth left out in the cold, it is difficult to see how we can do this, or why.

Back to the question of 'true' and 'warranted'. Rorty takes up a principle of warrantability given by Putnam,[66] which reads:

> Whether a statement is warranted or not is independent of whether the majority of one's cultural peers would *say* it is warranted or unwarranted. (Principle 2)

Translating '*say*' in the above as '*think*', the principle means that warrantability does not depend on majority opinion.

Rorty argues as follows: Even if a majority of one's peers reject 'S's statement, can it still be warranted? 'Well, a *majority* can be wrong,' says Rorty, and he even admits that, of course, "*p*" might be true'. But not unless there is 'some way of determining warrant *sub specie aeternitatis*, some natural order of reasons that determines, quite apart from 'S's ability to justify '*p*' to those around him, whether he is really justified in holding '*p*'. Of course he believes there is no such 'natural order of reasons', and, therefore, 'S's statement would remain unwarranted. 'Of course, "*p*" might be *true*,' Rorty grants; perhaps 'S' may be a prophet who somehow knows the truth. Many 'social movements and intellectual revolutions get started by people making *un*warranted assertions, assertions that begin to get warranted only as (in Putnam's words) "our norms and standards of warranted assertability ... evolve".'

Rorty's argument is of considerable interest. Firstly, he does find it makes sense to say a statement is true, even though it is not warranted, which means we can not only have a concept of truth, but even truth itself can exist, and exist even when not warranted. Secondly, even if the majority of one's peers reject a statement for what *they* believe to be lack of warrant; a minority, and 'S' himself, may think it sufficiently warranted. Thirdly, since the possibility of the evolution (or emergence) of norms and standards of warranted assertibility is admitted, it might also be admitted that they can be better or worse; but, then, the old question arises, what is our warrant for accepting these norms and standards as good norms and standards for establishing warranted assertibility? Finally, it is clear that truth and warranted assertibility are matters that transcend the current beliefs of even the majority of the members of the community. So much for Rorty's ethnocentrism.

A Resurrection

Rorty pits his 'ethnocentrism' against the views of Habermas, Apel and Wellmer, for whom 'truth claims "transcend the context

– the local or cultural context – in which they are raised"'.[67] Taking up a quasi-Socratic stance of ignorance, he writes, 'I cannot see what "transcendence" means here. I cannot even see what the point of taking my assertion as "making a truth claim" is'.

So, instead of rebutting the point about transcendence, Rorty questions the very idea of a truth claim. When he is said to be making a claim, he says he is 'informing my interlocutor about my habits of action, giving her hints about how to predict and control my future conversational and non-conversational behaviour', and 'inviting her to disagree with me by telling me about her different habits of action'. (She may, however, have the same habits and so might agree with him.) He may, he says, also be suggesting that he is 'prepared to give reasons' for his belief, or, in fact, be doing 'a thousand other things'.

He may be, but we are concerned here not with his entire autobiography but only with his 'conversational behaviour', which some other people's conversational behaviour refers to as making a truth claim.

Let us indulge in some conversational behaviour of our own. We will make no truth claim but will merely inform Rorty that, because of our very different habits, we totally disagree with him. He can have nothing against that. Our conversational behaviour goes like this:

1. Rorty may be doing ten thousand other things, but that does not mean that therefore he is not claiming truth when he asserts 'p'.

2. When, after informing his interlocutor, he says he is also prepared to give her 'reasons' for his 'belief', it would be interesting to know how Rorty would spell this out or,

as William James would ask, what its cash value might be. If Rorty's statement, 'It is likely to rain today,' tells her that he is going to buy an umbrella or going to stay indoors or to take a cab (which? how will she guess?), what, in terms of habits of behaviour, could amount to his 'reasons' for making this statement?

3. Is giving reasons different from giving information (about habits of behaviour)? Or is it giving more information about other habits of behaviour, so that my reason for saying, 'It is likely to rain today,' is to inform her that I scan the weather forecast every morning?

4. 'When I believe that '*p*', and express my belief….' This implies that he may believe that '*p*' without expressing his belief. He would then be informing himself about his habits of behaviour and giving himself hints about how to predict it and control it (a technique of self-control; Alcoholic Anonymous please note).

5. Normally, if we were to disagree with a person who said, 'It is likely to rain today,' we would say, 'No, it's not likely to.' Or: 'But it's bright sunshine', or something like that, but Rorty's interlocutor, playing his game, would say something like: 'Don't buy an umbrella.' Or: 'Don't stay at home.' No, not even that. She would perhaps *say* that it was not likely to rain, but this would not be anything about rain, it would be information about *her* different habits – that she arises at ten, drives a car, drinks only beer and reads philosophy (postmodern only).

Rorty should not be given credit for these views of his. They are not particularly exciting, nor even new. He has only fished them out of the godown of the pragmatism of William James and Dewey, polished them up with cheap polish and tried to sell them as his invention. Nor should I be given credit for my exposure (if such it is) of this shopworn poppycock. You will find it exposed in two essays of F. H. Bradley, 'On Truth and Practice' and 'On the Ambiguity of Pragmatism' in *Essays on Truth and Reality*.

Transcendence 'Baffles' Rorty

Rorty tells us on what point he agrees with Putnam.[68] He agrees with this statement of Putnam's: we occupy 'the position of beings who cannot have a view of the world that does not reflect our interests and values, but who are, for all that, committed to regarding some views of the world – and for that matter, some interests and values – as better than others'.

1. This statement, which Rorty 'wholeheartedly' endorses, speaks of a view of the world. But for Rorty, we have all along heard, a statement is never about the world or what happens in it (e.g. that it is likely to rain), but is about his own future activity, or rather, not even about his activity as such but only how we should predict and control it (however we understand *it*).

2. How does Rorty understand an idea, which he also agrees with, that some views are better than others? Are they, when expressed in writing, more beautiful, or when spoken, more pleasant to listen to? Or are they more exciting (which would appeal to Rorty)? Or are they, perhaps, better in the way of being *truer*?

Putnam's statement is quite compatible with the thesis of Habermas and others that truth claims 'transcend the context … in which they are raised'. Of course it is true that one's view of the world or of anything *reflects* one's interests and values. Truth is one of the values reflected or, better, aimed at. If a primitive tribesman says that rain falls when the gods weep, or when the members of a certain religion say that their dead visit the earth during certain months, their interests and values are reflected, and the content of what they are saying is believed by them (unless they are in a joking or deceiving mood) and claimed to be true. They may also give their own explanations of their beliefs and furnish their own warrants for them. They would be upset and angry if you doubt them, for they would expect you to agree with them. They would not be satisfied or pleased if you were to try and pacify them by saying, 'But these beliefs of yours only reflect *your* interests and values and concepts of truth.' 'Oh no!' they would retort, 'it is really so.' They would want to justify their beliefs to you who are of a different culture, and you too, on your part, if you had a strong missionary strain in you, would try your best to justify to them your view of the world. It is in this sense that their and your views are said to be 'context-transcendent'. It all 'baffles' Rorty, which is not really surprising since, though it is all quite elementary, he started to run before he walked — even to leap and to war-dance, so that he finds ordinary walking almost impossible.

If a claim is context-transcendent in this sense, so is its evaluation. This means firstly, we are not bound to accept the beliefs of a community, simply because the community believes them, to be true — true in their own way. Secondly, we could have good reasons and evidence to show that the community's views are mistaken; and thirdly, we could, in principle, show the community its errors.

Anyone who makes a statement has a number of interests, even interests in making the particular statement. He may want to impress you with his erudition, or to further a cause, or just to make conversation (in the ordinary sense), or whatever. But the only interest we are here concerned with is the interest of claiming truth, and involves the recognition that all the other interests are irrelevant and, if not seen to be such, are likely to interfere with the objectivity of the claim. 'It can be objective that an interpretation or an explanation is the correct one,' says Putnam, '*given* the interests which are relevant in the context;' relevant to the question of truth, of course. Rorty 'wholeheartedly' agrees with this statement of Putnam's. He further declares, 'I do not think that I have ever written anything suggesting that I wish to alter ordinary ways of using "know", "objective", "fact", and "reason"'; he only gives, he says, a 'philosophical gloss' on ordinary speech. It is for my reader to judge whether it is a gloss or a defacement.

'Mild Ethnocentrism'

A glance at some of Rorty's views on morality will again raise the question of his being a relativist or not.[69]

According to Rorty, a staunch postmodern, you cannot ask, 'Is ours a moral society?' for that would resurrect the dreaded ghost of Archimedes. To answer such a question, he supposes, would require us to stand outside of our society and in some 'larger community called "humanity" which has an intrinsic nature'. This would raise the universalism spook which has given philosophers no end of trouble but has been laid by post-modernism. Morality, for Rorty, is only the 'voice of ourselves as members of a community'. He agrees with the thesis of Sellars and Oakeshott, that 'the core meaning of "immoral action" is "the sort of thing *we* don't do"' as against the sort of thing which animals and 'people of other families, tribes, cultures, or historical epochs' do. This ignores the fact that moral language always carries the further idea that we disapprove of other people doing such things and would want them not to do them. In fact, social reformers always take their stand on the fact that their own society should do things which are not being done, or desist from doing what is being done.

Of course, on Rortyian lines, people of other cultures and even of families other than ours within our own community could well say, 'But *we* do these things. We burn those who disagree with us, we throw people to the lions, we cut off their hands if they steal a loaf of bread, we subject our females to genital mutilation, and so many other things; and we are no more immoral than you are.' Reformers and 'social revolutionaries' who protest against 'immoral' practices in their own society are, thinks Rorty, 'protesting in the name of the society itself against those aspects … which are unfaithful to its own self-image'. But why do they think this self-image worth protecting? If they were true Rortyians they would be bored by it and welcome change. If our society, which, by the norms which it now accepts, is regarded as a fairly decent, honest society, should turn into a corrupt, ruthless one, would the few remaining 'decent' people bemoan the transformation and protest, or should they, following the Sellars-

Oakeshott-Rorty combine, accommodate themselves to the new society?

In any case, we are not talking about a society whose members protest against certain of its prevalent norms; the issue is about different societies, each having its own set of norms peculiar to itself and different from the set of norms of any other society. There is no super-community, Rorty says, 'which stands to my community as my community stands to me'. To each its own; communities and their respective norms are incommensurable.

Even if the notion of a super-community, a *human* community as such, having an image of itself, may seem too unrealistic, there is no reason why societies cannot have and share in common the idea of humanity. Except postmodern prejudice, there is nothing against such a possibility, particularly since Rorty himself can visualize 'the *ideally* liberal society' whose 'ideals can be fulfilled by persuasion rather than force, by reform rather than revolution, by free and open encounters'. Can you not detect, in Rorty's words, a tone of proselytizing fervour? Is he really saying that this can be one kind of society among others having totally opposite ideals, and that we of the liberal societies (or, at least, we who believe in the ideally liberal society) would and should accept this quite comfortably?

Some nine years later, Rorty writes:

> Traditionally, the name of the shared human attribute that supposedly 'grounds' morality is 'rationality'. Cultural relativism is associated with irrationalism because it denies the existence of morally relevant transcendental facts. To agree with Rabossi one must, indeed, be rational in this sense... Philosophers like myself ... see our task

> as a matter of making our own culture – the human
> rights culture – more self-conscious and more powerful,
> rather than demonstrating its superiority to other cultures
> by appeal to something transcultural.[70]

I see in this once again a strong proselytizing strain. Otherwise why should we strive to make the human rights culture more powerful? Isn't there a strong desire in Rorty's words that all societies should become like ours?

To talk of human rights culture while dismissing the idea of humanity (an idea which transcends the concept of particular human beings) is incomprehensible. If within a society, different flourishing sub-social cultures can transcend their sub cultural ideas and think in terms of a human rights culture (as Rorty urges and therefore believes to be possible), it should be equally possible to believe in a human rights culture to which societies, communities and cultures can subscribe. In neither case is there a necessity for the existence of a larger society 'over and above' these various societies, communities and cultures. The hesitation to acknowledge the human rights culture to be superior to other cultures is only a piece of prejudice and false modesty, trying to make out that we are super-liberal, or a piece of sheer deception about what, in our hearts, we really and justifiably believe.

Rorty maintains that 'it seems enough to define moral progress as becoming like ourselves at our best', 'people who are not racist, not aggressive, not intolerant', who are 'always willing to hear the other side, to think out all the implications, and so on'.[71] To which audience is this addressed? Not to *us*, surely, for we know and accept all this, even when sometimes we are not at our best or unless there is some danger of backsliding. Surely then to the members of societies that are still groping in moral darkness. It seems, then, that there is an ideal concept – call it humanity or what you will – which even *we* are not always able to exemplify in our actions, a concept by which all societies could be graded on the path of progress. Cultures are not incommensurable.

What light does this discussion throw on whether Rorty is a relativist or not? To think that 'everyone ought to share our beliefs because our beliefs are rational, true and objective', is 'pernicious ethnocentrism'; Rorty thinks it 'dangerous'. He calls his own view 'mild ethnocentrism', the view that 'being true, rational, or objective is always a matter of *our* procedures for justification coupled with the realization that' these are 'no more grounded than those of other cultures.'[72] From what I have shown above, it is plausible to argue that Rorty's words implicitly suggest that he is in fact dangerously near the pernicious and dangerous type of ethnocentrism. Guignon and Hiley see in him an 'ethnocentric with tolerance instead of dogmatism' and a 'pragmatist comfortable with contingency and solidarity instead of theories'.[73] But Rorty, and Guignon and Hiley too, have to explain how the mild and the dangerous types of ethnocentrism can be reconciled in the same philosopher's mind. Rorty of course, with his 'extraordinary gift for ducking and weaving and laying smoke',[74] would refuse to engage in any 'fruitless' controversy or acknowledge that there is need for any kind of reconciliation.

'Catch Me If You Can'

In spite of Rorty's craving to find or say something new and exciting, we see repeatedly in each of his publications, the same stale stew, cooked over twenty-five years ago, once more warmed up and served without even a fresh dressing: the world does not decide between alternative language games, we never have truth but only warranted justifiability, there are different vocabularies, philosophy (Rortyian style) is one of them, traditional controversies are pointless, we want something new – on and on it goes.

We are told that from 'the outset Rorty has been aware that his vision of pragmatism threatens to lead to charges of relativism'.[75] Indeed, most of his views do present that appearance. But due to his 'profound rejection of the traditional philosophical project', he 'can be dismissive of relativism', because it is an item which figures in that project. Rorty in fact thinks relativism is 'inextricably entangled in misguided philosophical baggage'.[76] 'Not having any epistemology,' writes Rorty, about a philosopher like himself, 'a fortiori he doesn't have a relative one'.[77] A mere denial, of course, amounts to nothing. Often a person is not a good judge of what he himself is. Someone who rejects, profoundly or superficially, the traditional philosophical project, bag and misguided baggage, cannot either be a pragmatist (whatever be his version of it) or pass judgement on relativism, for pragmatism and relativism exist within that tradition. Not only does he pass judgement on it, he says it is 'easy to refute'. One 'would merely use some version of the self-referential argument used by Socrates against Protagoras.'[78] Most philosophies, however diverse or even mutually antagonistic, claim Socrates as their patron saint. Rorty pays a compliment to the founder of the traditional philosophical project. Our master-contortionist finds it easy to turn himself inside out.

References

1. Brandom, R. B. (Ed.), 2001, pp. xvi-xvii.
2. Rorty, R., 1983, p. 6.
3. Rorty, R., 1989, p. 9.
4. Heal, J., 'Pragmatism and Choosing to Believe' in Malachowski, A. R. (Ed.), 1990, p. 102.
5. Ibid., p. 102.
6. O'Grady, P., 2002, p. 108.
7. Conant, J., 'Freedom, Cruelty and Truth' in Brandom, R. B. (Ed.), 2001, pp. 275-77.
8. Rorty, R., 'Response to Bouveresse' in Brandom, R. B. (Ed.), 2001, p. 151.
9. Rorty, R., 'Universality and Truth' in Brandom, R. B. (Ed.), 2001, p. 7.
10. Rorty, R., 'Response to Bouveresse', op. cit., p. 151.
11. Rorty, R., 1989, p. 5.
12. Davidson, D., 'Truth Rehabilitated' in Brandom, R. B. (Ed.), 2001, pp. 66, 73.
13. Heal, J., op. cit., pp. 103-4.
14. Ibid., p. 104.
15. Davidson, D., op. cit., p. 72.
16. Rorty, R., 1998, p. 74.
17. Rorty, R., 1983, p. 186.
18. Guignon, C. & D. R. Hiley (Eds.), 2003, p. 9.
19. Ibid., p. 11.
20. Rorty, R., 1983, p. 178.
21. Ibid., p. 318.
22. Ibid., p. 319.
23. Rorty, R., 'Response to Bouveresse', op. cit., p. 152.
24. Rorty, R., 1983, pp. 96-97.
25. Guignon, C. & D. R. Hiley (Eds.), 2003, p. 8.
26. Rorty, R., 1983, p. 11.
27. Guignon, C. & D. R. Hiley (Eds.), 2003, p. 9.
28. Ibid., pp. 9-10.

29. Rorty, R., 1989, pp. 11-12.
30. Ibid., p. 16.
31. Rorty, R., 1983, p. 322.
32. Rorty, R., 1989, p. 6.
33. Ibid., pp. 12-13.
34. Rorty, R., quoted by Festenstein, M. & S. Thompson (Eds.), *Rorty – Critical Dialogues*, 2001, p. 142.
35. Rorty, R., 1998, p. 72.
36. Ibid., p. 72.
37. Putnam, H., 'Richard Rorty on Reality and Justification' in Brandom, R. B. (Ed.), 2001, p. 81.
38. Rorty, R., 1998, p. 73.
39. Ibid., p. 6.
40. Ibid., p. 7.
41. Ibid., p. 71.
42. Ibid., p. 72.
43. Ibid., pp. 51-53.
44. Guignon, C. & D. R. Hiley (Eds.), 2003, p. 24.
45. Rorty, R., 1998, p. 7.
46. Guignon, C. & D. R. Hiley (Eds.), 2003, p. 24.
47. Rorty, R., 'Universality and Truth', op. cit., p. 14.
48. Ibid., p. 17.
49. Rorty, R., 1989, p. xiii.
50. Guignon, C. & D. R. Hiley (Eds.), 2003, p. 24.
51. Ibid., p. 24; quotation from Rorty, R., *Consequences of Pragmatism*, 1982, p. 166.
52. Rorty, R., 1989, p. 4.
53. Ibid., p. 20.
54. Sorell, T., 'The World from Its Own Point of View', in Malachowski, A. R. (Ed.), 1990, pp. 11-12.
55. Rorty, R., 1989, p. 19.
56. Elstain, J., 'Don't Be Cruel' in Guignon, C. & D. R. Hiley (Eds.), 2003, pp. 143-44.
57. Rorty, R., 1989, p. 20.

58. Rorty, R., 1983, pp. 330-31.
59. Rorty, R., 1998, pp. 56-57.
60. Rorty, R., 'Universality and Truth', op. cit., p. 2.
61. Ibid., p. 4.
62. Rorty, R., 'Response to Habermas', in Brandom, R. B. (Ed.), 2001, p. 57.
63. Rorty, R., 1998, p. 22.
64. Rorty, R., 'Universality and Truth', op. cit., p. 9.
65. Ibid., p. 9.
66. Rorty, R., 1998, pp. 49-50.
67. Rorty, R., 'Universality and Truth', op. cit., pp. 9-10.
68. Rorty, R., 1998, pp. 43-44.
69. Rorty, R., 1989, pp. 59-60.
70. Rorty, R., 1998, p. 171.
71. Ibid., pp. 5, 52.
72. Guignon, C. & D. R. Hiley (Eds.), 2003, p. 27.
73. Ibid., p. 28.
74. Ibid., p. 30.
75. Ibid., p. 17.
76. O'Grady, P., 2002, p. 110.
77. Rorty, R., 'Objectivism, Relativism and Truth' (1991) quoted by O'Grady, P., 2002, p. 110.
78. Rorty, R., *Consequences of Pragmatism* (1982), quoted by O'Grady, P., 2002, p. 110.

Chapter 13

The Wonderworld of Feminism

'...many small knowledges, and each of them dangerous'

Samuel Butler, *The Way of All Flesh*

Although feminists are very close to postmodernism and endorse most of its notions, they have their own ways of expounding them and they also have some interesting peculiarities of their own.

Feminists are, of course, much concerned about socio-ethical matters, particularly those that affect women and what they refer to as the marginalized sections of humanity. 'Feminist ethics is grounded in a commitment to ending the oppression, subordination, abuse and exploitation of women.'[1] This at once suggests that their treatment of ethical and other related issues is not philosophically disinterested but is coloured by their commitment.

Feminists believe they have much to say in many areas that is different from, and often opposed to, traditionally held views, specially those held by mainstream Western philosophers. The most important areas are knowledge and reasoning. Feminists are greatly concerned, and rightly so, about the kind of knowledge generally called 'science', which includes the positive sciences such as physics, biology, astronomy, psychology and sociology. Of these, physics is generally considered to be the most exact.

Two of the essential ingredients of science are its neutrality or objectivity and the necessity of justification.

Neutrality and objectivity are often held by feminists to be synonymous, but objectivity is sometimes acclaimed and sometimes denigrated because it means different things to them at different times. Neutrality, because of its association with the Archimedean Point, is always dismissed as impossible and therefore absurd. Objectivity's other name is impartiality; it is the absence of bias. Feminists claim that objectivity, as conventionally understood (that is, as understood by objectivists), is not real objectivity and not really impartial. According to the high priestess of feminism, Sandra Harding, Standpoint Feminist Epistemology differs from Standpoint Empiricism in that the latter accepts the objectivist notion of objectivity and only wants to improve on it by more rigorous and careful investigation, whereas Standpoint Epistemology challenges this conventional scientific model. Both groups, of course, want objectivity of some kind. However, Evelyn Fox Keller, feminist mouthpiece, bemoans the fact that feminists themselves are tempted to 'abandon their claim for representation in scientific culture' and 'return to a purely "female" subjectivity, leaving rationality and objectivity in the male domain'; by 'rejecting objectivity as a masculine ideal', feminist relativism 'lends its voice to an enemy chorus and dooms women to live outside modern culture' and so 'exacerbates the very problem it wishes to solve'.[2]

Neutrality or the Fear of Being Nowhere

'Are the sciences neutral with respect to social issues and social values, their harm or benefit arising solely from the uses to which knowledge … is put?' ask Fox Keller and H. Longino.[3] Their answer is, they are not, and this, they think, is the same as saying that they do not respect social and cultural values. Where does impartiality come in?

The 'dominant view' until the 1960s was, we learn, that 'science consisted of logical reasoning applied to observational and experimental data acquired by value-neutral and context-independent methods', but in 1960 many 'historians and historically minded philosophers (that is, themselves and worthies like Kuhn and Feyerabend) 'decisively challenged this vision'. Scientific observation is 'never innocent', but is always 'influenced by theoretical commitments' or is 'theory-laden'.[4]

Objectivity or The Wanted-Unwanted

When feminists rail against objectivity they are against what they call the 'conventional conception of objectivity'. According to one view, it is not that it is 'too rigorous or too "objectifying"'… but that it is *not rigorous or objectifying enough* … too weak to accomplish even the goals for which it has been designed, let alone more difficult projects called for by feminisms'.[5] It may be pointed out that objectivity is not something that is 'designed' by scientists as if it is part of a scientific procedure. It is a basic presupposition: without it science cannot hope to pursue its goals of understanding and acting upon the world.

Harding writes that from the viewpoint of Standpoint, conventional standards are weak because they advance 'only the "objectivism" that has so widely been criticized', that is, the standards are weak because they are objectivism's standards and objectivism is rejected by feminists. Objectivism, Harding says, 'too narrowly operationalizes the notion of maximizing objectivity.'[6] This 'conception of value-free, impartial, dispassionate research is supposed to direct the identification of all social values and their elimination from the results of research, yet it has been operationalized to identify and eliminate' only certain values and interests, that is, those of African-Americans, of women and of those who are the victims of racism and sexism. If these are excluded, then they will not 'be identified within a community of scientists' who 'benefit – intentionally or not – from institutionalized racism and sexism.'[7]

Whether this is so or not is a question of fact and has nothing to do with the nature and true meaning of objectivity. No fault is found with 'value-free, impartial, dispassionate' research as such in that part of science which is 'controlled by methods of research' and 'methodological rules'. So, as far as the crucial issue of our discussion is concerned, that about objectivism's too weak concept of objectivity, nothing is done to establish its weakness as such. In fact it is that very objectivity or impartiality itself, which, according to Standpoint, is used only in the methodological part, which is sought to be extended to the results of research. Besides, there is confusion here. The impression given is that somehow, after the research is completed, the social values and interests of certain groups have been identified and eliminated from the results. What, of course, is meant is that these values and interests have been ignored at the *start* of the research and have, therefore, not appeared in the results. That this is what is meant is clear from what follows.

It is contended that objectivism, due to its blindness, looks upon the methodological part only as truly scientific; the part 'in which problems are identified ... hypotheses are formulated, key concepts are defined', is 'thought to be unexaminable within science by rational methods'.[8] This is sheer nonsense. In any case, even in this co-called 'context of discovery', the same concepts of objectivity or impartiality have surely to operate, and that is exactly what our author is (without realizing it) demanding.

Objectivists are said to 'claim that objectivity requires the elimination of all social values and interests from the research processes and the results of research', but, says Harding, 'not *all* social values and interests have the same bad effects upon the results of research.'[9] It is, then, admitted that some do, and those are precisely the ones that are likely to prejudice the results and make them agree with 'already formulated hypotheses' (hypotheses which you want, willy-nilly, to be confirmed), and so spoil the integrity and impartiality of the research. For example, it is the interests and wishful thinking of the astrologers that have to be kept out if you are researching into the truth or fraud of astrology. It is not 'democracy-*advancing* values (italics mine) that generate,' as it is suggested, 'less partial and distorted beliefs', for this worthy motive is extra-scientific; but what would generate such beliefs are those values which may perhaps be called democratic: seeking truth as widely as possible and researching without bias or distortion. Nothing is wrong with the objectivist's conception of objectivity, it is the Standpoint conception that is mistaken because thoroughly confused.

Some feminists claim that the notion of objectivity is 'so hopelessly tainted by its use in racist, imperialist, bourgeois, homophobic and androcentric scientific projects' that it 'should be abandoned altogether.'[10] However, 'there is not only one legitimate way to conceptualize objectivity'; it is 'transformed into "strong objectivity" by the logic of Standpoint epistemologies'.[11] This is one of the standard feminist-postmodernist ploys. Unable to maintain their stand regarding a concept, they switch to alternative definitions, which, of course, leaves the discussion about the matter as originally defined high and dry.

This 'strong objectivity', which conceptualizes objectivity in a different and, presumably, more acceptable way, 'retains *central* features of the older conception'(italics mine).[12] So, our old friends are there all right, safe and sound – impartiality, etc., and Harding adds, 'might should not make right in the realm of knowledge production.' 'Understanding ourselves and the world around us requires understanding what others think of us and our beliefs and actions, not just what we think of ourselves and them.' This is objectivity carried much further than even we had thought. It is comforting to know that there are goals common to both science and Standpoint. The 'appeal to objectivity is an issue' not only between feminists and non-feminists, but also 'within each feminist … agenda', for there are 'many feminisms, some of which result in claims that distort the racial, class, sexuality, and gender relationships in society'. So you see, partiality and distortion is not the privilege of those who benefit from racism and sexism. The last sentence of the article from which these gems are selected is disturbing: 'The notion of objectivity is useful in providing a way to think about the gap that should exist between how any individual or group wants the world to be and how in fact it is.' *Should* exist? Do they really want the gap to be perpetuated?

So, we now know what strong objectivity is. Some earlier statements need to be examined. The argument for strong objectivity that we have so far considered is that in conventional science practices, impartial research was restricted to that part of science which is 'controlled by methods of research' and not extended to the 'context of discovery', but a page earlier, Harding includes much more under strong objectivity. It 'requires that the subject of knowledge be placed on the same critical, causal plane as the objects of knowledge', that 'objectivity-maximizing procedures be focused on the nature [of what?] and/or social relationships that are the direct objects of observation and reflection must also be focused on the observers and reflectors – scientists and the larger society whose assumptions they share.'[13] 'This is because culture-wide (or almost culture-wide) beliefs function as evidence at every stage in scientific inquiry', that is, even in the part called the 'context of inquiry', 'the selection of problems, the formation of hypotheses, the design of research ... the collection of data ... decisions about when to stop research, the way results of research are reported, and so on'. Even, believe it or not, the 'organization of research committees', whatever those are, is considered part of the research.[14] Perhaps even their salaries.

The 'context of inquiry' here includes so much that it is not clear what is left for the other part. Surely, apart from the last-mentioned item, everything else would generally be considered to be part of 'methods of research'. Except where scientific knowledge is employed in the tackling of a social or civic problem or problems affecting individuals, even the selection of a problem of research is determined by the nature of the subject matter and the stage the science has so far reached. Whatever the reason for selecting the subject matter of a research project, an impartial and dispassionate approach is the core of the 'objectivity maximizing procedures'.

That scientists themselves, the observers and reflectors, and even the 'historically located social community whose un-examined beliefs its members are likely to hold "unknowingly"', 'must be considered as part of the object of knowledge' along with what would ordinarily be called the object of research (e.g., the behaviour of an animal species or of a gas), is simply bizarre. If there were to be any doubts about the competence of the researcher or any suspicion that he is likely to be influenced by community factors extraneous to the investigation at hand, you could institute a separate inquiry into these matters. Trying to pursue the two different inquiries within the same research would be something like watching yourself (not your image) in a film you are watching; someone else can watch a film and also simultaneously see you watching it, but *you* can't do this. Harding's requirement is part of the confused postmodernist rejection of the distinction between the subject and object of knowledge.

Towards objectivity, as towards other things, feminists take an ambivalent attitude. They either accept and claim it but want to improve on the conventional concept of it or they challenge it and recommend a substitute.

'Spontaneous feminist empiricists' (a name probably coined by Harding) hold that sexist and androcentric results in research are due to 'insufficient care and rigour in following existing methods' and hence urge greater care and rigour along the same lines. They 'try to fit feminist projects into prevailing standards of "good science"', but, says Harding, even when the dominant conceptions 'are most rigorously respected', they 'distort results of research'. Standpoint theorists, of whom she is the high priestess, produce 'stronger standards' to 'maximize objectivity'.[15] In doing so, of course, they change the very concept of objectivity. 'From the perspective of Standpoint epistemology', writes Harding, 'even rigorous pre-feminist methods of testing hypotheses is *far too weak a strategy*'[16] to maximize objectivity, because pre-feminist science does not make it possible for the voice of the oppressed to be heard and is only concerned in protecting itself from the intrusion of politics, whereas 'all knowledge attempts are socially situated'.[17]

Whether the voice of the oppressed gets to be heard or not is a question of fact; our question was about the strength or weakness of 'the methods for the testing of hypotheses' (notice 'testing'), and whether you are concerned about the oppressed or anybody or anything else is beside the point. This is an instance of another standard trick: try to make the reader forget what we were talking about and slip on to something else – the track-changing game.

Even if certain research projects would achieve greater 'objectivity' by starting from the lives of the oppressed, this requirement would be entirely irrelevant to an immense amount of research in problems about the natural, non-human world. Feminists are constantly thinking that the social sciences constitute the whole of science, whereas they constitute a very small part of it. (This may be called 'the mouse's point of view'.) Against 'the most fundamental assumptions of the scientific world-view and the Western thought that takes science as its model of how to produce knowledge', Standpoint, which challenges this, 'sets out a rigorous "logic of discovery" intended to maximize the objectivity of the results ... thereby produce knowledge that can be *for* marginalized people...'[18] Asserting that the problems of the marginalized, grave as they are, form the sum of scientific problems and the notion that Western science is '*for* the use only of dominant groups in their projects of ... managing the lives of marginalized people'[19], are two of the hobby-horses that feminists ride all the time.

Let us consider some of the features in which Standpoint epistemology claims to differ from Conventional empirical epistemology:[20]

Conventional Epistemology	Standpoint Epistemology
A1. The subject or researcher is 'invisible, disembodied', having 'no determinate historical location'.	B1. The subjects 'start from some particular set of lives' and 'conceptual frameworks' are of a 'particular historical moment'.

The researcher is disembodied only in the sense that, as long as he is assumed to be adequately trained and reasonably competent in his subject, and as long as he takes all the standard precautions to avoid being swayed by personal factors, inclinations, likes and dislikes, which are extraneous and irrelevant to the task at hand; that is, as long as he is impartial in the only sense that matters, his personal biography has no connection with the research and, in

304 • Human Reason and Its Enemies

this sense and this sense only, he has 'no determinate historical location' and is 'invisible'. It is absurd to suggest that he is not located at a particular place doing a particular piece of research from a particular point of view at a particular time according to – not *any* conceptual framework but – one that is appropriate to the particular inquiry.

A2. The subject is 'different in kind from the objects of the study' which are 'located in determinate space/time co-ordinates'.	B2. Subjects are 'not fundamentally different from the objects of study.'

The point that is sought to be made is so vaguely stated that it cannot be meaningfully answered. What kind of difference is visualized? Different in what way? If the subject (that is, the investigator) is investigating, say, a new animal species or the behaviour of a gas, he is certainly very different from these in several ways, including location in space. If he is researching into a historical event, he is located differently from it even in time. If he is inquiring into gravitation or the theory of evolution, these have no space/time location, though, of course, he has.

Harding, trying to clarify, adds that even objects of natural science are not fundamentally different from the researcher for they, too, are objects of knowledge, 'appearing to scientists only within specific scientific traditions and local cultures'. Even if, for the sake of argument, we don't dispute that objects assume a certain character by becoming objects of knowledge and that as 'objects-of-knowledge' they are not fundamentally different from each other, even so, the difference between them and the researcher is not obliterated, particularly because he is not himself a part of the phenomenon under investigation. Even if a scientist were trying to understand himself, *as the object of investigation*, he would still be different from himself *as the investigator*.

A3. Knowledge is 'produced by' 'individuals or groups', not by 'cultures, genders, races, or classes'.	B3. 'Historical moments' and 'communities and not individuals' produce knowledge.

As usual, these contentions are too obscure to be commented on.

Are communities not groups? Are races or classes not made up of individuals? If individuals were to be eliminated, would historical moments and communities float around on their own? And genders too?

A4. Knowledge 'is to be consistent and coherent' and 'the subject of knowledge must be homogenous, unitary, coherent'.	B4. 'These subjects are multiple, heterogeneous, and conflicted.'

One has reached a point where one feels that the ground beneath one's feet is shifting. When Harding talks of 'subject' she seems to mean object, for how could subjects (that is, researchers) be homogenous or heterogeneous, unitary or multiple, coherent or conflicting? And if she means objects, then what does she mean by saying they are 'conflicted'? How can objects be in conflict if they are not fundamentally different? We soon learn what is meant. But before that it may be pointed out that, a little later, the subjects are said to be 'contradictory'. Are 'conflicted' and 'contradictory' synonyms? Contradiction is a logical relation between propositions; neither objects nor persons (subjects) can be contradictory. Even bitter enemies cannot be, though they can be in conflict. Conflicted? Who knows? There are 'gaps between the values and interests of women's lives' and 'those that have organized the dominant conceptual frameworks'. These, then, are the things that are conflicted. These gaps are 'crucial', for the 'most fruitful feminist problematics have emerged out of the gaps' and, it seems, feminist standpoint must keep focusing on these gaps and (as we have noticed earlier) must see to it that the gaps should continue to exist for feminist survival. So, now we know what feminist standpoint is. It is multiple, heterogeneous and contradictory – or conflicted.

It is clear that while feminists reject objectivity as ordinarily understood, the objectivity that they want means simply the representation, in research, of women and marginalized groups. You hear this repeatedly. '"Subjugated" standpoints are preferred because they seem to promise more adequate, sustained, objective ... accounts of the world'[21] and, says Harding, 'selecting problematics' from 'women's lives can provide more reliable "grounds" for knowledge'.[22] Women 'occupy a privileged epistemic standpoint' for seeing 'the partiality of a dominant androcentric and sexist world view'.[23] In these quotations, 'objective' (used approvingly) and 'partiality' (used pejoratively) bear conventional meanings – the absence and presence, respectively, of bias that could distort reality. 'Objective' does not bear the extended meaning given to it by feminists. Try as hard as they might, they cannot get rid of the conventionally accepted requirement of good research. Whether this actually obtains in current research or not is not our concern here. We are only concerned with the mess that feminists create over the concept of objectivity.

Let's look at another instance of track-change. Rae Langton writes, 'Women are actively hurt' by the idea that objectivity 'is the stance of the traditional male knower' and that this objectivity is taken to mean that 'things are independent of us, and their behaviour is … determined by their natures'.[24] Both the points are resisted by feminists, the latter because of their congenital hostility to essentialism.

Langton, however, concedes that 'when it comes to practical matters, our actions will of course need to accommodate the natures of things, if we are to achieve our practical goals,' and, 'thus understood, objectivity seems to be an innocuous enough collection of epistemic and practical norms governing one's reasoning about the world'.[25] This implies that in our *theoretical* reasoning about the world, objectivity is not so harmless.

One would naturally suppose that in theoretical reasoning, since women are hurt by the idea that objectivity is a stance only of the male knower, they would argue that it is equally the stance of female knowers. One may agree that objectivity is about how *mind* (presumably both male and female) conforms to the world. But instead of following this line, Langton jumps on to a different track to talk about 'objectification', that is, 'the ways in which *the world* conforms to the mind', meaning thereby nothing very

308 • Human Reason and Its Enemies

startling but simply the 'process in which the social world comes to be shaped by perception, desire and belief'.[26] (Note that this talk is only about the social world, but there is really no need to restrict the point to that world, for even the physical world can be changed, at least by our desires.) This is objectification. Langton, quoting Marilyn Frye, writes that the male so 'manipulates the environment' and also the 'perception and judgment' of woman that 'the course she chooses will be such as coheres with his purposes'. This objectifying of woman is 'where seeing women as subordinate *makes* women subordinate' (italics mine), and then, having perpetrated this wicked transformation, men somehow 'believe that women are in part submissive … by nature'.

But this, Langton assures us, 'is quite illusory'. Having said that, however, we are told that 'under conditions of oppression, that belief' (that women are submissive by nature) 'will be a true belief', that is, they truly are submissive by nature! The argument seems quite conflicted! But, whether they are or not, the starting point of this excursion was not whether women are objects by nature or whether men believe that they are objects by nature or they are made objects by men or men believe that they are made objects; the starting point was whether *objectivity* – the belief that things are independent of us – was a stance of only the male knower, an idea that hurt women. Feminists (perhaps un-consciously) spin such a rigmarole that they are apt to forget the starting-point; they would be surprised to find how sound other people's memories are. Feminists are also skilled users of what might be called the Protagoras *techne*.

Of Science or the Feminist Spinning Wheel

'... if shape it can be called that shape has none'

John Milton, *Paradise Lost*

Feminists adopt a superior attitude when it comes to science. Science 'embodies a strong androcentric bias', asserts Fox Keller, and continues, patronizingly (or matronizingly), that it could 'benefit scientists to attend closely to feminist criticism'.[27] Feminists state that 'there is not just one legitimate way to conceptualize objectivity, any more than there is only one way to conceptualize freedom, democracy or science'.[28] These conceptions, as conventionally held, are very different from the way feminists understand them. According to Donna Haraway, the Trumpet Voice of Feminism, there is even 'no single feminist standpoint' because there are many dimensions to their visions. The goal, however, seems to be one: 'better accounts of the world, that is, "science"'.[29] While we must be grateful for this assurance (because we were not quite sure), the earlier statements are typical examples of a standard strategy to avoid being pinned down to a consistent response to our queries, the strategy of changing shape. Call it the Protean operation.

In feminist discussions of science we find, as elsewhere, a polymorphous character. Either science as such is rejected and something, we know not what, is substituted for it, or science, as we know it, is accepted but sought to be improved upon, or there are said to be two rival sciences, the old and the new. To be called 'scientific' is, we know, a stamp of respectability, so however different this new somewhat may be from the old science, it has to be called science.

We may remember Fox Keller and Longino telling us that in 1960 the dominant view that scientific knowledge consisted of logical reasoning applied to data resulting in a 'single, unified account', value-free and objective, of the world, was challenged. It should be realized that logical reasoning as such was not challenged. We are told that the claim made by Genevieve Lloyd, the Woman of Reason, in her famous *The Man of Reason,* is not about the nature of reason but about what has historically been construed by philosophers as reason, namely 'the thing we call Reason'.[30]

Feminist ideas about reason will be considered later. There is, in feminist writing, a continuing wavering between science, thought of as an exclusively male activity, and two sciences, a male and a female science.

Haraway has told us that the goal of science is a better account of the world. Longino accepts 'the central goals of science' to be 'producing empirically adequate, objective, explanatorily powerful theories', and, although as a loyal feminist, she goes on to talk of contextual values, it is interesting to know what she has to say about them: the goals of science 'are best served not by ignoring or suppressing contextual values, but by making them explicit and subjecting them to critical scrutiny'.[31] So, entirely contrary to the general feminist position where theory is supposed to be (perhaps exclusively) determined by social values, they are now, according to Longino, to be critically scrutinized. And why so except to avoid bias and achieve objectivity — conventional objectivity? She wants knowledge claims to be subjected to 'critical assessment from as many different angles as possible' in order to discover errors and limitations'. This is exactly what scientists, even male ones, do in the interests of objectivity.

I shall first dispose of some of the more trivial feminist criticisms of science.

In highly charged rhetoric, the Trumpet Voice proclaims that the history of science is 'tied to militarism, capitalism, colonialism, and male supremacy'; everything 'in the interests of unfettered power' from satellite surveillance to home video; just one 'unregulated gluttony'.[32] Harding, more restrained, tells us that 'at the heart of science' there is 'a kind of lawlessness' institutionalized by the conventional notion of objectivity, which refuses to 'theorize any criteria internal to scientific goals for distinguishing between scientific method' and things like 'torture or ecological destruction'.[33]

Since these are just factual claims, they do not have to be considered here. They are, as is usual when feminists are enraged, highly exaggerated. Even if science is tied to militarism, etc. (as if it is also not tied to medical relief and so on), this does not show that science as such reflects social, cultural and other similar values, nor does it negate the claim that the harms and benefits of science arise 'solely from the uses to which knowledge ... is put'. It is difficult to see why or how the conventional notion of objectivity is expected to furnish criteria to distinguish scientific method from torture and ecological destruction. It is also difficult to see how such criteria could be internal to scientific goals, which, as we have been told by the Trumpet Voice, are the giving of 'better accounts of the world'. One would have thought that scientists were capable of distinguishing between science, and torture and ecological destruction!

Deep down within them, feminists want to prove that science is inherently flawed because, by its very nature, it is biased against women and other groups and therefore not objective as claimed by the dominant view. Not knowing how to do this, they catch at any straw and go to any lengths to make good their claim. Since reason is considered to be the core of science and philosophy, reason has to be denigrated. But instead of straightforwardly pointing out where it has gone wrong, it is attacked obliquely. Thus, it is said that philosophers' conceptions of reason have tended to align it with 'cultural conceptions of masculinity' and conceived it as 'superior to intuition and emotion which the cultural imagination has associated with femininity'.[34]

This is cited only as the philosophers' view of reason; whether it is so or not, others are not obliged to accept it. Nor need we believe that reason is, in every sense, superior to intuition and emotion. All that we need to hold is that, as far as science (and, indeed, any intellectual discipline) is concerned, reason is, not a superior, but the only faculty that can do the work and achieve objectivity, which, if intuition (that is, non-scientific intuition) and emotion were resorted to, would be compromised. Nothing in Lloyd's 'influential line of argument' has remotely shown that there is some inherent defect in reason, which therefore fails to achieve objectivity, or that intuition or emotion should be substituted for it. Whether reason is male or female or mammalian or of the *homo sapiens* brand is, as usual, a red herring.

Other red herrings about reason and science slither about in feminist literature. We are told that even in 'explicitly gendered inquiries' in the social and life sciences, there have been 'gaps' in 'understanding' when 'researchers exclude women and gender as a subject of inquiry'; and 'systematic distortions' occur when gender differences are 'encapsulated in terms of stereotypes'.[35] Even granting, for argument's sake, the truth of these contentions, what they amount to is that such lacunae make the inquiries inadequate and distorted and so produce one-sided results. They do not show bias in the 'logical reasoning' applied to the data.

'It is possible to think', write Fricker and Hornsby, 'that the male philosophers who have addressed the question have not always subsumed everyone with their "we's" and their "our's"', and this makes one question whether their 'generic conception is the ... neutral one that their universal claims would require'.[36] It is unclear what this sentence means, starting as it does with 'it is possible to think'. Are male scientists also as guilty in this as male philosophers are said to be? Why are we talking of philosophers all of a sudden? In any case our authors' charge against the philosophers has misfired. That the conception of neutrality does not match their universal claims is, as far as feminists are concerned, not a serious defect, since they have a 'suspicion of *any* universal claim' because human subjects are 'socially ... diverse beings' (italics mine).[37] They do not fault the male philosophers (and scientists too) for not matching their conceptions with their universal claims; they fault them for making universal claims. Further charges refer to 'gender inequalities in the training, representation and recognition of women in the sciences', to the allegation that women were 'rarely admitted to the major scientific academies and universities ... until the last fifty years'. So, this defect has been rectified ten years before the feminist challenge to scientific objectivity! It is also admitted that women, even so far back, had 'growing representation in graduate programmes'.[38] Due to 'unfair employment practices', writes Fox Keller, 'almost all scientists are men' (which is because, as we shall see later, all humans are men and all women mammals), yet problems taken up in the health sciences are 'focused primarily' on techniques to be used by women. However, Fox Keller is good enough to admit that 'this kind of criticism does not touch our conception of what science is, nor our confidence in the neutrality of science'. Coming to the design and interpretation of experiments, she points out that 'virtually all of the animal-learning research is done on male rats (but males are rats, aren't they?), because there is the assumption that 'the males represent the species'.[39]

Fox Keller makes further admissions. 'Evidence for bias in the interpretation of observations and experiments is very easy to find in the more socially oriented sciences' and 'critiques are almost exclusively aimed at the "softer" … sciences' and so 'can be accommodated within the traditional framework' by the argument that these sciences are 'not sufficiently scientific'. She does not answer this; in fact, she admits that it 'is much more difficult' to find bias in the 'hard' sciences and asks 'scientifically minded' scientists (whatever that means) 'to make these "soft" sciences more rigorous'.[40]

It should be clear that none of all this touches the core issue of the neutrality and objectivity of science. I now proceed to deal with more serious and interesting challenges to conventional science.

Fox Keller and Longino point out that 'the development of scientific knowledge cannot be understood as a matter of accumulation, the addition of more detail or theoretical sophistication to a stable base'.[41] Quite correct. Because, as against foundationalism, there are no incorrigible and absolutely bedrock empirical statements that cannot be revised in the light of new discoveries and according to the criterion of comprehensive coherence. However, the next statement seems to show that our authors have failed to properly understand the full import of what they are asserting. 'Stability itself,' they continue, 'is temporary', as if science is rather wobbly – therefore not entirely reliable and not to be taken seriously. The reason for this so-called instability is that science is 'subject to periodic rupture in the course of what Kuhn termed scientific revolutions'.[42]

My earlier, full discussion of scientific revolutions should be enough to show that they constitute one of the merits of science and are in no way the cause of the alleged instability of science.

Alison Wylie grants the value of evidence and the 'ideals of objectivity' as 'the key features' of science, but speaks of their 'sociopolitical dimensions', which 'can be understood using the resources of ... post-positivist contextualism'.[43] Lynn Nelson and Longino admit that 'authoritative knowledge is evidentially grounded', but propose 'a quite fundamental reformulation of what counts as evidence and as epistemic agents (presumably, the scientists). Nelson argues that 'hypotheses are always embedded in networks of assumptions'.[43] This, if interpreted correctly, is a true statement and is in line with the idea that observation is 'theory-laden' (as correctly understood). I shall explain this presently. Instead of pursuing this line, Wylie runs off on to a diversion. She says agents are 'interdependent; they never produce ... knowledge in isolation from one another', and 'consequently evidence, and the knowledge based on it, should be regarded as a collective achievement'.[43] There is nothing to suggest that the pursuit of science must necessarily be a collective effort. There have been, as far as we know, significant individual scientific achievements. Considering the present advanced state of science, it may be conceded that, by and large, scientific work today demands collective effort. This talk about collective achievement is, like the voluble chatter of a conjuror or a dentist, an attempt to distract your attention from what is going on under your nose.

The next act is to jump to the conclusion that agents 'should be conceived as communities' in order to 'play a crucial role in determining what counts as an observation and what bearing it has on exploratory and generalizing knowledge claims'.[43] This is a (perhaps intentionally) clumsy way of saying that it is communities and not individuals that are the researchers and, further, that what counts as evidence and observation is determined by community norms or what communities think they are. Not only is knowledge produced by communities, as we have earlier heard from Harding, but it is also what communities think it is. This claim will be dealt with below under 'situated knowledge'.

Fox Keller and Gronthowski wish to prove male domination in a novel way.[44] In the 'traditional hierarchy of the senses', they write, 'the emphasis is accorded to the visual'; 'the logic of Western thought is too rooted in the visual', which shows an 'unwholesome' bias against the other senses because of 'the belief in vision as a "higher" and touch of "lower" sense'[sic.], vision being a 'peculiarly phallic sense'. The other senses, I suppose, are thus 'marginalized'. Since 'women find more pleasure in touch than in sight' and 'the prevalence of the gaze' (quoting the words of Luce Irigaray) is 'peculiarly foreign to female eroticism', the 'logic of the visual is a male logic' (Fox Keller and Gronthowski). Since this is the logic that operates and has always operated in science, science is fundamentally male and has to be excommunicated. The 'voyeur's theory' which reigns in science and which puts a 'strange emphasis on externality and the specular' is unacceptable to feminists because, as Irigaray says, 'women's desire does not speak the same language as men's desire'.

Feminists have also 'drawn a connection between the identification of nature as female and the scientific mind as male', which makes feminists 'question the very idea of scientific method capable of adjudicating the truth or probability of theories in a value-neutral way'.[45] The grounds for drawing these identifications are not revealed; it is a piece of fertile feminist imagination. Still, it shows that at least some feminists prize the concepts of value-neutral adjudication and of truth.

I take up the question of the theory-ladenness of observation. This is stressed by Fox Keller and Longino in their Introduction and again by Longino in her 'Feminist Philosophers of Science'.[46] Here we find a mix of truth and error. It is true that observation is theory-laden, but this has to be properly understood and, if it is so understood, Longino need not worry about protecting 'theory choice from subjective elements hidden in background assumptions'. 'It need not follow,' she admits, 'that scientific knowledge is impossible of attainment.' Applying 'feminist insight', she tells us that she has 'suggested' that 'scientific knowledge is constructed not by individuals applying a method to the material to be known but by individuals in interaction with one another in ways that modify their observations, theories and hypotheses, and patterns of reasoning'.

It is admitted that scientific knowledge, in spite of hidden subjective elements, *is* possible, which means that there are methods by which these elements can be ferreted out, exposed and discounted. Instead of clearly telling us what these methods are, she rambles on about the interaction between (probably female) researchers and how they modify observation, etc. Lost in this morass about individuals in interaction, she forgets to explore why and how they modify their observations, and so she misses the crucial point that this mutual modification is done in order to eliminate subjective bias and attain as much neutrality as possible. There is a methodology of doing this which male insight has discovered since the dawn of science. In any case, after all this modifying by interacting individuals, what next? Does application to observed data come into the picture or not?

There is nothing scientifically obnoxious in the fact that observation is theory-laden; indeed, it is absolutely necessary. It is to insist that without a hypothesis, framed by a researcher on the basis of his/her scientific knowledge, scientific training and *scientific* insight, the observation would be lacking in aim or direction and, hence, wasteful and unlikely to lead to any worthwhile result. This is totally different from saying that observation is influenced or determined by political, social or any other extra-scientific values and interests. It is precisely these that would militate against getting a fair and relevant observation. The theory that determines observation is one that is rationally developed in order to make the observation objective and unbiased and unlike a layman's observation, which would possibly be biased and certainly scientifically unprofitable. The hypothesis that the ICE super-fast German train met with a disastrous accident in 1998 because of a derailment due to a fractured rail was 'influenced' by the theory that fractured rails cause derailment and a much larger scientific theory about the way trains run on rails. The theory-laden hypotheses made engineers look along the track for a fractured rail some distance before the site of the accident. They found it and then inquired, again by framing hypotheses, into why the rail was fractured. They found the true causes. People ignorant about railway traction might have looked at the wrong places for the cause of the accident. If they were postmoderns and feminists, they would have looked for social factors like whether the passengers were mostly women and other marginalized persons; some might even have consulted witch doctors, depending on the culture they belonged to. And some might have declared that trains just do, like feminist discourses, run off rails. There are no 'puzzles introduced by the theory-laden nature of observation' nor are theories 'undetermined by data' in normal scientific procedure. Theories that guide observation are themselves founded on the basis of earlier observations; they don't fall from heaven.

Mary Tiles is an 'artful dodger' requiring the utmost vigilance on the reader's part not to be misled. Tiles maintains that 'the continued under-representation of women in science' is the result of a 'science culture' which has been 'the product of a distinctively male consciousness, embodying forms of rationality which are alien to women'.[47] In the sub-section entitled 'The Defence of Scientific Neutrality' of her essay 'A Science of Mars and Venus', Tiles begins like a lawyer by showing us the nature of science as seen by male scientists. She points out that even men themselves admit that 'political and economic concerns frequently influence the direction of science' and that research topics, in developed countries, are selected by white, middle-class males. But all this, these men say, is only about the direction, not the content of science; scientific results 'should be acceptable to anyone' because 'the ultimate standard of acceptability is empirical adequacy'. Even where wrong priorities discourage research on matters that concern women, the fault is said to lie, not with the *methods* of science, but with extra-scientific circumstances. Hence, science as 'a body of objective knowledge' is defended; its current *practice may not be* defensible.[48]

This is the case for the defence. The prosecution begins by stating that 'this distinction cannot be made as sharply as seems to be supposed', and builds up the case as follows.[49]

(I have to condense Tiles's long, meandering narrative not only because of constraints of space but also because we are otherwise likely to be entangled among the silken threads of the extensive and intricate web she has woven. She out-Protagorases Protagoras.)

Here is her submission: In the natural sciences, 'empirical adequacy provides an ultimate objective criterion', and 'between two competing theories, that which is empirically more successful ... should be chosen'. 'Empirical adequacy' means 'success'. The 'manifest success of science' is its 'ability to predict and control'. Since 'every human being in his [or her?] right mind (any rational person [that is, male?]) has an interest in increasing his technological control over his environment' and scientific success is precisely that capacity of science, it follows that this character of science 'should command universal respect' and 'everyone must and should respect and exclusively value' the 'technological control achieved by modern science', that is, modern science itself.

What Tiles is using is a sorites:

> Objectivity of science is empirical adequacy.
> Empirical adequacy is success.
> Success is predictability and control.
> Predictability and control imply that everyone should respect and value this predictability and control of science.
> Therefore objectivity implies that everyone should respect and value, etc.

Now, she wants to prove that science is not objective. Therefore, she should have tried to show that predictability and control *do not,* as a matter of fact, command universal respect, so that *by modus tollens* (a principle of male logic) it would follow that there is no objectivity – no objectivity in science. However, not subscribing to this logic, she does not follow this line but says, instead, that nothing makes it follow that 'everyone must or should respect and exclusively value the particular forms of technological control achieved by modern science.' This shows that Tiles has not understood the gist of her own argument. The argument, when it started, was not aiming to show that everyone should not respect and value these particular forms of control. If that is what she wanted to say, she could just as well have said it straight off without starting to tell us that in the natural sciences empirical adequacy produces an objective criterion and then going through three more steps of argument. In trying to show that we should not respect and value the technological control of science, the argument she goes through plays no part. She would have to find some other argument to prove her point.

In any case, every link in the chain is fragile. Empirical adequacy does not provide the ultimate objective criterion; it is what a science aims at. Success, as measured by predictability and control (that is, *practical* success) is not always or the only test of empirical adequacy. Science aims at theoretical truth, not merely practical success, and the ultimate criterion is comprehensive coherence. Tiles has done nothing to disprove the premises of her infructuous argument; in fact, she wants them to be accepted as true, her only claim being that they don't prove the conclusion about respecting and valuing, etc., etc.

Tiles now astonishes us by performing a somersault. Two pages after she puts forward the above argument, she suddenly turns round and asks 'whether an interest in technology is an intrinsically scientific interest'.[50] But neither the scientists nor we ever said it was; it was she who suggested it and we never agreed. 'Was this what was meant by the criterion of empirical adequacy?' she asks. We wouldn't have dreamed of saying such a thing. She blames Bacon and the Renaissance for shifting 'the *primary* focus of scientific attention away from contemplatively perceived truth to the goal of mastery over nature'. 'The pursuit of truth,' she bemoans, 'is no longer disinterested.' We are completely in sympathy.

Tiles has provided other arguments against the view that 'values play no role in determining the content of science'.[51] 'The strength of this claim,' she says, 'derives largely from the plausibility of the claim that laws such as the second law of thermodynamics, or of gravitational attraction', which are the laws of science's 'core theories', are not rejected by the critics of modern science like herself and her cronies. And such laws are 'independent of whatever factors may have conditioned the route' to their proposal. Tiles admits all this. What else could she do? But she insists that this 'misses the point of the more sophisticated critiques of science'. Danger: change of tracks likely! 'What is under attack' by these more sophisticated critiques is 'precisely exclusive attention on this conception of cognitive content'. That may be, but it is precisely this cognitive content that scientists and pro-science philosophers contend is value-free. Tiles has, once again, shied away from the point at issue, namely, that there are scientific laws (she has referred to them herself), at least in the 'hard' sciences, that are value-free and she has admitted them to be so, and which, therefore, prove that science is value-free. That the sophisticated critiques of science do not pay enough attention to this aspect of science is a totally different point and very regrettable.

We move on, then, to the more sophisticated critiques of science.[52] These critiques deny science can give us 'the whole truth on any matter'. This plain denial is made to sound profound by speaking of 'any law or theory which withstands tests devised in a certain way' instead of just saying 'science'. 'Devised in a certain way' simply means 'according to the standard methods of science'. The attempt is, of course, to trip you at every step. Anyway, let us proceed.

'The claim that science, including its content, is conditioned by interests and values' (that is, the feminist claim) 'is not the claim that content is determined by these conditions.' But that is what we were always given to understand was the claim. No, no; science is 'limited by them'. Our mistake was to take 'a partial truth, something which is not to be rejected', for the whole truth. Let me give an analogous argument. Ashok says, 'The dinner at the Taj was excellent,' but Beena answers, 'Not really, because the dinner was only a limited part of the whole show and you will agree that the whole show (that is, the rest of the show) was very poor, therefore you must admit the dinner was not excellent.' Ashok retorts, 'But I was talking only about the dinner; I am not concerned about the whole show; and the dinner *was* excellent.' Beena, shaking her head violently, replies, 'Ashok, you are talking with your usual male logic where, I know, you distinguish whole and part, but that is gender bias; we don't make these hair-splitting distinctions. So you see, it is you who have missed the point.' Turning to matters more serious than gastronomic, Ashok says, 'Science is independent of non-scientific values and interests in giving us scientific truths.' Beena, shocked, says, 'You are wrong, Ashok; science is limited by all sorts of other considerations, so what science gives us is not the truth, but only a partial truth and therefore not the truth at all.' Ashok: 'But I never said it gives the whole truth, whatever that might be; I said it gives scientific truth, and it does not do *that* partially, but completely according to its own principles.' Beena: 'This is male bias.' That science does not cover everything in life, is old hat. But what it does cover, it covers quite well. That, too, is old hat. Tiles herself says that her argument 'does not require rejection of scientific results'. Good, if reached by the impartial use of scientific methods. That is all that pre-feminist thinkers want. They are not after a worldview, a *weltanschauung*; that is the business of philosophy. If science claims to give it, it goes beyond its limits. Some scientists are guilty of this.

Our conjuror has now got a new act together.[53] It seems that 'the two-valued rhetoric of truth and falsity' is to be cut into two before our very eyes. Don't get scared. It is not to be cut up; only to be 'avoided' like a boring acquaintance. Tiles says, 'Now it is not at all clear that … the cognitive content of science is simply a sum of claims made in individual statements.' Who said it was? 'An integral component of the concept of *scientific* … knowledge is that it is … systematically organized. Laws do not merely function as true or false statements, but serve in the provision of explanations and in the organization and classification of phenomena. Theories impose a structure,' which is 'arguably part of the cognitive content of the theory. To claim that a theory is correct is … to make claims about the interrelations between laws and hence also between the phenomena to which they apply'. Laws 'are given their epistemological value, based on their theoretical, explanatory role rather than their mere empirical adequacy' (that is, according to their capacity to predict and control). Tiles sometimes speaks very cogently and reasonably. This is an excellent short account of science. So, you see, empirical adequacy, as understood by feminists, is not the *essence* of science or condition of its truth. Tiles now says, 'It would appear that place must be accorded at least to the notion of *epistemic value*.' So, after all, we are back to the idea that science is *not* value-free. We are also back to double-speak. The question is, 'Is it intentional or congenital?'

What is 'epistemological value'? 'Epistemological values,' explains Tiles, are a 'function … of explanatory ideals and conceptions of the goals of scientific endeavour,' and what is the goal of scientific endeavour if not truth – that very 'contemplatively perceived truth' which is, as we have earlier learned from the lady herself, different from mastery over nature? The equivocation can fool only fools. Truth is certainly a value, the intellectual or, if you prefer a more sophisticated word, the epistemological value. But it is not a social or political or any other value and interest whose influence on, and interference with, scientific inquiry and its methods was the issue under discussion. It is *these* values and interests that were considered to be threats to scientific neutrality and impartiality and objectivity in the search for truth. Epistemological value or, the same thing, truth, could not possibly be regarded by 'any human being in his right mind' as being a threat to truth or epistemological value itself. It is difficult to believe that feminists, who are so sharp, should not detect the equivocation.

Towards the end of her essay Tiles seems to have transformed into a new woman or, rather, into a pre-feminist woman.[54] 'The theoretical and explanatory endeavour of the natural sciences has been analytic and foundational' – 'the quest for fundamental laws, for basic constituents of matter ... by reference to which the characteristics of all more complex objects and phenomena are to be explained.' 'Disinterested science as puzzle-solving activity with a momentum of its own is quite understandable.' But then the feminist in her cannot be repressed. What is 'problematic is the relation of this autonomous activity', she says, 'to wider concerns'. But those wider concerns, whatever they are, were neither her concerns nor ours, when we embarked on this trip. Our joint and only concern was about the objectivity of science. On this, the position Tiles has tried bitterly to defend has been shown to have collapsed because it was erected on irrelevant and specious arguments, and now she has come round to admit that science is principally a theoretical, problem-solving and autonomous activity whose aim is truth.

Knowledge

Although, 'it may be tempting to think,' writes Sally Haslanger[55] (why tempting?), that feminists are not addressing mainstream epistemological issues, but doing something else, yet 'a significant amount of feminist writing explicitly undertakes to critique' such issues. She decides 'to make clear how a broad range of feminist work that is often deemed irrelevant to the *philosophical* inquiry into knowledge is in fact highly relevant.'

After giving several examples to show how males are overwhelmingly privileged in scientific activity, and how sexist and racist institutions are sustained, she asks, 'Should we conclude from this that "our" concept of knowledge is one that requires the knower to be male (or masculine)?' Of course not, such a suggestion is 'implausible', and she does not 'think that it has been part of feminist epistemology to defend' that sexism is built into the truth conditions of knowledge. This is heartening, because most feminists have been very vocal in pointing out that scientific practice is sexist, based on the belief, particularly among scientists, that knowledge, especially scientific knowledge, is inherently male. Feminists are forever striving to correct the belief – some of them even going to the extent of suggesting that knowledge itself should be abandoned.

Where traditional epistemology would ask, 'What is knowledge?', feminist research should rather ask 'what the point is in having a concept of knowledge' or better, 'what work …

could it do for us?' (We have learnt from Rorty that there are more things in heaven and earth that are 'pointless' than we had thought.) This approach is called 'an *analytical* approach'.[56] In what way is this approach better than the traditional one? Why should it be taken? Haslanger's next question: 'What concept (or concepts) would serve our well-conceived purpose(s) … best', whatever the purpose(s) might be? (It is unclear whether she is talking about knowledge or the concept(s) of knowledge.) So, instead of fixing on the object of inquiry and seeing what it is like, the new 'analytical' way of doing things is to decide what the object *should* be like, and then – what? We have already decided, in advance, what its nature should be, and there is nothing further left to be done. We are told that 'we must revise – perhaps even radically – our ordinary concepts and classifications of things'. Sure, but that is if our inspection of things (which are already taken to be there) demand such revision. But, according to the 'analytical' approach, we must first decide what we will call knowledge. On what basis do we decide? Our purposes? What purposes? We 'will have to be responsive to ordinary language', grants Haslanger, but 'there is also a stipulative element to the project: *this* is the phenomenon we need to think about; let us use the term "knowledge" to refer to it. In short … it is up to us to decide what to count as knowledge'. Haslanger takes away with one hand what she has, so sensibly, given with the other. Suppose, for some purpose, we need to think about insanity; we should refer to it as knowledge, a special kind of knowledge!

'Some of our purposes in having an epistemic framework are likely to be very basic animal purposes,' writes Haslanger in typical feminist style, which, in plainer English, means, in her own words, 'we need to have … information to help us get around in the world'. But, she wisely reminds us, knowledge does much more than this, and it 'is not, and has never been thought to be, simply true belief.' Sometimes Haslanger writes so very sensibly. But – we may remind her – according to the 'analytical' approach, we were not concerned about what knowledge or anything is. Isn't it up to us to stipulate whether knowledge is simply true belief or not, or even if knowledge needs to be true, or, for that matter, if knowledge is what non-analytical people call 'eating'?

Let us continue: 'Human Knowledge committees' (committees, presumably, connected with knowledge in some way) 'do more than facilitate the gathering and exchange of information: they draw lines of authority and power', and this and that, and decide public policy. In all this, which has really nothing directly to do with knowledge, knowledge is somehow involved. Therefore, it is held to be 'epistemically valuable' to decide what kind of knowledge we want. However, this is not epistemology as generally understood. We 'need to decide what kind of knowledge community is desirable', which, in turn, must 'involve political priorities and political choices'. 'Feminists have much to contribute in considering such priorities and choices'.[57] This is 'the broad range of feminist work' that, we were told, is 'highly relevant' to 'the *philosophical* inquiry into knowledge'. (In feminist and postmodern vocabulary, 'inquire' often means 'decide'.)

An objector may argue that a 'consideration of political goals is not appropriate in determining what constitutes knowledge' and that 'the *epistemic* status of such values as truth and coherence is not up for political negotiation' and, therefore, a 'feminist debate about the politics of knowledge is not relevant to determine what knowledge is.'[58]

'There is something right about this complaint,' grants Haslanger. (Didn't I say she speaks very sensibly sometimes?) But, she says, this 'only pushes the normative question back, for we define what's *epistemically* valuable in terms of the constitutive values of our epistemic practices'. 'What recommends our academic practice', that is, our practice of pursuing knowledge (for whatever reason) 'as opposed to some others?'

'To get a handle on this', our author, still, like a clever lawyer putting forward the opponent's case as strongly as possible in order to knock it down, turns to belief. It is claimed that belief '"aims at" the truth'; 'knowledge plausibly requires true belief' (plausibly!); therefore, 'to be a successful knower is, among other things, to represent the world accurately', that is, plausibly, truly. And so 'it appears that we can discover some constitutive epistemic values without reflecting on the social and political context of knowledge'. Could these, perhaps, be truth, objectivity and such like?

Now, Haslanger opens her own case. Her pleading deserves a place among the classics:

> It may be that some constitutive epistemic values (such as truth) can be discovered without a consideration of contextual values, while others require attention to social context. But before granting that even this small part of epistemology can proceed without attention to social and political matters, I think it is valuable to consider the basis for regarding truth as an epistemic value.

From regarding truth as a rather insignificant epistemic value, now we are to doubt whether it is an epistemic value or some other kind of value, or a value at all. We have now reached fundamental issues.

> After all, truth may be a constitutive goal of belief, but is there some reason we should see ourselves as committed to forming *beliefs* (as opposed to, say, acceptings)? Is there some value in being a *believer*?

Unbelievable! Why not be a painter or politician instead? The objector or complainant is so dumbfounded by Haslanger's advocacy that he has collapsed and has had to be carried out. Haslanger had herself said there was something right about the complaint; to get a handle on this she brought in belief and knowledge; she now asks whether it is worth believing anything. So, where are we? Have we got a handle on the matter? The argument, such as it was, has lost itself in the Bog of Irrelevance.

A similar misadventure follows soon after.[59] Our 'knowledge attributions seem to be [seem to be?] specifically oriented to evaluation of belief: in saying that S knows that 'p', I am saying that S has met certain cognitive/doxastic standards, with respect to the *belief* that 'p'; because truth is a constitutive goal of belief' and 'we take truth to be a primary condition for knowledge'. Once again, very sensible. 'After all,' Haslanger goes on, 'it is normally thought that knowledge is not simply true belief. Is there anything more? Traditionally, of course, the "something more"… has been justification. And controversies have raged over the nature of justification.' With this, one feels the ground is being prepared for either challenging the view that the 'something more' is justification or examining the true nature of justification. However, in Rortyian style, she proceeds, 'Pursuing the analytic strategy I outlined above, the prior question should be … why are we interested in justified true belief rather than simply true belief?' Because, dear, you have yourself just said that it was normally thought that knowledge was not simply true belief and wanted to know if there was something more, and, if so, what that might be. Feminists and postmoderns suffer from very short memories.

Next, Haslanger tries another line. Is justification a 'matter of fulfilling epistemic responsibility'? 'We might ask: What is the point of pursuing epistemic responsibility?' This is again Rortyian, but she suddenly wakes up: 'We should also ask: What counts as epistemic responsibility?' She then drifts off into talking about the self and its relation to others; tells us 'there's still the question why truth matters' and that it matters 'because we have certain capacities' whose exercise 'is intrinsically good'. She confesses, 'I haven't offered here a view about why justification matters', but it is heartening to know that she believes it does matter.

Pandemonium or 'Situated Knowledge'

'Chaos of thought and passion all confused'

Alexander Pope, *An Essay on Man*

A blast from the Trumpet Voice of Feminism declares, 'Feminist objectivity means quite simply *situated knowledge*.'[60] Let us explore 'situated knowledge'. Different groups in society live under different conditions and different relationships with each other. These generate different 'conceptualizations and perspectives', 'beliefs and theories' and 'standpoints'.[61] This is a purely factual claim and acceptable. Standpoint, however, 'denies that any questions asked by humans could be universal in the sense of expressing no particular historical values or interests,' writes Harding.[62] This statement, which seems to claim some privileged insight, is so vague that it could be acceptable to any non-standpoint person.

Every statement could be said to *express* some particular historical values and interests. Every speaker speaks from his present particular position and, unless he or she is mentally disadvantaged, has some particular reason for, or interest in, making the statement; every seriously made statement claims, as we have *all* admitted, epistemological value or truth; but all this is not the issue here. Surely, there are innumerable statements that are not *about* some particular value, historical, social, political, economic *et al.*, that relates to, or is held by some particular person in some period in history. Examples: Planets move in elliptical orbits, diamonds are hard, gravity is... Any statement which expresses something, expresses that something; the question is, whether it is true. This is crucial because what Harding and her friends are getting at, of course, is the claim that a statement's truth or falsity is determined only according to those values or interests that obtain within a certain culture or community at a particular point in time. This is the whole gist of situatedness, and this does not follow from what has been said about different perspectives, beliefs or theories of different groups or societies.

However much a statement may express some historical value or interest, in assessing its truth-value (whether it is true or false) the general principles of reasoning cannot be ignored, and these are not dependent on historical values or interests, although they have been discovered, formulated and developed historically and periodically, since the time of Aristotle. This view is referred to by Harding as 'the conventional universalist/absolutist' theory, and its rival is 'the relativist, perspectivalist and pluralist' one. Harding writes that Standpoint provides a 'theory of knowledge that stands in opposition to' both these opposed theories![63] Standpoint is full of surprises. This means that Standpoint theory stands in opposition to two contradictory theories and thus violates the Law of Excluded Middle.

According to what Harding calls 'conventional accounts', to acquire the status of knowledge, 'beliefs are supposed to break free of … their original ties to local, historical interests, values, and agendas' (that is, free of being 'situated'). But 'many feminists … now hold that it is not only desirable but also possible to have that apparent contradiction in terms – socially situated knowledge'. If the contradiction is real, Harding would, this time, be violating the Law of Non-Contradiction. Quoting Haraway, she writes: 'It turns out to be possible "to have *simultaneously* an account of radical historical contingency for all knowledge claims and knowing subjects … and a no-nonsense commitment to faithful accounts of a "real" world.'[64] There is no nonsense in Haraway's voice, but is she talking of two claims or two accounts of two claims? If the latter, there is no impossibility in having them both simultaneously; the question is whether they can both be true together, either simultaneously or otherwise. Harding, at any rate, thinks they can. Feminists' careless use of language is notorious.

Let's see what light Wylie throws on the issue. She says that the problem with Standpoint theory is that 'contextualizing moves of any kind lead inexorably to corrosive relativism; if knowledge claims are recognized to be … situated, it seems that there can be no ground for asserting their credibility, and no justification for claiming that any have epistemic authority'. Excellent, but 'neither horn of this implied dilemma', she writes, 'has been acceptable to feminists'. While they refer to science's capacity to 'provide reliable, probative knowledge of the natural and social worlds', non-feminists ask what 'probative' means – for the feminists.[65] Wylie continues, 'Feminists ... insist that "there are cultural *and* natural material causes for knowledge claims".'[66] Cultural or any other causes are never denied by objectivists; of course there are many reasons or causes for making claims. What is denied is that cultural factors, *as understood in the context of this debate,* should count as criteria for the *truth* of these claims.

Wylie, quoting Barad, goes on to say: 'The fact that scientific knowledge is socially constructed does not imply that science doesn't "work", and the fact that it "works" is not grounds for reverting to objectivist ideals that disappear [*sic*.] its essential contingency and contextual rootedness.'[67] Objectivists certainly do not deny that science works and works in the sense of being able to predict and control. The fact that it works is precisely the reason for saying that it is *not* socially constructed and for reverting to the objectivist ideals, which disentangle (or 'disappear') it from contingency and contextual rootedness.

Let's turn to Longino on situated knowledge. She explains that 'hypothesis testing' includes the 'subjection of putative data, of hypotheses, and of the background assumptions ... to varieties of conceptual and evidential scrutiny and criticism.'[68] This could be acceptable to objectivists as a correct and innocent account of scientific method, but spies are hiding in 'background' and 'varieties'. Every investigation works with certain assumptions, but it is the data and the nature and purpose of the investigation that will determine which assumptions need to be scrutinized and how far the scrutiny should go. In the absence of examples we cannot say what background assumptions Longino is thinking of. In the investigation of a specific problem, the entire background does not have to be scrutinized even if you can determine what the entire background is. What part or aspect of it has to be looked at is determined by the inquiry itself.

What does Longino mean by the varieties of scrutiny? Is a hypothesis regarding, say, a car accident to be scrutinized by the standard methods of science that look into such things *as well as* according to shamanism, numerology or other weird beliefs of some eccentric community? Longino's statement that 'conceptual criticism can include … investigation of the factual, moral, and social implications of background assumptions' is too vague and general to be meaningfully scrutinized and critiqued. If, for example, the implications of an inquiry into a case of corruption are that some big person's reputation might suffer, should the inquiry be called off? Should the matter be decided according to the particular society's perspective on corruption? From Longino's opaque and cryptic language one is quite mystified, but knowing *her* feminist background one may be justified in assuming that a sinister meaning lurks behind her words.

Longino proceeds, 'Background assumptions … most frequently are invisible to the members of the scientific community … and because unreflective acceptance of such assumptions can come to define what it is to be a member of such a community … effective criticism of background assumptions requires the presence and expression of alternative points of view.' With this we have left *terra firma* and are floating somewhere among the clouds. It now seems that we were not talking about the background assumptions of the subject matter of an investigation but about the background assumptions concerning the investigators themselves. This is all terribly confusing and the confusion is further compounded by the words, 'This sort of account allows us to see how social values and interests can become enshrined in otherwise acceptable research programmes.'

We have now risen to an altitude that makes us dizzy. How does this sort of account allow us to see the enshrinement of social values in research programmes, particularly if these programmes are otherwise acceptable? If they are otherwise acceptable on scientific grounds, nothing more is required to be 'enshrined' in them. If certain assumptions have to be explored in the interests of 'empirical adequacy' (that is, getting the maximum amount of relevant data), why are 'alternative points of view' required? What alternative points of view? 'Scientific knowledge, on this view,' writes Longino, 'is an outcome of the critical dialogue in which individuals and groups holding different points of view engage with each other.'

So, come along everybody, Western scientists, shamans, allopaths, homoeopaths, physicists, Christian scientists, architects, jerry-builders, chemists, witch doctors, oncologists, ayurveds, FRCSes, *narivaids,* engineers, magicians, *babas, dadas,* gutter-inspectors, Oshoites – as many as can enter the Ark. The more the merrier or messier. Let's all have a critical dialogue, if we can, about, say, why there were floods in Mumbai in July 2005. If we can't, let's toss up as to who can.

Now we are told that 'even though context-independent standards of justification are not attainable' (who said they were not? Only you did!) 'community level criteria can ... be invoked to discriminate among the products of scientific communities'. So, we *are* talking about scientific communities; we thought we were talking about the community at large whose moral, social, political and other ideas and norms had to be taken into account by the 'agents' or researchers and 'enshrined' in research programmes. If we were all the time talking about scientific ideas and norms, where was the need for all this going up the mountain just to come down on the same side? Is there one scientific community or many such communities, and if many, how are they distinguished? According to their different disciplines and subject matter, or in some other obscure way? We seem to be in a hopeless snarl.

Referring to the view that different social conditions would produce different beliefs and standpoints, Diemut Bubeck (not a feminist sympathizer) writes, 'This process of proliferating standpoints can be continued until one reaches ... *either* each person's unique social condition [which] warrants her or his unique standpoint; *or* the group oppressed by all possible systems of oppression must be identified as having the epistemically most privileged standpoint, and hence the most cutting edge critique of everyone else's theory.'[69]

To the first alternative, Bubeck gives two valid answers.[70] 'The position is arguably a *reductio* of standpoint theory.' What is one's individual standpoint? One has several standpoints, 'defined either by different points in time in her life, or by various standards of her personality, or both'. The question is, how far down you will go in doing complete justice to the idea of Standpoint. Further, even 'individual, let alone sub-individual, standpoints can only generate stories rather than theories, since no general claims beyond one's own particular experience can be made'. A statement about a particular case is not a theory and hence cannot be a Standpoint theory.

My answer to Bubeck's second alternative is that such a comprehensive identification would lack internal consistency and involve conflict. Since systems of oppression are vastly different, a group oppressed in every possible way is extremely unlikely even if theoretically possible. One single standpoint being thus very unlikely, a grading and a choice would have to be resorted to if systems of oppression are to be at all effectively dealt with. This would inevitably require general principles of reasoning of the male variety, which the Standpoint people despise.

It is interesting to learn from Wylie that the High Priestess of Feminism, Sandra Harding, characterized Standpoint theory, in the 1980s, 'as an unstable position located dialectically between feminist empiricism and various forms of feminist postmodernism'. Her arguments are a clear exposition of the case against 'situated knowledge'. 'She argued that if feminist Standpoint theorists were consistent in maintaining their central contextualizing insight – that all knowledge is "situated and perspectival", and all science "irreducibly social" – they must accept the thoroughgoing relativism of a postmodern stance that abandons or, at least, regards with ironic scepticism all claims of epistemic privilege.

If, on the other hand, Standpoint theorists are committed to the claim that feminists' (or women's) standpoints are epistemically privileged, they often [and must] revert to justificatory arguments that invoke transcendent epistemic standards (of rationality or credibility).' However, after being so critical – and rightly so – of Standpoint, later, she 'renewed her interest in Standpoint theory.'[71] Only her interest, or her allegiance too? If the latter, it would be worth knowing her arguments against her own earlier arguments against Standpoint.

Justification

When feminists talk about justification they do not mean to discuss the way in which a statement or theory is to be established, the kind of reasons or facts that can be cited in its support. They keep harping on the question of what problems ought to be taken up for investigation and into what areas the search for facts has to be conducted. And all this is to be done with feminist interests in mind and with an aim to avoid male bias. This is not, of course, a logical or epistemological inquiry. Although they talk in general terms, as if they are concerned with all the sciences or science as such, they are really exclusively interested in social problems, and that too the problems of women and marginalized people. It is, of course, not the job of science to select, from the host of problems these people face, the ones which should be addressed from a socio-political point of view. Feminists, again, do not have a purely theoretical scientific interest in the problems they choose to take up.

Their interest is centred round identifying and solving the practical problems of oppressed and disadvantaged groups, particularly the victims of male injustice. Thus, their scientific interest is, though nobly motivated, extremely narrow. It is true that in selecting the problem that should be tackled, it is necessary to make a wide and in-depth study of the situation. This would 'justify' the subject matter of the research. (Feminists are never quite sure, nor can we be, as to what 'subject' is supposed to refer to – to the subject matter of the research or the researcher.)

The first need, says Alison Jaggar, is to 'distinguish justified moral claims' from 'subjective desires', that is, you must not just take up what concerns your personal desires and fancies. Fair enough. Next, you must 'eliminate covert bias on the basis of race, gender and any other axis of domination' and 'take care not to discredit or disregard the moral narratives, vocabularies' of women and marginalized persons. Fair again. And not disregard 'women's style of thinking'.[72] No, not fair at all. If women and marginalized people do indeed have their own peculiar styles of thinking in the sense of using principles of reasoning and methods of investigation which are different from the ones men use, then they should certainly be discredited and disregarded. This is not to say that men's principles are superior to those of women or marginalized groups; it is to insist that there cannot be different and antagonistic principles of reasoning if that is what 'styles of reasoning' means.

Some feminists, however, believe that 'traditional conceptions of moral justification' are 'a deceptive rhetorical device that adds a ring of magisterial authority to philosophers' rationalizations' of oppressive practices. If rationalizations, that is, false and motivated attempts at justification, are acknowledged, it implies that true and rational justifications are also possible, but some philosophers are so disgusted with both justification and rationalization, that they have 'abandoned the traditional project of moral justification' altogether.[73]

The baby is thus thrown out with the bath water. (It was an old Western practice for the whole family to use the same water in the tub for each one's bath. The baby's turn came last, by which time the water was so murky that the baby was invisible. There is a telling parallel here.) Justification and reasoning are pitted against 'an ethic of caring'. The latter 'does not *emphasize* justification' (emphasis mine). The question, however, is not one of emphasis. 'Postmodernist feminists insist on the multiplicity of possible narratives', not truth claims, and hence have no need of justification. 'Some feminists, however, are still concerned that feminism be able to justify its moral claims'; therefore, 'rather than abandoning the project of moral justification, we are working to reinterpret it in terms that are less covertly elitist and authoritarian and more transparent and democratic.'[74] We, in turn, applaud the endeavour and wish them god-speed.

'Styles of Reasoning'

> 'I have no other but a woman's reason.'
>
> Shakespeare, *The Two Gentlemen of Verona*

Genevieve Lloyd writes: 'Our trust in a Reason that knows no sex has … been largely self-deceiving.'[75] Fox Keller and Longino, referring to Londa Schiebinger, write:

> Mammals, she observes, are grouped together and demarcated from other animals by a distinctly female function – the presence of mammary glands defines the mammal as the genus of nurturing mothers. By contrast, humans (*Homo sapiens*) are grouped together, and distinguished from other mammals by their intelligence.

The effect of this taxonomic structure on perceptions of gender is obvious (women are mammals; men are human).[76]

Reading this delightful passage one really begins to believe that female logic is indeed different from male logic. Is it necessary to unravel the confusion or sophistry? The taxonomic truth is that all species whose females have mammary glands are classed as mammals, including their males. The human species is one whose females have mammary glands; therefore human beings, female and male, are classed as mammal. So, both men and women are mammals. Humans, including women, are distinguished from other mammals by their intelligence (though this is not quite correct because animals are intelligent too). Women are humans too, therefore women are distinguished from other mammals by their intelligence. Therefore, along with men, women are intelligent. The feminists' wilful distortion of the correct position is patent.

'In the late 1960s, when feminist ethics began, it consisted mainly of applying the resources of traditional moral philosophy to ... topics that philosophers, almost exclusively male, had previously ignored', but in the 1980s, feminist ethics 'turned its attention to the tools themselves' and, 'by careful analysis', 'exposed what seemed to be male biases in the very concepts and methods of traditional philosophical ethics'. These tools are 'tools of articulation, interpretation, and analysis that appeared to reflect their male standpoints, despite a presumption of abstract universality'. Feminists not only 'sought to introduce specifically female moral perspectives,' but also 'to forge conceptual and methodological tools that reflected women's standpoints'.[77]

We would next expect to hear more about these new tools, but, instead, we slide off into something about the 'correlation between gender and moral orientation'. Let us see if there is anything about tools in the writings of Carol Gilligan, who is now referred to at length by our author, Marilyn Friedman.

According to Gilligan, writes Friedman, 'males are characteristically concerned with substantive moral matters of justice, rights, autonomy, and individuation.' So far no sign of tools. 'In their moral reasonings', males 'tend to rely on abstract principles and to seek universality of scope. Women, by contrast, are more often concerned with substantive moral matters of care, personal relationships' and 'tend to avoid abstract principles and universalist pretensions and focus instead on contextual detail and interpersonal emotional responsiveness'.[78] Even now nothing about new feminist tools; only male tools to be avoided.

So, we learn that the subject matter that men and women 'tend' to be concerned about, is different for each party. The only reference to tools is what is said about abstract principles and universality of scope. I shall have more to say about abstract principles and universality later. For the present, one may ask whether, even in dealing with care, etc., women don't use abstract principles at all. When they 'focus on' this or that, does not focusing include classifying and analysing the data? And when they so often complain that men ignore the problems of women and other groups, don't they (feminists) demand 'universality of scope'? Why is seeking universality a male crime?

With the mention of care ethics the dikes are breached and in rushes a torrent of rhetoric against 'traditional justice-oriented moral theories'. Don't you know that 'women have distinctive traits … not necessarily inferior to those of men; sometimes even superior'? Women have 'diverse methodological strategies' such as the 'legitimation of the personal point of view, defense of the role of emotion' and a 'relationally oriented moral psychology'. These, ladies and gentlemen, are the new feminist tools that were to replace the old male ones of articulation, interpretation and analysis.[79]

Feminists are generally cultural relativists, maintaining that only ideas and principles peculiar to a particular culture or community operate as norms for assessing truth-claims (that is, when they are in the mood to talk about principles and truth). Longino gives 'criteria' necessary to achieve 'the transformative dimensions of critical discourse'. 'Scientific knowledge', she says, 'is an outcome of the critical dialogue in which individuals and groups holding different points of view engage with each other' in 'an interactive dialogic community'. The community's inquiry 'is productive of knowledge to the extent that it facilitates transformative criticism'.[80] We must keep remembering that Longino is talking of a scientific community, but the continuing confusion of thought and vagueness of language never allow us to keep distinct the ideas of a scientific community (which is only a pompous way of talking of scientists) and the community at large, so that the social values and interests which, on the objectivist view, ought to be kept out of scientific discourse (unless we are talking specifically about *them*) keep slipping in either explicitly or surreptitiously. If all these devious undercurrents are kept in mind, there is nothing in the four criteria that Longino gives which would support cultural relativism. The criteria are:[81]

1. 'There must be publicly recognized forums for the criticism of evidence, of methods, and of assumptions

and reasoning.' Surely, such forums could not be meant to give opportunities for all sorts of people to air their views – scientists, doctors, lawyers, shopkeepers, sportsmen, etc., whatever be the phenomenon under investigation. What is 'publicly recognized' supposed to mean?

2. 'The community must ... tolerate dissent' and 'its beliefs and theories must change over time in response to critical discourse taking place within it.' This, of course, is an essential character of scientific procedure as long as we are talking of a scientific community. Of course the larger community in which the scientists, like any other professionals, live and work, must tolerate (if you like) and facilitate what their scientists are doing, as long as it does not harm the community. There is nothing very relativist or feminist in all this.

3. 'There must be publicly recognized standards by reference to which theories, hypotheses and observational practices are evaluated and by appeal to which criticism is made relevant to the goals of the inquiring community.' Once again, as in the first point, 'publicly recognized' needs to be questioned and so also 'inquiring community'; and, as the next sentence shows, we are justified in expressing our doubts. 'With the possible exception of empirical adequacy, there needn't be ... a set of standards common to all communities.' Which communities is Longino now talking about? Scientific ones or socio-political ones? If the former, then the empirical adequacy that is said to be common, is the only relevant criterion or standard. But

empirical adequacy is not, as feminists seem to suppose, success in prediction and control, but (in her own words) 'cognitive virtues such as accuracy, coherence' and suchlike. Again, due to mental confusion, she calls them 'social virtues' because they meet the 'technical or material needs' of society and its members. Feminists are haunted by communities, societies and their members.

4. Consensus among communities 'must not be the result of the exercise of political or economic power'. Naturally. It must be the 'result of critical dialogue in which all relevant perspectives are represented'. The inclusion of 'relevant' just about saves the sentence from slipping into the usual nonsense where every kind of opinion prevalent in a society is supposed to be represented in a scientific inquiry. Feminists are also obsessed by the idea of 'consensus'; consensus can be the result of an arbitrary or expedient decision, or of having reached the truth. Surely, in a scientific inquiry it is the latter sort that we want; the emphasis should be on reaching the truth, and consensus will follow.

It should be clear that apart from the vagueness and confusion enshrined here, all the four criteria are harmless and pose no threat to the objectivity and universality of Reason. Nor are they very original, whatever is original in them being eccentric.

Alison Jaggar, also speaking of 'conceptual tools' being 'biased in favour of the privileged', makes six points:[82]

1. In the mainstream tradition, 'moral subject', supposedly the researcher, 'reflects a specific social type … a Western male head of household … probably white,' whose

'motivation and style of reasoning' are 'ascribed to all rational moral subjects, despite the overwhelming empirical evidence that many people have different motivations and employ alternative styles of reasoning'.

2. People whose thinking deviates from that of the Western male 'are presented as deficient in moral authority'.

3. 'The sphere of moral reason is arbitrarily limited so as to exclude matters of intimate and family relations.'

4. Hence 'there is no conceptual space for criticizing many practices oppressive to women'.

5. 'The foregoing points together entail that the mainstream conceptions ... deny the conceptual resources that would permit women' and other oppressed groups to 'express their own moral perceptions in their own terms'.

6. 'Despite the impartiality and universality claimed', the conceptions 'are in fact self-serving and circular because they rationalize' their own views 'while silencing dissenting voices'.

The six-point answer to Jaggar is as follows:

1. Every one of these six points makes factual claims which, even if true, do not remotely touch the question of 'conceptual tools' in the sense of principles and methods of reasoning.

2. Jaggar, like all feminists, speaks of 'styles of reasoning', not principles of reasoning, and 'styles' is too imprecise to be taken seriously.

3. The very assertion of bias and rationalizing imply that the notions of impartiality and rational arguing make

sense and are taken to be possible; therefore, bias can be corrected and rationalizing avoided.

4. Who stops women and oppressed groups from criticizing oppressive practices or including intimate and family relations in moral discourse? If anything does stop them, it cannot be a principle of reasoning or a method of acquiring data.

5. We are not told what are the conceptual resources and tools of reasoning that are denied by the mainstream tradition. Whatever they might be, how can that tradition deny them? If they are used relevantly and cogently, they cannot be denied; they could be questioned and assessed (by the tradition in its own terms) if only they would reveal themselves.

6. What are the oppressed groups' 'own terms'? If they are only moral assessments of a social situation, they are not tools of reasoning, which is what we are currently concerned with. If they are meant to be principles and methods of reasoning different from and opposed to those used by the oppressors, then we are once again up against the old, troublesome and for-ever-unanswered question: how can the two parties engage in what Longino calls a critical dialogue or any kind of dialogue? They would be reduced to a Rortyian 'conversation'.

In short, Jaggar's six points do nothing to damage the mainstream traditional style of reasoning or establish a better one. Jaggar ends on a surprising note. Referring to the 'dominant tradition of Western ethics' as the master, the last sentence of the essay says: 'Rather than scrapping the master's tools, many feminist philosophers are working to transform them so that we may build a moral household that has no head or master.' 'Even as it changes' the dominant Western tradition, 'feminism simultaneously contributes to that tradition'. And how does it do so? Neither by adding new tools to it nor by transforming old ones; it 'exploits' the tradition by using something from it, using the 'values of representation, consent, self-determination, respect, equality, and freedom', which are 'squarely founded on moral and political ideals of modern Western social thought'.[83] So, feminism contributes by taking something away for itself. In any case, we seem to have forgotten that we were talking of 'conceptual tools', tools of articulation, interpretation and analysis (as Friedman would remind us), which have nothing to do with self-determination, respect, equality or freedom founded on modern Western or on any other political thought. Feminists have a lot of wind but short memories.

Feminists also use the phrase 'models of reasoning'. Jaggar writes, 'Subjects who are usually constituted by their membership in different collectivities, especially collectivities that stand to each other in relations of dominance and subordination, are likely to have disparate moral viewpoints', and 'such disparities and inequalities create obstacles to projects of imaginative identification and even to productive discussion. To recognize these obstacles is to challenge mainstream assumptions that there is a single correct model of moral reason.'[84] The last sentence does not follow from what has gone before, nor from what follows. 'Empirical discourse allows people to raise questions such as: *For whom* is this situation problematic and what criteria are *used to* identify "those affected"? In whose terms is the situation described, and what is *highlighted* and what *obscured* by those terms? What are the *interests* and *values* at stake and how do these change if the problem is *re-described? Who is responsible for addressing the situation?* [85] All the words I have italicized show that they concern neither models, nor reasoning, nor models of reasoning. All that they show is that members of different collectivities or groups, when faced with a particular social situation, are likely to view it and to deal with it in a way that would be advantageous to themselves. Take the case of encroachments on pavements. Members of the dominant class will see them as a nuisance to their free movement and as unhygienic and aesthetically offensive. They will want them to be removed. The pavement dwellers, on the other hand, will consider them as necessary for their survival, will not see them even as a nuisance and will see the attitude of the dominant class as inhuman. They will resist any attempt at eviction. Where, in all this, does 'models of reasoning' come in?

Social matters affect different sections of society differently and so will be described 'in their own terms', that is, as the matter affects them. If, however, the matter has to be thrashed out between the two groups with any hope of a solution satisfactory to both parties, it cannot be done by challenging mainstream assumptions of a 'single correct model of moral reasoning'. If different groups insist on their 'own terms' in the sense of their own peculiar principles of reasoning, 'productive discourse' is impossible.

Mainstream philosophers do not insist that there is a single 'model' of reasoning. B. Bosanquet, in his *Logic or the Morphology of Knowledge*, has considered different forms of reasoning suited to different kinds of subject matter (empirical, mathematical, moral, philosophical, etc.), but these differences have nothing to do with differences of gender, class, race or ethnicity. That these and other such considerations should be excluded from discussion or research is the only single model mainstream philosophers want.

It is interesting to see what two feminists, Elizabeth Spelman and Maria Lugones, write in a paper entitled 'Have we got a theory or you?':

> ...only when a genuine and reciprocal dialogue takes place between 'outsiders' and 'insiders' can we trust the outsider's account. At first sight it may appear that the insider/outsider distinction disappears in the dialogue, but ... all that happens is that we are now both outsider and insider with respect to each other. The dialogue puts us both in a position to give a better account of each other's and our own experience.[86]

The distinction of outsider and insider remains only in the sense that, due to the use of the *same* principles of reasoning, each outsider *understands* the view point, the concerns, the fears and the suggestions of the other and so becomes an insider, with the result that there is some chance of jointly solving the problem.

Bubeck makes the following points: First, that 'knowledge is "produced" jointly, through mutual listening and talking (although the oppressors will have to do a lot more listening than the oppressed)' and second, that 'the relations within which knowledge arises are cooperative rather than antagonistic.'[87] This seems to accord with what Jaggar herself arrives at. After telling us that 'the remedy for existing bias' is not 'to replace one singular model that covertly represents moral rationality as bourgeois and masculine with another singular model ...', she writes that 'individual rationality is no longer defined by the possession of specific motivations and values or by the utilization of a particular style of moral thinking; instead, it consists in proficiency in those interactive skills and virtues necessary to participate as an equal in productive moral discourse.'[88] What do these interactive skills and virtues depend on except the principles of reasoning common to the dominant and the subordinate?

Where 'Standpoint theory goes wrong,' says Bubeck, is 'in its endorsement of the antagonistic model,' for 'why should it not be possible for potential knowers of various social positions to try to disentangle truth from distortion *in discussion with each other?*' It may be argued that oppressors would not want to surrender the advantages of their privileged positions. This 'may be true as a rough *sociological* generalization' (italics mine), says Bubeck, 'but it does not exclude the possibility of oppressors being morally and politically motivated by considerations and interests other than those they would be expected to have in virtue of their own social position'.[89] There is no reason to suggest that the members of the dominant social group, in my example of encroachment, would find it impossible to consider the justice of the subordinates' case. Conversion and change of heart do occur, and where they do occur it is, at least in part, due to the give and take of arguments and reasons.

Universals

Feminists, following postmodernism, are anti-universalists and anti-essentialists.

Since 'human subjects are socially concrete and socially diverse beings, feminists encourage suspicion of any given universal claim', say Fricker and Hornsby.[90] But for Fox Keller, a 'task of a feminist theoretic in science' is 'to distinguish that which is parochial from that which is universal in the scientific impulse, reclaiming for women what has historically been denied to them', and she even wants to retain, rather than abandon, 'the quintessentially human effort to understand the world in rational terms'. However, she adds that we must attend to 'the features of the scientific project that belie its claim to universality'.[91] Fox Keller is obviously performing a delicate balancing feat. Jaggar says that most feminists do not recommend that the bourgeois masculinity model should be replaced by a 'characteristically feminine' model, because there is no 'generic woman' or 'generic human'.[92]

In spite of frequent denials and dismissals, universals are constantly used and hankered after in feminist literature. Society, writes Friedman, 'has failed to appreciate ... what is distinctly valuable in *women's* character traits', and despite the feminists' 'reluctance to generalize about the moral perspectives of all women', 'the conviction is widespread among feminists' that 'women are more rationally oriented than men'. In the 1980s, many feminists resisted generalizations about '"women" without qualification' and began to articulate differences due to sex, race, class and religion, ethnicity, nationality and age. But they are slow to realize that each of these is a universal, and Friedman rightly points out that accordingly, 'We might well need lesbian ethics, black womanist ethics and so on.' However far down the line one may go, one simply cannot escape universals and generalizations if one is to propound any kind of theory, however minimal.

Jaggar, who rejects generic woman and generic human being, has written just a page earlier, 'Feminists do not deny that moral subjects are alike on some level of abstraction, but their consciousness of the many false humanisms … as universal truths of human nature motivates them to highlight human differences over human commonalities.'⁹⁵ Indeed a rather modest objective.

You could say about feminism, what Sir Thomas Beecham said about a Bruckner symphony – that he had found in it many miscarriages and false pregnancies. To which one could add some still births and two-headed monsters.

References

1. Friedman, M., 'Feminism in Ethics – Conceptions of Autonomy' in Fricker, M. & J. Hornsby (Eds.), *Feminism in Philosophy* (Cambridge, 2000), p. 205.
2. Fox Keller, E., 'Feminism and Science' in Fox Keller, E. & H. E. Longino (Eds.), *Feminism and Science* (Oxford, 1996), p. 31.
3. Fox Keller, E. & H. E. Longino (Eds.), op. cit., p. 1.
4. Ibid., p. 1.
5. Tiles, Mary, 'A Science of Mars or Venus' in Fox Keller, E. & H. E. Longino (Eds.), op. cit., p. 237.
6. Harding, S., 'Rethinking Standpoint Epistemology' in Fox Keller, E. & H. E. Longino (Eds.), op. cit., p. 245.
7. Ibid., p. 245.
8. Ibid., p. 245 and for all quotations in this paragraph.
9. Ibid., p. 246.
10. Ibid., p. 246.
11. Ibid., p. 247.
12. Ibid., p. 247.
13. Ibid., p. 244.
14. Ibid., p. 244.
15. Ibid., pp. 238-39.
16. Ibid., p. 241.

17. Ibid., pp. 241-42.

18. Ibid., p. 242.

19. Ibid., p. 242.

20. Ibid., pp. 243-44.

21. Haraway, D., 'The Science Question in Feminism' in Fox Keller, E. & H. E. Longino (Eds.), op. cit., p. 255.

22. Harding, S., op. cit., p. 242.

23. Wylie, A., 'Feminism in Philosophy and Science' in Fricker, M., & J. Hornsby (Eds.), op. cit., p. 175.

24. Langton, R., 'Feminism in Epistemology' in Fricker, M., & J. Hornsby (Eds.), op. cit., p. 135.

25. Ibid., p. 135.

26. Ibid., pp. 138-40.

27. Fox Keller, E., 'Feminism and Science', op. cit., p. 28.

28. Harding, S., op. cit., p. 247.

29. Haraway, D., op. cit., p. 258.

30. Fox Keller, E. & H. E. Longino, op. cit., p. 4.

31. Wylie, A., op. cit., p. 177.

32. D. Haraway, op. cit., p. 253.

33. Harding, S., op. cit., p. 247.

34. G. Lloyd's view voiced by Fricker, M., & J. Hornsby (Eds.), op. cit., p. 2.

35. Wylie, A., op. cit., pp. 168-69.

36. Fricker, M. & J. Hornsby, op. cit., p. 2.

37. Ibid., p. 2.

38. Wylie, A., op. cit., p.168.

39. Fox Keller, E., op. cit., pp. 29-30.

40. Ibid., p. 30.

41. Fox Keller, E. & H. E. Longino, op.cit., p. 1.

42. Ibid., p. 1.

43. Wylie, A., op. cit., p. 177.

44. Fox Keller, E., & C. Gronthowski, 'The Mind's Eye' in Fox Keller, E. & H. E. Longino (Eds.), op. cit., p. 187.

45. Longino, H. E., 'Feminist Philosophies of Science', in Fox Keller, E., & H. E. Longino (Eds.), op. cit., p. 264.

46. Ibid., pp. 271-72.
47. Tiles, M., op. cit., p. 223
48. Ibid., p. 224.
49. Ibid., pp. 224-25.
50. Ibid., pp. 227-28.
51. Ibid., pp. 225-26.
52. Ibid., p. 226.
53. Ibid., pp. 226-27
54. Ibid., p. 230.
55. Haslanger, S., 'What Knowledge Is and What It Ought to be', in Tomberlin, J. E. (Ed.), 1999, pp. 459, 463.
56. Ibid., pp. 467-68.
57. Ibid., pp. 468-69.
58. Ibid., pp. 469-70.
59. Ibid., pp. 471-72.
60. Haraway, D., op. cit., p. 253.
61. Bubeck, D., 'Feminism in Political Philosophy' in Fricker, M. & J. Hornsby (Eds.), op. cit., p. 187.
62. Harding, S., op. cit., p. 242.
63. Ibid., pp. 242-43.
64. Ibid., p. 236.
65. Wylie, A., op. cit., p. 176.
66. Ibid., pp. 276-77. Wylie quotes from Barad, 'Meeting of the Universe Halfway', p. 162
67. Ibid., p. 177, quoting Barad.
68. Longino, H. E., op. cit., p. 272. This is the reference for the entire discussion of background assumptions.
69. Bubeck, D., op. cit., p. 188.
70. Ibid., p. 189.
71. Wylie, A., op. cit., p. 176.
72. Jaggar, A., 'Feminism in Ethics' in Fricker, M. & J. Hornsby (Eds.), op. cit., p. 234.
73. Ibid., p. 241.
74. Ibid., p. 241.

75. Lloyd, Genevieve, *The Man of Reason*, 1984, p. ix.

76. Fox Keller, E. & H. E. Longino, op. cit., p. 7.

77. Friedman, A., op. cit., pp. 205-6.

78. Ibid., p. 206.

79. Ibid., pp. 207, 211.

80. Longino, H. E., op. cit., pp. 272-73.

81. Ibid., p. 273.

82. Jaggar, A., op. cit., p. 234.

83. Ibid., p. 242.

84. Ibid., p. 236.

85. Ibid., p. 237.

86. Quoted by D. Bubeck, op. cit., p. 193.

87. Bubeck, D., op. cit., p. 193.

88. Jaggar, A., op. cit., p. 237.

89. Bubeck, D., op. cit., p. 194.

90. Fricker, M., and J. Hornsby, op. cit., p. 2.

91. Fox Keller, E., op. cit., pp. 31-32.

92. Jaggar, A., op. cit., p. 237.

93. Friedman, M., op. cit., pp. 207, 209.

94. Ibid., p. 210.

95. Jaggar, A., op. cit., p. 236.

Postlude

Vanitas Vanitatum

'...all these, upwhirled aloft,
Fly o'er the backside of the World far off
Into a limbo large and broad, since called
The Paradise of Fools.'

John Milton, *Paradise Lost*

In this essay, I believe I have been, in an insignificantly small way, 'an under-labourer in ... removing some of the rubbish that lies in the way of knowledge'. Locke, about three hundred years ago, writes about what he calls a 'sanctuary of vanity and ignorance', the state of learning in his day:[1]

> Vague and insignificant forms of speech, and abuse of language ... and hard or misapplied words, with little or no meaning, have, by prescription, such a right to be mistaken for deep learning and height of speculation, that it will not be easy to persuade either those who speak or those who hear them, that they are but the covers of ignorance, and hindrance of true knowledge.

With uncanny prescience, Locke has also described the new sanctuary of the postmodern era. It is not so much ignorance that animates postmodern discourse as a perverse desire to destroy ('deconstruct'), coupled with arrogance, a good amount of

360 • Human Reason and Its Enemies

deliberate sophistry with genuine intellectual confusion – all of which I have tried to show.

However, at the end of my labours I get the uncomfortable feeling that I might have totally misunderstood the worthies whom I have (as they say nowadays) critiqued. For it is difficult to believe that such renowned scholars and thinkers, whose tomes are published by reputed publishers and bought in large numbers, devoured and alluded to by so many, could seriously purvey such unacceptable views, often sought to be supported (even while disclaiming to do so) by specious or muddled arguments. Are they joking? I have begun to wonder. Are they taking us for a ride? Perhaps some day one of them, maybe the great 'ironist' himself, will tell us that postmodernism was just a (language) game and what fools we were to be taken in by a spoof, a sort of 'Cogito Ergo and All That'. I can hear Rorty's snorting laughter, 'Didn't fall to it even after reading the funny stuff written by our scientific experts in a light-hearted vein?' 'Where was your sense of humour, you stodgy old fogies?' say Kuhn and Feyerabend. 'Really!' cries Appleyard, 'you deserve to be made to stand in the corner with fool's caps on your silly heads'. Yet, in others there is such a tone of passionate conviction and supercilious smugness, that it is difficult not to take them seriously.

Thackeray (W. M., not B.) ends his famous novel with these words: 'Come children, let us shut up the box and the puppets, for our play is played out.'[2] Our game (language game?) has also come to an end; let us put away the pieces with which we have been having such a rollicking time – ethnocentrism, cultural relativism, incommensurability, assorted tools, vocabularies, the Archimedean point, Standpoint epistemology, historical situatedness, edifying philosophy and, of course, the language game itself. And then there were all the 'vanities' which abound in traditional philosophy and which our postmoderns kindly brought to our attention – triviality, hollowness, pointlessness. The greatest of the 'vanities' – 'vanity of vanities' (*vanitas vanitatum*) – is traditional philosophy itself.

Into the box, along with all the other puppets and vanities, we should put ourselves. For ethnocentric postmodernism does indeed regard human life as a puppet show in which we act according to the ideas and norms of our community, unable to reason and deliberate or take an objective stand without bias. Nor are the community ideas and norms established or altered by conscious and purposeful thought. We are 'programmed'. These ideas and norms, which determine our actions, just happen to be there, and, if they change, they just happen to change. In postmodernism you have only happenings; there is not even a puppeteer.

Has postmodernism (along with the epistemic wing of feminism) passed into the limbo of philosophical curiosities? I suspect so. Did the one-time exciting novelty die of sheer boredom? Let us, before the burial, give it a last salute, for, while it irritated us and, in the gadfly tradition of Western philosophy, pricked us into rethinking our basic positions, it did also bring some mirth into our staid philosophizing. For 'every time a man smiles – but much more so, when he laughs – it adds something to this Fragment of Life'.[3]

References

1. Locke, J., 'The Epistle to the Reader', *An Essay Concerning Human Understanding.*
2. Thackeray, W. M., *Vanity Fair.*
3. Sterne, L., *Tristram Shandy.*

Bibliography

Books

Abbey, R. (Ed.), 2004, *Charles Taylor* (Cambridge University Press).

Appleyard, B., 1993, *Understanding the Present* (Picador).

Aristotle, *De Anima*.

Audi, R., 2001, *The Architecture of Reason* (Oxford University Press).

Baldwin, T., 2001, *Contemporary Philosophy – Philosophy in Europe Since 1945* (Oxford University Press).

Blanshard, B., 1948 (2nd Imp.), *The Nature of Thought* (George Allen and Unwin, 1939).

Bosanquet, B., 1931 Imp., *Logic* (Oxford University Press, 1911, 2nd ed.).

Bosanquet, B., 1928, *The Essentials of Logic* (Macmillan, 1895).

Bradley, F. H., 1928 Imp., *The Principles of Logic* (Oxford University Press, 1883).

Brandom, R. B. (Ed.), 2001, *Richard Rorty and his Critics* (Blackwell).

Carnap, R., 1937, *The Logical Syntax of Language* (Routledge and Kegan Paul).

Chalmers, A., 1990, *Science and Its Foundation* (Open University Press).

Collins, H., & T. Pinch, 1998 (2nd Ed.), *The Golem* (Cambridge University Press, 1993).

Feyerabend, P., 1987, *Farewell to Reason* (Verso).

Fricker, M. & J. Hornsby (Eds.), 2000, *Feminism in Philosophy* (Cambridge University Press).

Guignon, C. & D. R. Hiley (Eds.), 2003, *Richard Rorty* (Cambridge University Press).

Habermas, J., 1998 Imp., *Metaphysical Thinking* (Polity, 1995).

Harré, R. & M. Krausz, 1996, *Varieties of Relativism* (Blackwell).

Keller, E. Fox, 1992, *Secrets of Life, Secrets of Death* (Routledge).

Keller, E. Fox & H. E. Longino (Eds.), 1996, *Feminism in Science* (Oxford University Press).

Kuhn, T., 1970 (2nd Ed.), *The Structure of Scientific Revolutions* (University of Chicago Press, 1962).

Levinson, R. & J. Thomas (Eds.), 1997, *Science Today* (Routledge).

Lloyd, G., 1984, *The Man of Reason* (Methuen).

MacIntyre, A., 1985 (2nd Ed.), *After Virtue* (Duckworth).

MacIntyre, A., 1988, *Whose Justice? Whose Reason?* (Duckworth).

Malachowski, R. (Ed.), 1990, *Reading Rorty* (Blackwell).

Murphy, M. C., 2003, *Alasdair MacIntyre* (Cambridge University Press).

Nicholson, L. J. (Ed.), *Feminism/Postmodernism* (Routledge N. Y.).

Norris, C., 1990, *What's Wrong with Postmodernism?* (H. Wheatsheaf).

Norris, C., 1991 rev., *Deconstruction – Theory and Practice* (Routledge, 1982).

O'Grady, P., 2002, *Relativism* (Acumen).

Putnam, H., 1995 Paper, *Words and Life* (Harvard University Press, 1994).

Putnam, H., 2003, *The Collapse of the Fact/Value Dichotomy* (Harvard University Press).

Quinton, A., 1978 Paper, *The Nature of Things* (Routledge and Kegan Paul, 1973).

Rorty, R., 1983 rpt., *Philosophy and the Mirror of Nature* (Blackwell, 1980).

Rorty, R., 1989 rpt., *Contingency, Irony and Solidarity* (Cambridge University Press, 1989).

Rorty, R., 1998, *Truth and Progress* (Cambridge University Press).

Sokal, A. and Bricmont, J., 1998, *Fashionable Nonsense* (Picador).

Sorabji, R., 1993, *Animal Minds and Human Morals* (Duckworth).

Stebbing, L. S., 1950 ed., *A Modern Introduction to Logic* (Methuen, 1930).

Stebbing, L. S., 1955 rpt., *Thinking to Some Purpose* (Penguin, 1939).

Taylor, C., 1997 2nd rpt., *Philosophical Arguments* (Harvard University Press, 1995).

Teichman, J. and G. White (Eds.), 1995, *An Introduction to Modern European Philosophy* (Macmillan).

Tomberlin, J. E. (Ed.), 1997, *Philosophical Perceptions 13* (Blackwell).

Toulmin, S., (2003), *Return to Reason* (Harvard University Press).

Waugh, P., 1992, *Postmodernism* (Arnold).

Waugh, P., 1992, *Practising Postmodernism, Reading Modernism* (Arnold).

White, S. K. (Ed.), 1995, *The Cambridge Companion to Habermas* (Cambridge).

Wilson, J. Cook, 1926, *Statement and Inference* (Oxford).

Wolpert, L., 1992, *The Unnatural Nature of Science* (Faber and Faber).

Journal

Bradley Studies, Vol. 10, Nos. 1 and 2, Autumn, 2004.

Index

Abbey, Ruth 44, 176-78

Appleyard, Brian 132

Aquinas, St. Thomas 161, 188-89, 192-93, 197

Archimedean point Ch. 10, 45-46, 82, 85-86, 141, 183ff, 197-200, 263, *see also* neutrality

argumentation *see* discussion

Aristotle 161-63, 187-88

Aristotelianism 188-89, 191-92, 196-98

Augustinianism 188, 191-92, 196-98

Ayer, Alfred Jules 42

Baldwin, Tom 23-24

Barthes, Roland 16

Berlin, Isaiah 212-14

bias *see* objectivity

Bloor, David 145

BonJour, L. 40-41

Bosanquet, Bernard 99-100, 351-52

Bouveresse, Jacques 11, 105

Bradley, F. H. 91, 99

Bricmont, Jean *see* Sokal, Alan

British empiricist tradition 27

Bubeck, Diemut 338-39, 352-53

Carnap, Rudolf 41-42

Chalmers, Alan 148-49

Claxton, Guy 146-47

Cohen, Stewart 58-61

coherence theory 68, 243

conceptual schemes *see* frameworks

Cook Wilson, John 97, 100

correspondence theory 242-43, 246

cultural relativism Ch. 9, 114-22, 228-31

Davidson, Donald 24, 243, 245-46

deconstruction 82

Deleuze, Giles 11, 20

Derrida, Jacques 16, 24

Descartes, Rene 16, 24, 26-27

discussion 11, 124-25

Dreyfus, Hubert 46-55, 174-75

Enlightenment 12-15

epistemology Ch. 4

feminism Ch. 13
    and Enlightenment 14-15
    and knowledge 36, 327-32,
        334
    and universals 353-55
    on epistemology 303-06
    on justification 340-42
    on neutrality 295-96, 319-22
    on objectivity 295-308, 315-
        22, 332-33
    on reasoning 310, 312-13,
        342-53
    on science 309-27
    on values see 'objectivity'
        [above]
    on women in science 306-08,
        319-20
Feyerabend, Paul 130-37, 244-45
Fish, S. 184, 186
Flax, Jane 22-23
Foucault, Michel 12-14, 16, 24, 240
Fox Keller, Evelyn 141-45, 295-96,
    316-17, 353-54
Fox Keller, Evelyn and Helen Longino
    296, 314-15, 317, 342-43
frameworks see traditions
Frazer, Sir James 120, 122
Freye, Marilyn 308
Fricker, Miranda 29
Fricker, Miranda and Jennifer
    Hornsby 313, 353
Friedman, Michael 344-45, 354

Gadamer, Hans-Georg 71-76
Galileo 65-66, 135-37, 254-55,
    271-73

Gilligan, Carol 344
God's-eye view see Archimedean point
Gronthowski, Christine 316-17

Habermas, Jurgen 75-77, 122-26, 210-
    12
Haraway, Donna 309-10, 333, 334
Harding, Sandra 296-307, 311, 334,
    339-40
Hare, R.M. 221
Haslanger, Sally 327-32
Heal, Jane 237-8, 244-45
Heidegger, Martin 24, 48
hermeneutics 44, 74, 243
Hornsby, Jennifer see Fricker
humans and human nature 215-23
Hume, David 161-63

incommensurability see reasoning
Irigary, Luce 149-50, 316

Jaggar, Alison 341-42, 347-55
Jethmalani, Shirley 18-20
Joachim, Harold 98
justification see warranted assertibility
justification, moral 218-22, 340-42

Kant, Immanuel 12
Klein, Peter 37-38
knowledge Ch. 5, 44-45
    among animals 36-40
    and logic 41-43
    and neutrality 45-46
    and reality 45-48, 174-76
    as justified true belief see

justification
  its tools 343-45, 347-50
  objectivity of 84-86, *see also
    under* feminism *and* Rorty
  'situated' 332ff
Kornblith, Hilary 39-40
Kuhn, Thomas 64, 137-41

Lacan, Jacques 16
Langton, Rae 307-08
language and truth *see under* Rorty
language games 32-35
Lloyd, Genevieve 65, 310, 312, 342
logic 41-43, 112-13, 261-62
  laws of, 19-20, 113
Longino, Helen 335-38, 345-47 *see
  also* Fox Keller
Lugones, Maria 352
Lyotard, Jean-Francois 15-16,
  28-30

MacIntyre, Alasdair 13, 15, 20-22,
  68-70, 105-14, 159-73, 187-
  200, 203-05, 223-24
metanarratives 16
Midgley, Mary 131
moral concepts 203-10, 212
moral reasoning 219-22
moral relativism 201-13
moral skepticism 215-18
morality and culture Ch. 11

Nelson, Lynn 315
neutrality of reason 45-46, 185-86

Nietzsche, Friedrich 16, 18-21, 24, 240
Norris, Christopher 12

objectivity, feminist style *see under*
  feminism
observation 317-19
O'Grady, Paul 41-44, 61, 93-96,
  127, 156-58, 178-79, 220

perception 100-103
philosophy Ch. 3, 11-12, 15, 234-
  39
Plato 201, 213
pragmatism 70, 281-83
Putnam, Hilary 206-10, 212-14,
  226-28, 258-59, 273, 283-85

Quine, Willard 52, 61-64
Quinton, Anthony 104

rationality Ch. 7 *see also* thinking
reasoning
  feminists on 342-53
  in morality 219-21
  models of 350-52
  objectivity of 84-90 *see also
    under* feminism *and* Rorty
  salient features of 90-100, 103-
  04
relativism 75-76, 228-31
  and incommensurability 65-7
  and traditions/frameworks 158-
  62, *see also* traditions *and*
  moral relativism
  and truth 156-58

epistemological and ontological
154-58
Rorty, Richard Ch. 12, 24, 31, 65-
68, 104
and language 33-35, 244, 254,
262-63, 269-71
and philosophy 234-39
and pragmatism 272-74, 280-
83
eel-like qualities of, 237-38
on common human nature
265-66, 287-89
on 'conversation' 247-50
on objectivity 257-62, 283-85
on science 267-70
on solidarity 266
on the Galileo-Bellarmine
controversy 254-55, 271-73
on truth 240-42, 262-64,
280-83
on universals 264-65
on 'vocabularies' 225-26, 254-57
on warranted assertibility 77-
79, 274-80
philosophical theses of 238-39
relativism and 'mild ethnocentrism'
of, 285-90

Sartre, Jean-Paul 20-21, 24
Schiebinger, Londa 342
scientific research 296-306, 312-14
science Ch. 8
alternative sciences 48-55, 61-64
and feminism 141-44 see also
feminism
and reality 46, 174-76

and 'revolutions' 138-39
and skepticism 48ff
neutrality of, 45-46
postmodern critique of, 146-48
Rorty on see under Rorty
science denigrated 130-35,
309-27
utility of, 57-58
skepticism about science 48ff
Socrates 20, 198
Sokal, Alan and Jean Bricmont 149-
50, 152-54
Sorabji, Richard 101
Sorell, Tom 185-86
Spelman, Elizabeth 352
Spinoza, Baruch 199
Standpoint 296-99, 302-06, 334,
339-40, 353
Stebbing, L. Susan 91-92, 98
'supersession' 174-76

Taylor, Charles 26-28, 44-47, 50,
114-22, 174-78, 215-23
Teichman, Jenny 20
thinking see also reasoning 15-20
and perception 100-103
challenged 104-05
culturally relative 58-61 see also
cultural relativism
Tiles, Mary 319-27
Toulmin, Stephen 83-86
Toynbee, Arnold 17
traditions 43-44, 68-70, 156-74
truth 15-17
and frameworks 155-59

and traditions 68-70, 108-10, 159-73, 187-97
as contextual 58-61
universals 264-65, 353-55

values 201-02
value judgements 226-28

'vocabularies' *see under* Rorty
Warnke, G. 71-73
warranted assertability 77-80, 274-80, 340-42
Waugh, Patricia 12-17
Williams, Bernard 185-86, 207-08, 273
Wittgenstein, Ludwig 16, 32
Wylie, Alison 315-16, 334-35